1936

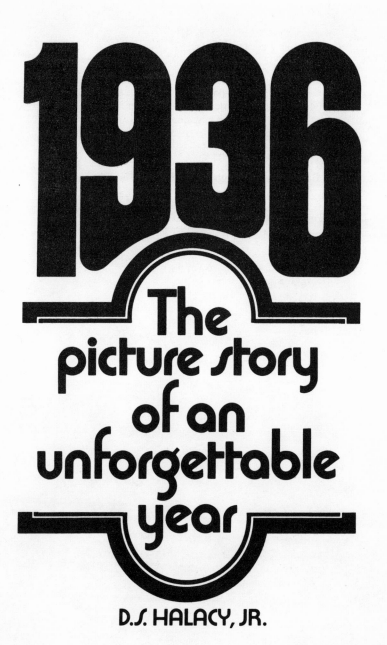

1936

The picture story of an unforgettable year

D.S. HALACY, JR.

ARLINGTON HOUSE·PUBLISHERS

NEW ROCHELLE, N. Y.

Copyright © 1963 D. S. Halacy, Jr.

Library of Congress Cataloging in Publication Data

Halacy, Daniel Stephen, 1919-
    1936: the picture story of an unforgettable year.

    Reprint of the ed. published by Monarch Books, Derby,
Conn., under title: Encyclopedia of the world's great
events: 1936.
    1. History--Yearbooks--1936. I. Title.
D410.5 1936.H3 1974   909.82'3   74-11061

ISBN 0-87000-283-X

CONTENTS

Introduction

Every year is of course important to those who live it; perhaps the current year is the most vital to us now, as was the year 1 to others. The year we are born and the year we die are big years in our lives and there are others in between that loom large in our individual memories. Considered objectively, though, some years stand out sharper than others and 1936 is such a year in our recent history.

It was a big year for two reasons: both for the events themselves that happened during its 366 days—it was Leap Year, remember?—and for the fact that it was a year of transition, a bridging from one way of life to another. It was a year that saw one war end and another start, while the organization formed to prevent such things watched helplessly from the sidelines, and all signs pointed to the coming of an even bigger war.

Yet there was the hint, too, of closer ties in the world as the globe shrank because of cultural, economic and communication improvements. "One World" was still a dream, but at least there were more of us dreaming about it.

In preliminary discussions with the publishers, as to just what this book should be, it was tentatively decided to present, as complete chapters, a number of varied "big stories" of the year—stories that needn't have any connection with one another. But almost at the outset it was evident that such seemingly unrelated events as the fleeing to England of the fearful Lindberghs and the romance between Edward and Wallis were actually interlaced not only in time but with respect to place and people as well.

Lawyer Sam Leibowitz, who was called in on the Lindbergh kidnaping case, was the same man who defended the Scottsboro Negroes, who came to trial for the last time in 1936. Jesse Owens would win four gold medals and have his name engraved in Berlin more lastingly than Adolf Hitler, and the same Jesse would come triumphantly back to America and figure in the political battle between New Dealer Franklin Roosevelt and Governor Alf Landon.

The same sort of dovetailing held for the Olympic Games and the rise of Hitler to ever-greater power; Mussolini's trampling of Ethiopia and the trial of the Scottsboro Boys; or even John L. Lewis' unions and the Spanish Civil War. From that war firsthand would come Hemingway's *For Whom the Bell Tolls,* a book whose title might well be the theme for the year 1936. "No man is an island," John Donne had said three centuries before. His statement was truer in 1936 than it had been when he said it.

The war in Spain embroiled not just that country, but Italy, Russia, Germany, Portugal and others, including Mexico, France and England. What was happening to the Jews in Germany in 1936 was a concern to Jews—and others— in America. Even little Haile Selassie, who in 1936 seemed truly forgotten by the world he begged to save him, would one day be restored to his lost throne because even though it is not strictly true that there are no islands left at least they are ever fewer.

With this important awareness, then, and insofar as the happenings of the year can be isolated, what follow are eleven "big stories" of 1936 told briefly and simply. Another chapter covers the remaining important events in capsule form—things like aviation and art, crime and disasters, business and entertainment. Some births and some deaths are recorded and some figures are mentioned.

But this book is neither a definitive history nor a rigorously quantitative almanac. The libraries already abound in volumes of this sort and the reader searching for the statistical fact and the considered evaluation had better look on those shelves. What we have here is, hopefully, a reliving in a few hours of today an important year from our recent past, a year that looks even bigger in retrospect than it did as we suffered and enjoyed it at the time. It was a most interesting year, remember?

Things were looking up a little by 1936 but we weren't yet out of the woods. In New York two veteran editors at E. P. Dutton declined a year-end bonus of $2.50, on principle, and were promptly sacked. President Roosevelt was hitting a snag or two and the AAA had been abolished by the Supreme Court. But unemployment insurance was in on a national scale and Social Security deductions were imminent.

One daily newspaper raised its price to an exorbitant 3 cents a copy and 22,000 readers angrily stopped buying it. Walter Johnson did his best to prove that the dollar was going farther elsewhere by pitching a silver one across the Rappahannock River on the birthday of the Father of Our Country. The ads in the magazines held out the lure of luxurious retirement on $100 a month, and in San Quentin several inmates tried to guarantee *themselves* an income by forging money with the prison photo lab equipment!

Veterans finally got their World War I bonus, and an enterprising college boy went on strike for a bonus for wars he might have to fight in the future. J. P. Morgan figured in a profiteering investigation into his firm's World War I activities. Uncle Sam was plugging the sale of Savings Bonds that would one day pay the holder $4 for $3, but an oldster out in California had a different plan for prosperity. The Townsend Plan, following on the faltering heels of Huey Long's "Share the Wealth" and Upton Sinclair's "End Poverty in California," would give the retired $150 a month just so they spent it all before the next payment.

We were still a nation on wheels—some said the only nation that *drove* to the poorhouse. You could buy a Plymouth —"the most beautiful of all three!"—for $510 if you had it. If you chose a Chevrolet you could ante up an extra $20 dollars and get "knee action" springing. Willys had introduced a compact model for only $375 and it offered 35 miles to the gallon. For the fastidious, Du Pont auto polish would send a set of gold initials for the car door. The price was just 6 cents.

In the air, sportsman Howard Hughes set a new cross-country speed record of 260 miles per hour, and plane builder Donald Douglas was marketing a new model called the DC-2 that hurtled across the sky at three miles a minute. "Wherever you are," Douglas said, "you can be anywhere else tomorrow!" And to get you there in good shape he was building sleeper planes.

Some aircraft, unfortunately, came to grief. Among those killed in crashes were restaurateur Fred Harvey and his wife. Another kind of aircraft, the huge German dirigible *Hindenburg*, gave watchers a scare when it floated aloft on its first flight. But what seemed to be smoke pouring from the huge inflammable gas bag turned out to be only dust accumulated during the long construction period. All of aviation was soon to be faced with a speed barrier, and one

9

eminent authority announced that planes would never fly faster than 575 miles per hour. Who in his right mind would want to go that fast anyway? The electronics people were tinkering with an unwieldy contraption called television but not making much progress. Rudy Vallee was a big name in show business, and he made headlines when boss George White clobbered him in an argument.

Among the songs Americans were singing was an import called *Gloomy Sunday* that was doing big things for suicide. Nelson Eddy and Jeannette MacDonald purveyed a happier music, and a Negro singer debuted in New York with a broken foot. Her name was Marian Anderson.

Charlie Chaplin and Paulette Goddard has just finished *Modern Times,* a movie that poked fun at our industrialized society. Now they climbed aboard a steamer for what might develop into a honeymoon cruise. Shirley Temple continued her winning ways, but for variety there was an H. G. Wells thriller, *Things to Come,* with all sorts of fantastic predictions such as space ships, a war that would return us to the cave, and the like.

Entertainer Eddie Cantor, trying to do something nice, gave an essay prize to a personable young farmer; took it back when it turned out that the winner had copied his entry out of an old book. A young author named Ayn Rand had written a book called *We the Living,* and there was another one with a catchy title, *Gone With The Wind.* There was a newcomer in the ranks of the columnists, a Mrs. Eleanor Roosevelt who wrote a feature called *My Day.*

Boxer Joe Louis thought life was just one round of fighting after another until a German named Schmeling knocked him out. And Sonja Henie, the tiny blonde on skates, decided she'd cut more ice as a professional. Fiorello La Guardia was singlehandedly running our largest city and a gentleman named Orville Wright was belatedly asked to join the National Academy of Sciences now that it seemed pretty sure that his flying machine really had flown at Kitty Hawk 33 years ago.

Motherhood was in the news. Scientists had come up with a method of planting a fertilized egg in a "host" mother, and some writers said if it worked with animals why not with humans? Margaret Sanger was getting absolutely nowhere in her sales pitch to Mahatma Gandhi on birth control, and in America Ann Hewitt Cooper was suing her

10

mother for having Ann sterilized without her knowledge. Richard Loeb, who with Nathan Leopold had murdered young Bobby Franks for kicks, was killed himself by a prisoner who accused Loeb of perversion. One of Bring-'Em-Back-Alive Frank Buck's bull elephants tore his keeper into four bloody pieces and was executed as a murderer. And another killer, named Hauptmann, went to his death, too.

Remember these things that happened? Think back, too, on what you were doing in the days of the big stories we've selected—the stories of the Big Year of 1936.

I

The New Deal

Franklin Delano Roosevelt, the man who was America's thirty-second President, and who would be the only one elected four times, was born January 30, 1882, on his family's estate at Krum Elbow on the Hudson River. He was an eighth-generation descendant of the pioneering Claes Martenszan van Rosenvelt who settled in New Amsterdam about the middle of the seventeenth century. President Theodore Roosevelt was descended from the same family.

Young Roosevelt graduated from Harvard in 1904 and from Columbia Law School in 1907. For three years he practiced law in New York City, and then entered politics. A delegate to the New York State Democratic Convention in 1910, he later won the election that year as state senator, despite the fact that his was a predominantly Republican district. As an opponent of Tammany Hall, he was re-elected in 1912.

In 1912 he was a delegate to the Democratic National Convention and supported the nomination of Woodrow Wilson as President. The following year Wilson appointed Roosevelt Assistant Secretary of the Navy, a post he held for two terms with the Wilson administration.

In 1920 Roosevelt supported Al Smith as a presidential nominee, and when Smith was defeated, Roosevelt wound up as vice-presidential candidate along with James M. Cox for President. This ticket met with defeat at the polls, and in 1921 Roosevelt was dealt a worse blow when he contracted infantile paralysis.

Even though he lost the use of both legs, Roosevelt continued actively in politics. In 1924 he again championed Smith unsuccessfully. In 1928 Roosevelt ran for governor of New York State and won while Smith was defeated by Hoover. So popular was Roosevelt in his new post that he was re-elected in 1930 by the largest majority yet recorded in New York. Prophetically included in his policies were

13

unemployment insurance, farm relief, old age pensions, reforestation and public utility regulation.

In 1932 Roosevelt was nominated for President of the United States to run against a luckless Herbert Hoover, and swept into office with an electoral vote of 472 to 59 and a popular majority of some seven million. He won in all states but Connecticut, Delaware, Pennsylvania, New Hampshire, Maine and Vermont. In 1933, prior to his inauguration, he narrowly missed death when an assassin fired at him and killed Chicago's Mayor Cermak instead.

In 1905 Roosevelt had married a distant cousin, Anna Eleanor Roosevelt, who was Teddy Roosevelt's niece. Born in 1884 in New York City, Mrs. Roosevelt was privately educated and received an honorary degree in 1929 from Russell Sage College.

Active in politics and in welfare work, she was an enthusiastic horsewoman and tennis player. She became a noted humanitarian, writer, lecturer and radio speaker, and was a strong asset to her husband's career. The President and Mrs. Roosevelt had five children—James, Elliott, Franklin, Jr., John and Anna—plus several grandchildren.

Despite leg braces and wheelchair, the big, exuberant boss of the New Deal continued as the smiling, confident head of his party. It was adviser Raymond Moley who had suggested the term "New Deal," probably borrowing from the title of Stuart Chase's book.

In 1936 the New Deal was now in its fourth year and Roosevelt had become its personification. Far behind were the bold "first hundred days," and many of the wild dreams of the new breed of Washington planners were now an accepted part of the American scene. Leading off in 1936 was perhaps the most revolutionary scheme yet—that of Social Security. Citizens now had numbers, to the professed horror of some detractors of Roosevelt. These numbers, they prophesied, would one day be steel "dog tags" slung about the necks of the populace or tattooed on its servile arms.

How had the nation fared thus far? In the three years of Franklin Delano Roosevelt's presidency the national income had jumped $30 billion. The national debt was up, too, climbing from $16 billion in 1932 to more than $28 billion in 1936. The dollar's value was officially pegged at 59.06 cents under the Gold Reserve Act, but the banks had been reopened. There was a new Federal Reserve Act. And there was the *Federal Register*, too; the country's first official newspaper.

Washington, D.C., was a far different place than the town vacated by Herbert Hoover, and though Walter Lippmann wrote that the discredited Republican had actually anticipated many of the reforms FDR put into practice, few of the party in their right minds could agree. The capital was still a ferment of starry-eyed liberal planners whose idealistic fervor gave one lady reporter the feeling that they were drunk half the time.

Roosevelt himself was saint or sinner depending on where you sat. The "little man" was apparently solidly for him, and there were, of course, more of them. At the Presidential Birthday Balls FDR stood out as a brave man who had whipped a tough handicap, and focused attention on the worthy fight against infantile paralysis.

Mrs. Roosevelt was a tireless worker for causes herself. Right in Washington she exposed the shocking conditions in the National Training School for Girls, where one wayward girl gave birth to her child in a cell. On a broader scale she worked with national youth groups. With boundless energy she traveled ubiquitously, and the *New Yorker* cartoon of a miner deep in the bowels of the earth exclaiming, "For gosh sakes, here comes Mrs. Roosevelt!" was hardly stretching the truth.

The White House rang continually with the laughter of youngsters, including Sistie and Buzzie and tiny Sara. Roosevelt enjoyed cronies like those of the "cufflink gang" which had started him in politics. He loved to go down to the sea, and was an inveterate fisherman who landed sailfish off the Florida coast and a 27-pound "mystery fish" for the Smithsonian to puzzle over. Like other citizens, he sweated over his income tax forms and the $15,000 bite out of his $75,000 salary.

Hale and hearty, he traveled up and down the land to receive the honors bestowed on his massive head by a grateful nation. Among them were countless degrees, typified in a Litt.D. from Rollins in Florida and the rarer Doctor of Jurisprudence conferred on him at Temple University. Originally planned as an LL.D., the honor was upped since the President had scads of those already. In his doctoral robes, Roosevelt had this to say about education:

15

No group and no government can properly prescribe precisely what should constitute the body of knowledge with which true education is concerned. The truth is found when men are free to pursue it. Genuine education is present only when the springs from which knowledge comes are pure.

Also on the agenda was the dedication of a fine new library at Temple. It had been completed by the PWA at a cost of some half-million dollars. He dedicated the Theodore Roosevelt Memorial addition to the American Museum of Natural History in New York and also the new $625,000 chemistry building for the government-maintained Howard University for Negroes.

All was not sweetness and light, of course. Among those who sniped at the leader were turncoat Democrats like one-time Happy Warrior Al Smith, who in January told a meeting of the American Liberty League that the New Deal was socialistic, and that he was seriously considering taking a walk from the party. The same month, a meeting of Jeffersonian Democrats in Macon, Georgia, was appealing to Governor Talmadge to lead the U.S. out of New Deal Communism. Talmadge now referred to Roosevelt scathingly as "that cripple in the White House."

Criticism ranged from the appraisal by Governor Gifford Pinchot of Pennsylvania that though Roosevelt was a wonderful radio speaker he was a flop as a business executive, to warped threats like that from a retired engineer:

Franklin Delano Roosevelt
Communist and Destroyer of Private Business
Warm Springs, Georgia
You ——— I warn you if you destroy my business I will strangle you with my own hands. May your soul be exterminated in Hell.

Investigators ferreted out the sender of the note and he was judged "sane but eccentric" and sentenced to ninety days in the Federal House of Detention.

The press was largely anti-Roosevelt and attacked him in articles, editorials and cartoons. Among these last was the classic by Peter Arno showing a group of wealthy people gaily on their way to a newsreel theater "to hiss Roosevelt." The President took this easily in his stride, scribbling

"Grand!" across a copy of the cartoon timorously shown him.

In another, a Helen Hokinson clubwoman addressing an audience of ladies said, "Of course we must draw some sort of distinction between wishing to overthrow the government and not liking the present administration," and still another cartoon in the *New Yorker* had a wealthy businessman telling his lady friend: "And if Roosevelt is not elected, perhaps even a villa in Newport, my dearest." More vicious were drawings like that of Roosevelt made up as Hitler and admiring himself in a mirror.

To businessmen, Roosevelt was anathema. Many considered him just another Stalin, only worse. Hadn't he recognized Communist Russia? These gentlemen found daily solace in papers like the New York *Herald Tribune,* and made jokes about the psychiatrist in heaven being rushed to attend God who thought *He* was *FDR!*

Of far more concern to the President as the year 1936 began was the Supreme Court. Anti-New Dealers applauded the Court and it was said that signs on automobile bumpers now read, "Save the Constitution!" where once they had said, "Repeal the 18th Amendment!" as business cheered what administration officials called the body with a building of marble and a heart to match.

In the eyes of the New Dealers this august body was simply "nine old men" who were effectively hatcheting much of the reform legislation Roosevelt was pushing for. In decision after decision the court snipped away at the alphabet world of Washington. NRA, the National Recovery Act, was already a casualty. The Blue Eagle was ignominiously done in by the "sick chicken" Schechter case and it was little consolation to New Dealers when the Schechter brothers failed in their poultry business in 1936.

Now the far-reaching Triple-A Agricultural Adjustment Act was torpedoed 6 to 3. Soon to go would be the Guffey Coal Act and the Municipal Bankruptcy Act. Under fire were administration of the Securities Exchange Commission and minimum wage laws. A current joke was that the Supreme Court was upholding the Constitution not only strongly, but weekly.

Near Ames, Iowa, six black-robed effigies were hanged in protest against the justices who had voted against AAA. Roosevelt was working on more effective methods of curb-

17

ing the Court, including limiting its powers, increasing Congressional power or possibly forcing the retirement of tired old men over seventy. There was another possibility, too, that of packing the court with New Deal sympathizers.

Refreshingly, TVA, the mammoth Tennessee Valley Authority that was to change the way of life for many Southerners, according to New Deal planners, got a clean bill of health from the Court in an 8 to 1 ruling. This to the keen discomfiture of Wendell Willkie, who saw TVA as the most useless and unnecessary of all the administration's "alphabetic joy rides." Willkie was president of Commonwealth and Southern Power Company.

But generally the courts continued to hack away at Roosevelt. Senator Hugo Black and his investigating committee had seized wholesale batches of telegrams sent and received by corporations, law firms and individuals who opposed the New Deal. Among these was the outspoken Hearst Press. Now the court granted an injunction against this procedure. The Railroad Retirement Act, too, was invalidated. During 1935 and 1936, federal judges handed down no less than 1,600 injunctions against federal laws. Some suggested that girls were not taking advantage of the Leap Year because they feared even that was unconstitutional.

There were other problems, too. The heady intoxication of the new order was beginning to wear off in a morning-after hangover. The strange collections of politicians, idealists, brain trusters and career civil servants bickered among themselves, and with the President.

Hugh Johnson's disenchantment was an example, and he wailed about Felix Frankfurter and his "Happy Hot Dogs," calling the distinguished Harvard professor the most influential individual in the country. It was bad enough that college professors had invaded Washington, some thought, but even worse that they had brought their senior classes along with them.

The Senate repealed the Bankhead cotton act, the Kerr-Smith tobacco act and the potato act. It passed an extension of the Neutrality Act, and the Soil Conservation Bill. Congress was listening to J. P. Morgan concerning his organization's actions during World War I, and evidence was produced showing that it had received $30 million in commissions for munitions sales to England. For the thirteenth time in history, court impeachment proceedings succeeded, and Federal Judge Halsted L. Ritter of Florida was removed from his job for misconduct despite his protestations and those of his sister, Mary Beard, the historian.

Tragedy stalked, too, in the untimely death of William Randolph Dyness, a WPA administrator for whom a homestead colony had been named. Dyness met death in the crash of the airliner *Southerner* in Arkansas.

There were other casualties. Major-General Johnson Hagood, Commander of the 8th Corps Area of the Army, was unhappy about the small amount of money the services were receiving. He was vocal in his complaint, and Congress asked him to tell it his feelings. Assured that he was speaking off the record, Hagood unburdened himself in part thusly:

I am not familiar with the various pockets in which Uncle Sam keeps his money, but I understand there's budget money which is very hard to get, PWA money which is not so hard to get, and then there is a vast quantity of WPA money which is very easy to get for triflng projects but almost impossible to get for anything worthwhile.

It's harder for me to get five cents to buy a lead pencil than to get a thousand dollars to teach hobbies to CCC boys. At the present time there is a vast flow of silver spreading out all over the country like mud. For God's sake put some of it in stone and steel!

Two months later, Congress published Hagood's harsh words despite assurances to him to the contrary. President Roosevelt could see no other way open to him but to order the General summarily relieved of his command. Later he was given command of the 6th Corps Area, but retired after a day of duty.

If the Army suffered, at least the CCC did some good. Needed forest work went on; helpful dollars were sent home by corps members to aid needy families; 35,000 illiterates learned to read.

The "hobbies" that Hagood mentioned were certainly being taught, and in fact the term "boondoggle" was born out of the WPA's work in idle-time training of the jobless. In New York, training specialist Robert Marshall told newsmen that he taught his charges "boondoggles," an old term for handicrafts like the making of webbed belts from bits of rope, and the like. It was a catchy term, and it caught on with the press, who henceforth applied it to most make-work programs of the New Deal.

Relief was a giant millstone around the neck of a country trying to regain its feet. The total number on the rolls or directly benefited by relief was estimated as high as 25 million, and Roosevelt could not escape the title of "Old King Dole," especially from those who saw in the WPA and other projects federal vote-buying on a grand scale. Galling, too, was a claim that one reliefer in seven was an alien, and that some three million foreign nationals were being supported.

It was inevitable that cries of "Police state!" would go up, with warnings not to put off until tomorrow anything that could be done today since by then taxes would be higher or there would be a law against it. But the picture was not all that bleak, and with understandable pride, the President pushed a button that put into operation Norris Dam 500 miles away, another "practical symbol of the better life" promised the country and now actually being delivered.

Senator Norris' Rural Electrification Act went through, with a price tag of $40 million. The private utilities might tear their hair, but it was certainly true that many who had never before seen an electric light read by one now and ironed clothes with the same convenient power. Across the land the government stood ready to tackle any project of benefit to its people. In Beaufort, North Carolina, local planners thought long and hard before proposing a most interesting one: a bomb shelter, to be built by the WPA, that would protect Beaufort residents against attack by hostile aircraft.

As Roosevelt's enemies pointed out, there was rampant fraud in WPA and other projects. Checkers asked one woman why her husband hadn't shown up on his government job for the last three days. The startled woman protested that her spouse had been dead for a year. A check of one area disclosed seventeen dead men on the rolls, and a caustic press suggested prodding those with shovels in their hands.

Sensibly, the government agreed that there was indeed chiseling, deplored it and welcomed help in stamping it out. Anti-New Dealers claimed the biggest danger lay in the fact that many people now declined "honest" work because it was harder and didn't pay enough. Others said they had been ousted to make way for New Deal friends and relatives. WPA boss Harry Hopkins himself was embarrassed by

the revelation that his sister had moved into an adminis-
trative position and she was removed. He protested that
there was no politics in relief, and perhaps found little relief
in politics either.

While TVA and Norris stood as monuments to Roosevel-
tian vision, there were large-scale flops as well. The visionary
Passamaquoddy power project that was to use tidal power on
the Maine-Canada border was a pet of the President. After
the expenditure of $5.5 million in PWA funds, "Quoddy,"
as Roosevelt called it, was dropped. Detractors referred to it
as "Passa the bucky." The same fate befell the Gulf-Atlan-
tic Canal across Florida. This bold WPA project also spent
some $5.5 million before it, too, was abandoned, with op-
ponents crying it would have ruined Florida's water supply
and made a desert of the southern half.

Another project that seemed to be in doubt was the
"Shelter Belt" out West, where 80 percent of the trees had
already died and wrangling was going on as to what to do
now. Cynics wondered if grass wasn't what was needed,
rather than trees.

But no one could dispute the fact that public works were
changing the appearance of the country and surely some of
the changes were for the better. Civic centers and post offices were built, streets were paved and ditches dug. And
one phase of the WPA the government could point to as an
unqualified success. The Federal Art Project hired more
than 5,000 artists in practically every state, and in a creative binge these men and women were producing the adorn-
ment for public buildings.

Close to 700 murals had been painted, including a George
Biddle masterpiece covering 600 square feet of wall in a
new Department of Justice building. Titled simply, "The
Sweatshop and Tenement of Yesterday Can Be the Life
Planned with Justice Tomorrow," the painting typified a
wave of social awakening in government-sponsored art. Ap-
propriately, one of the downtrodden "sweatshop seamstres-
ses" in the mural was none other than Frances Perkins, Secretary of Labor and first lady cabinet member in our history.

Actors, too, were taken under the government wing. Along
with the first U.S. official newspaper there was also the WPA
Federal Theatre "Living Newspaper" whose principals acted
out such drama-filled events as *Triple-A Plowed Under*
and *Injunction Granted*.

With the growing interest in "social man," typified in the

21

federal projects to record and preserve folk tales and tunes, and in the homestead projects that were Eleanor Roosevelt's pride and joy, capital seemed to be taking a back seat in this new world of the New Deal. Reedsville, West Virginia, was the First Lady's pet project. Here a small group was set up in government-built housing and started out on "cottage-labor" projects. Tying in with the burgeoning of electric power, Reedsville assembled vacuum cleaners, and Mrs. Roosevelt was the recipient of the first one off the production line.

Despite the New Deal, or because of it, business was prospering. The Dow-Jones averages were up to a healthy 147. In 1936 business was up almost 15 percent over the preceding year. Metal prices were up, and automobile production increased 20 percent. Steel averaged $28 a ton, with the industry fighting off John L. Lewis with one hand and the Attorney-General's prosecution with the other.

The automobile business was doing well enough for Chrysler to hand out Valentine's Day presents totaling $2.3 million to its workers, and at Christmas General Motors raised wages 5 cents an hour and paid another $10 million in bonuses. Home builders, with federal loan assistance, were coming up with neat homes for $2,500 with long-term, low-interest payments.

In the fall the football industry's receipts showed a gain of 15 percent, and many wondered how the entertainment world could do so well. Many people had nothing to do but go to the movies or sports events, but how could they afford it?

In 1936 there were millions of unemployed. William Green, head of the American Federation of Labor, came up with the depressing statistics that despite all the government's efforts there were 12,626,000 unemployed in January of 1936—and there had been only 13,100,000 in 1933. More than a million lost jobs in the first month of 1936, and Green blamed industry for labor's plight.

The Bonus Army was a symptom of the times. Its marchers camped in Washington, and Roosevelt treated them with kindness. "Hoover sent the police," someone said, "and Roosevelt sent his wife." Heretofore Roosevelt had vetoed the bonus. Now the pressure was too great and in 1936 he vetoed it on principle but made no fight as Congress mustered the two-thirds majority to pass the bill. The national debt would be increased by $2.5 billions more, by the time the "baby bonds" had been paid off by the babies of the day. Bonds were mailed in June and by December 75 percent of them had been cashed.

Schoolteachers, some of whom had been getting less than $700 a year when Roosevelt took office, received slight pay raises, the increase balanced somewhat by a drop in their number because of the decline in enrollment in lower grades. This was the result of a drop in the birth rate. At the other end of the spectrum, however, adult education boomed.

There were strikes across the country, especially on both coasts in the shipping industry. Despite an occasional feud with John L. Lewis, the President seemed a staunch friend of labor. To business, at least in the form of the Chamber of Commerce, he tendered the back of his hand by ignoring its convention.

Such measures as the administration's 33-1/3 percent corporate surpluses tax were blasted by Raymond Moley, who had been a trusted adviser to the New Deal in happier days. And Roosevelt's brand of economics, in which he deplored more efficient means of production as harmful to the general welfare, stunned business and many economists alike. But despite this radical approach, Lord Keynes, a British theorist, found Roosevelt a "disillusioningly naïve economist."

Business, however, continued to prosper. One firm, Radio Corporation of America, relied on the good services of the former chairman of the Securities Exchange Commission for profitable deals. Joseph P. Kennedy, a successful businessman and politician with homes in New York, Palm Beach and Hyannis Port for his brood of nine youngsters, stepped easily from SEC to RCA. Sewell Avery was defending his job, and his $100,000 salary, as the head of Montgomery Ward. Income tax took $30,000 of that, Avery complained, and if he saved all the rest, the government would take all but $12,000 when he died!

Despite the claims of men like the ousted General Hagood, the United States was felt to be militarily strong. Down in the Philippines, for example, General MacArthur pointed to the growing strength of that country and foresaw a force strong enough to beat off any possible invasion.

Spain was beginning a civil war, and its effects already included those on Germany and Russia. Russia was an enigma to the United States, and careful investigation was pursued in this country for spies. One was caught in New York—trying to spend a phony $100 bill! On the West

23

Coast, an ex-sailor named Harry Thomas Thompson was arrested as a $500-a-month spy for Japan. His contact was Toshio Miyazaki, a student at Stanford, now fled. Investigators turned up the fact that a Japanese of that name had been a member of the Japanese Embassy in Washington earlier.

Cordell Hull's Reciprocal Trade Agreements were in line with a philosophy of "trade or fight." There was one small snag, in the raising by Roosevelt of the tariff on Japanese cotton cloth by 42 percent. Done to protect U.S. farmers, it worried the Japs.

The farm picture was bleaker. Despite the fact that prices were up, and cotton was doing well, corn had a disastrous year and there seemed no compromise between terrible floods like those at Johnstown and in Texas, and droughts that blighted whole sections of the country. Roosevelt's crop control bill went through Congress to a whopping victory of 267 to 97, but it was impossible to legislate rain where it was needed.

To take the place of the invalid AAA was the Soil Conservation and Domestic Allocations Act. Roosevelt urged a moratorium on farm foreclosures until impoverished landowners could get government loans, but it took time for his plea to reach the grass roots. The "farm holiday" movement swept the country, culminating in one gang kidnaping a judge and threatening to hang him for refusing to stop foreclosures. When he fell on his knees and begged God for "justice to all men," the farmers settled for shredding his clothes and smearing grease on him before turning him loose.

The farmers were getting 92 cents for wheat that had brought a pathetic 33 cents in 1933, but there were jokes rampant about how good the 1936 crop looked as it went by in the gale. A dust storm fantastically reached as far east as New England! As one writer put it, the hardest thing to keep down on the farm was the farm itself.

In one section of the West a survey showed as many homes deserted by despairing farmers as were still occupied. The "black blizzards" had created pathetic bands, including Okies and Arkies and Alabama sharecroppers who headed West and became fruit tramps.

California police were patrolling the eastern borders of the state to keep out the indigent, and Colorado's National Guard clashed with officials of New Mexico as the latter sought to ban cheap labor from Colorado. It was this economic turmoil that led to tragedies like the Scottsboro Case that blotted the pages of justice, and trials such as those Steinbeck would chronicle in *The Grapes of Wrath.*

The spring floods hit even at the capital itself, and when the Potomac rose 26 feet at Washington, government buildings were sandbagged for protection. Close to 200 people died in Eastern floods that were only a prelude to further rampages in 1937 when nearly a thousand would die and hundreds of thousands be made homeless.

So bad were conditions that from 1931 to 1936 there were more people leaving the United States than immigrating to it! Only in 1936 was this trend checked and the normal influx again begun, due in part to those fleeing oppression in Hitler's Germany that year.

Henry Agard Wallace, the half-mystic, half-agriculturist who was as strange a hybrid as many a farm product he had worked on, was convinced that the Western United States was turning into a desert. Soberly he suggested that the day was coming when the country must look to federal aid in certain profound adjustments to be made. The opposition, aghast at the Secretary's weird goings-on with the White Russian "Guru" who was his teacher, and at some of the bright young "liberals" like Alger Hiss toiling diligently in the Department of Agriculture, said, "If the drought is a calamity, what is Wallace?"

Michigan's Republican Senator Vandenburg caused a commotion when he asked for a list of recipients of AAA payments in excess of $10,000. He had heard, he said, of a farmer getting $219,000 during a two-year period for *not raising* 14,500 hogs, and another who collected $168,000 for *not planting 7,000* acres of cotton.

There was much weeping and wailing for the poor little pigs that "Lord Corn Wallace" had slaughtered, and when an Indian prince killed a thousand oxen and ten thousand sheep for a feast he was accused of thinking he was the AAA.

Secretary Wallace said he hated to take busy clerks off the task of disbursing checks, which so far totaled nearly $300 million, but under pressure he delivered the lists. It turned out that some individual payments had been more than a million dollars. A Puerto Rican syndicate got $961,-000 for sugar it didn't raise, and a British-controlled farm in the Southern U.S. took in $177,000 for cotton that never

25

saw the light of day. Not qualifying for the $10,000 figure, but turned up anyway, was Allan Hoover, son of the preceding President, who collected some $4,000 on a California farm. Smith and other disenchanted Democrats were pushing harder than ever for repudiation of FDR and the selection of a "genuine" Democrat to nominate.

To add to the farmer's woes was a mechanical cotton picker looming on the horizon, touted to do in one day a season's work for a man. Brain child of Daniel and Mack Rust, the new product of the machine age did seem able to put a human to shame and these ousted individuals were gathering up handfuls of rocks to pelt the creature. In light of the President's public antipathy toward increased production efficiency, there was justification for the many farmers who fervently hoped the cotton picker wouldn't work.

Despite all these farm woes the nation faced, there was hope. Two years earlier the President had stumped the farm country prior to election time and "Roosevelt Rain" had followed many of his visits. Now it was drawing near to another election time. Could the greatest New Dealer of them all repeat?

In 1936 Earl Browder claimed a membership of more than 600,000 in the organization he headed—the American Communist Party. In March the Columbia Broadcasting System stirred up the wrath of enemies of the party by giving Browder time on the air to voice his views, listing the program simply as "Talk." Defending itself, CBS said this was merely in line with its general policy of giving expression to different philosophies. This argument was echoed by many, including Harold Ickes, the one-time Republican who now headed the Department of the Interior.

"Why are we so bent," Ickes said, "on forbidding the advocacy of theories the absurdity of which should be apparent to all if they were allowed freedom of expression? Communism is merely a convenient bugaboo with which to frighten those who are in their political childhood."

Al Smith, no youngster politically, felt differently. "There can be only one capital, Washington or Moscow," he said. "There can be only one atmosphere of government, the clean pure fresh air of free America or the foul breath of communistic Moscow."

There were more who thought the real danger was not the Communist but the Fascist. David Dubinsky of the Garment Workers Union, accused of sending money to Spanish

Communists, was one of these. To men like him, Hitler was the real danger, along with his emulators in the U.S.

Among those whose "isms" were on the far right were Father Coughlin, whom Roosevelt called "the mad priest," and Gerald L. K. Smith. It was a confused and confusing picture at best, since not only America but also Germany and Spain and Russia must be taken into consideration. The fight between left and right would grow hotter as the presidential campaign progressed through the long dry summer. Another issue would take on more importance, too—that of the Negro.

The Negro in politics was a touchy problem. Traditionally the Republicans could look back at Lincoln; the Democrats, with the South and its "white supremacy" to consider generally, made the best of an awkward situation. Men like Jimmie Byrnes of South Carolina had got themselves in hot water with constituents by standing up for the rights of a Negro. There were Negroes at the Democratic Convention, and two famous figures in sports would highlight the campaigning. Mrs. Roosevelt's ideas of equality would be both a tribute and a trial to the party. And the Democrats' own double standard would show embarrassingly.

With Jim Farley as National Chairman and Emil Hurja heading up the most complex intelligence service yet known in a campaign, the New Dealers swung into action. Timing his trip to coincide with the Republican Convention, Roosevelt swung West to speak at Little Rock, then Houston and Dallas. Not long after he left the Arkansas capital came word of the flogging to death of a Negro, and the subsequent flogging of white sympathizers.

Gerald L. K. Smith did his best to hurt Roosevelt by exploiting the American Liberty League meeting in the South, at which vicious pamphlets featuring a picture of Mrs. Roosevelt with two Negroes were circulated. Investigation revealed that among the contributors for the Liberty League get-together were wealthy Northern Republicans.

Later Smith formed a weird coalition with Father Coughlin and Dr. Francis Townsend. Almost sanctified by his elderly followers in California, Dr. Townsend headed a new and unknown element in the electorate. With the promise of $150 a month to pensioners, the good doctor had his flock militantly, if irreverently, singing:

27

Onward Townsend Soldiers
Marching as to war,
With the Townsend Banner
Going on before.
Our devoted soldiers
Bid depression go,
Join them in the battle,
Help them fight the foe.

Cynics said he had taken in one million dollars and ten million suckers, and the New Dealers were concerned. Townsend was even hailed into a Congressional investigation, from which he stalked angrily, saying he would not return unless under arrest. But the threat of the Townsendites waned, and after much wrangling and pseudo secrecy, the coalition "Union Party" convened and nominated Senator William Lemke of North Dakota for President and Thomas C. O'Brien of Massachusetts as his running mate.

Rabble-rousing Huey Long, the Kingfish from Louisiana, had been assassinated, so his visionary "Share the Wealth" program was no longer a threat to the New Deal. And Governor Floyd Olson of Minnesota, whose farm-labor bloc had been a thorn in Roosevelt's side, died in 1936 and was no longer a possibility for nomination.

But there was Norman Thomas, perennial candidate of the Socialist Party, with vice-presidential candidate George O. Nelson of Wisconsin. Socialism was big that year, and the Socialist Labor Party nominated John Aiken of Massachusetts and Emil Teichert of New York. The Prohibition Party, meeting where else but Niagara Falls, picked Dr. D. Leighton Colvin of New York, and war hero Alvin C. York of Tennessee.

The Communists nominated Earl Browder for President and James Ford, a New York Negro, for Vice President. Kansan Browder ran afoul of the law several times and wound up with the martyrdom of twenty-six hours in jail in Terre Haute, Indiana, for vagrancy. While Browder languished, however, his alert attorney barricaded himself in a radio station and read the campaign speech!

Undoubtedly the strongest figure at the Republican Convention was Herbert Hoover himself. The ovation he received was so great and so long that a postponement of the business at hand was necessary. Many of the party would have run Hoover again, but it was not to be.

The terrible days of 1929 were still too fresh in the minds

28

of the American people. Wags pointed out that Hoover had been a big gun all right, but that he was fired in 1932. About all that was left for a man who had been chased by an elephant was a life membership in the Explorers Club. So Hoover had to content himself with stumping against the Democrat's Roosevelt. He had considered all the ideas that FDR had put into practice, the Ex-President said, but rejected them rather than put free men into shackles.

Besides Hoover, the Republicans passed over Senator Vandenburg and Colonel Frank Knox. Senator Borah tried to throw his hat in the ring and caused a "tidal wave of popular approval similar to a gnat falling into a bathtub." Acid-tongued H. L. Mencken, long an ardent Roosevelt hater had cockily said, "If they can beat Roosevelt at all they can do it with a Chinaman, or even a Republican." The folly of using the Chinaman approach was pointed out, considering the already sad state of U.S.-Japanese relations; the convention at Cleveland picked a Republican: Governor Alf Landon of Kansas.

Honest and forthright, if not inspiring, the man with a sunflower in his buttonhole claimed he was not beholden to anyone. He was promptly dubbed "No-Man's Landon," and Roosevelt's friend John L. Lewis scoffed mightily and found the Midwesterner "as inane as a watermelon that's been boiled in a washtub!" Even some irreverent Republicans were heard to say, "Elect Landon and we'll sleep nights —even his speeches make you drowsy."

"The Democratic Party is about to run out of alphabet," Hoover suggested. "But the Russian alphabet has thirty-four letters." Another Republican cried, "If Roosevelt is elected grass will grow in the streets," and someone else added "Yes, and the WPA will cut it, too!"

The Communist issue was back in the picture and Roosevelt countered it at Syracuse as a red herring. Nonetheless, he firmly repudiated the Communists, and in August ordered J. Edgar Hoover to investigate the party. In August, too, Secretary of State Hull prevented the entry into this country of William Gallacher, Communist Member of Parliament from England.

Now it was time for the Democratic National Convention in Philadelphia and Roosevelt admirer Ray Clapper found that the party which had come to nominate the great idealist for another term as President sank to the lowest common denominator, "which is plenty low," he added.

29

But some of it was high-toned. Lily Pons sang, and as Roosevelt entered Franklin Field he spotted poet Edwin Markham, whose *Man With The Hoe* might well have typified the WPA. Greeting the aging poet, Roosevelt was knocked down in the crush, his speech flying into the mud. The next five minutes were the worst he ever experienced, Roosevelt would say later, but he went doggedly on to the platform and an acceptance speech that thrilled the thousands of faithful. Later he ran into a group of American Legionnaires, donned an overseas cap and joined them in *Pack Up Your Troubles in Your Old Kit Bag*. The press would note wistfully that Landon didn't sing.

Like Roosevelt, another Democrat went home stronger than he had come. Tom Pendergast took over as party boss in Kansas City on the strength of the job he did at the convention.

Many would work from now until election day for the New Deal's leader. Fortunately not many of them botched the job as did Joe Louis. Speaking in Paterson, New Jersey, for the Democrat local candidates as well as for Roosevelt, the Brown Bomber forgot what town he was in, and to mention the party he was plugging. He wasn't, he ruefully admitted later, as good a speaker as he was a hitter.

Another Negro figured in politics. Jesse Owens, who had swept the Olympics in Berlin, took a brief fling at personal appearances on the night club circuit and then announced his availability for aiding the Republican cause. This was irksome to Democrats since they had been carrying Jesse as a nonworking page in Ohio at $3 a day.

Republican hopes ran higher than they had for the last four years. The *Literary Digest* predicted not just a win for Landon, but a landslide. It had been correct in 1932 when Roosevelt swept into the White House, and Landon backers seized upon this encouragement and even increased the odds. The Gallup Poll differed, however, and if you asked Jim Farley he said that only Maine and Vermont could go Republican and he wasn't sure about them.

In October Al Smith was haranguing listeners with the word that the New Deal had failed and the advice to vote for Landon. Roosevelt calmly called the increasing debt an "investment in humanity," and promised that in a year or two the budget would be balanced and the debt wiped out.

Roosevelt cheerfully accepted the nomination as candidate, not only of the Democratic Party, but also the

American Labor Party. Labor contributed some half-million dollars to the campaign, most of it coming from the new power in labor, John L. Lewis.

Asked for last-minute comments, Al Smith said confidently, "We'll soon be out of the woods." A gracious Eleanor Roosevelt viewed a torchlight parade and confided, "I find this kind of politics very delightful!"

It was up to the voters now, up to each man to weigh the past four years and peer into the four ahead and be guided accordingly. On November 4, the electorate spoke and the dreams of Republicans were dashed to bits in a Democrat wave that washed over the entire country, except for two states.

"As goes Maine, so goes Vermont!" jeered the Democrats, tallying the electoral vote in the largest ballot ever for a presidential election. Beaten into the ground, the GOP shook its head and staggered home. Conspicuous in his loneliness, Massachusetts Republican Henry Cabot Lodge was elected to the Senate.

So smashing was the defeat that a man like William Randolph Hearst could say, "Perhaps Roosevelt has given essential democracy a new lease on life." Gloating Jim Farley was in a magnanimous mood, allowing that, "No individual and no corporation on the level with the people need fear Mr. Roosevelt's second term. There is no thought of reprisal."

Father Coughlin, apologizing as profusely for epithets like "scab" and "liar" as he had been vehement in his use of them against Roosevelt, announced that he was quitting the radio. Mencken seemed whipped.

Right after election payroll deductions began coming out of wages, but there was no tattooing or even dog tags—only a harmless-looking card and a 1 percent bite out of the check. The New Deal, and a new way of life, were definitely in and everyone knew it. Franklin Delano Roosevelt, still a cripple in a wheelchair, was the strongest man in the United States.

In November he journeyed aboard a warship, the *Indianapolis,* to South America and demonstrated his popularity there. In Rio de Janeiro, he was greeted and hailed by 300,000 Brazilians, and in Buenos Aires half a million Argentinans repeated the gesture. Speaking at the opening of the Inter-American Conference for the Maintenance of Peace, Roosevelt prophetically advised a shoulder-to-shoulder attitude for mutual benefit in case of aggression coming from the Old World. Only the death of Roosevelt bodyguard, August Gennerich, of a heart attack in Buenos Aires, and a vocal outburst against the President by an extremist at the Conference marred the goodwill trip.

Roosevelt steamed back home toward the end of the year, bracing himself the best he could for the trials that 1937 would bring. It had been a big year, a year that made it possible for bigger ones that FDR would dominate.

BIBLIOGRAPHY

The Politics of Upheaval—Schlesinger
The New Age of Franklin Roosevelt—Perkins
The Secret Diary of Harold L. Ickes
Watching the World—Clapper
The Future Comes—Beard
The New Deal and World Affairs—Nevins
A New Deal for Youth—Lindley

II

John L. Lewis

Early in 1936, police in Washington, D.C., cracked down on traffic violators. Among those bagged was a scowling, craggy-eyebrowed labor leader named John Llewellyn Lewis. For doing 42 miles an hour in a 30-mile zone, Lewis paid a $10 fine and blew out of town. It would take more than a safe-driving campaign to curb this massive Shakespearean voice of the working man, for John L. Lewis, tagged by one writer as a "miner prophet," would roar across this election year like an avenging angel.

"No backward step!" was his motto, and he had started to move forward with a momentum that had been long in the coming but now could not be stopped. Here was a man who could ask in apparent wonderment, "What makes me tick?" Whatever it was, the 230-pound package was about to explode.

Unless you mined coal or were a student of the U.S. labor movement, Lewis seemed to have burst upon the scene full-blown. Actually he was a 56-year-old veteran who for seventeen years had bossed the United Mine Workers, biggest of the many AFL unions.

In addition, he was vice president of the AFL itself and already beginning to rip that august body apart at its staid 50-year-old seams. For Lewis was father and midwife to something called the Committee for Industrial Organization.

Born in Lucas, Iowa, on Lincoln's birthday in 1880, Lewis was the first child of Thomas and Louisa Lewis. The elder Lewis had come from the coal mines of Wales five years earlier. Active in the pioneering Knights of Labor, Tom got himself blacklisted when John L. was just two years old.

For fifteen years the family moved from one town to another until finally the elder Lewis was able to return to Lucas and enter the mines again. Joining him were John L. and brother Tom. After nine years of mining, including the

33

sickening task of helping dig out the bodies of 220 miners caught in the Hannah, Wyoming, explosion, John L. forsook his pick for a variety of jobs that included managing an opera house and finally led to labor leading.

In 1906 he was Lucas' delegate to the United Mine Workers convention and his destiny was beginning to be shaped. A year later he married schoolteacher Myrta Bell and with her help began to build on the grade school education that was all he had acquired. Foreswearing drinking and poker, he devoted his nights to study.

The family went from Lucas to Panama, Illinois, and on to Springfield. His reading of Shakespeare and the other great poets was beginning to rub off and John L's spellbinding oratory as a lobbyist in Springfield attracted attention to the fledging. Under the wing of the great Sam Gompers, Lewis became an organizer. As early as 1913 he made an abortive attempt to capture the steel industry.

There were other failures, as well. Too early, young Lewis challenged his boss and benefactor for leadership of the organization Gompers had founded in 1886. Gompers beat him two to one, but in 1924 Lewis laughed last as he helped move William Green in as president.

Within the UMW Lewis was far more successful. With loud and pompous oratory, brash skill and ruthless coups, he moved up the ladder until only President Frank Hayes stood above him. Like Lewis, Hayes admired poetry. Unlike him, he was a tippler. The communist William Z. Foster accused Lewis of calculatingly letting Hayes drink himself right out of office so that John L. could move in. In return Lewis cried "Communist!" at Foster and any others who challenged him, using the epithet indiscriminately and effectively. In 1919, not yet forty years old, John L. Lewis took command of a union half a million strong.

Off to an awkward start when his strike was outlawed by President Wilson's reminder that the war was still on, "I will not fight my government, the greatest government on earth," Lewis swore solemnly, on December 7, 1919. On another December 7, twenty-two years later he would face a similar big decision.

His troubles continued for the next twelve years and it took a hand of iron plus the glossing over of most democratic principles to remain head of the UMW. "No backward step!" he had sworn, but union membership plummeted in the twenties. Besides the government and the operators he had to fight enemies within the union. "Lewis must go!" was their battle cry, and in 1924 he almost went.

In the years from 1920 to 1932 John L. Lewis was a faithful Republican. He plugged for safe-and-sane "business unionism" and considered Herbert Hoover a statesman of the highest caliber. A one-time statistician, Lewis had had to dig deep in a literature rivaled in extent "only by that of the German war guilt" and he amassed the knowledge to write a book, *The Miners' Fight for American Standards*. In it he advocated the free play of natural economic laws in the production and distribution of coal, a thesis that left him wide-open to attack by many unionists and made him cry fervently, "Would that mine enemy had written a book!"

In 1932 Lewis was getting a salary of $12,000 a year. He was one of the most hated men in labor and had seen his membership drop to a pitiful 20 percent of what it had been when he took over. And in 1932 he voted for Hoover. If his man had won John L. Lewis might have been finished as a labor leader. Instead, his future was assured with the election of the candidate Lewis refused even to visit along with other UMW leaders prior to the Democratic victory in 1932.

Part of the New Deal that swept in with Franklin Delano Roosevelt was the National Industrial Recovery Act. Like a man grabbing at a last straw, Lewis seized on Section 7-A of NRA, the part that gave workers the right to select a union of their choice.

With the literally last dollars of the UMW treasury, Lewis descended on the coal fields with Section 7-A in one hand, a UMW button in the other and the shouted slogan, "President Roosevelt *wants* you to join the union!" on his lips.

The slogan became a cant, and miners even sang it:

> In nineteen hundred and thirty-three
> When Mr. Roosevelt took his seat,
> He said to President John L. Lewis,
> In *union* we must be!

By 1934 this windfall blown Lewis' way by the New Deal gale had packed the UMW with a membership of more than 400,000. Lewis enlisted the aid of Senator Joe Guffey of Pennsylvania with a "little NRA" for coal. The miners got raises, and so did their boss.

John L. was making $25,000 a year by 1936 and he was a power to reckon with. He was as American as "a flung pop bottle at the ball game," and only a little less popular than Joe Louis or Shirley Temple. In fact, he was being touted now as the Jack Dempsey of labor, a fabled John the Giant Killer.

With Mrs. Lewis and the two children, Kathryn and John L., Jr., Lewis lived in fashionable Alexandria in an authentic colonial house that George Washington's physician had built. He rode in a Cadillac V-12, and his chauffeur was clad in whipcord. Though he might display a miner's pick in his home, it was twenty-five years since he had swung it and now he dined with the top people.

True, some of the old-time socialites like Mrs. Fleming Holland in Alexandria did not accept him. That haughty lady had even refused to sit at the captain's table on an ocean liner because Lewis was there. But in Washington John L. was a sought-after dinner guest.

In 1936 the coal miner who had once killed a dangerous mule named Spanish Pete with a spike blow to the head and later fought off five steel company toughs in Aliquippa, Pennsylvania, achieved the distinction of having his picture on the cover of *Time* magazine and causing more than one subscriber to cancel his subscription.

Anonymous leaflets accused Lewis of being a red, and at the same time John Frey of the AFL was reminded of Mussolini. Lewis himself admitted he was being helped by the Communists because it was "a good rule to work with anyone who will work with you." His hair had turned from red to a kind or iron-rust color, and only the eyebrows still flamed. But the voice was more colorful than ever. Still pompous and even bizarre at times, it had the volume and range of a full orchestra and lyrics that spanned from alley to Bible.

A lesser man's cup would have been running over, but Lewis was only beginning to fight. He still saw labor in the pathetic role of "Rachel crying in the wilderness" and determined to do something about it. He had already flung down the gauntlet to the AFL, the organization that had nurtured him.

In 1936 Lewis had more than half a million followers, and more than two million dollars in his treasury. He wasn't satisfied, but he wanted to be fair about it. Like the Texas rancher, he didn't want *all* the land, only what bordered his. Starting with his UMW, the new CIO had captured seven more unions: the International Typographical Union, the Amalgamated Clothing Workers, the International Ladies' Garment Workers, the United Textile Workers, the Oil Field, Gas Well and Refinery Workers, the United Hatters, Cap and Millinery Workers, and the International Union of Mine, Mill and Smelter Workers.

This seeming motley crew was a revolutionary idea in unionism. Samuel Gompers had created the "craft" union in his AFL, and his successors had preserved this form. Members of the AFL were skilled craftsmen, a snobbish clique who looked down their noses at the unskilled worker.

Dan Tobin, boss of the Teamsters had a descriptive name for these lesser beings; he called them "rubbish." The craft idea of grouping all men of a particular trade resulted in "horizontal" unionism, with as many as twenty-five different unions represented in a business like the auto industry. Lewis had dreamed a fantastic dream of "vertical" unionism to replace this unwieldy arrangement. Instead of twenty-five craft unions, he would substitute *one* huge industrial union!

Already claiming that 40 percent of labor was back of him, Lewis grandiosely envisioned as many as forty million members for industrial unions, and he saw their leader each time he studied his mirror.

Understandably, William Green and his cohorts were appalled. In January of 1936 the Executive Council of the AFL sat in Miami and ordered Lewis to dissolve his ridiculous Committee for Industrial Organization. As one writer saw it, acceptance by the parent AFL of Lewis' CIO would have been tantamount to Bishop Manning of the Cathedral of St. John the Divine hocking the church and starting to convert the heathen of the Orient!

From Washington's Constitution Hall, Lewis curled his lip and thundered that members of the Executive Council would all be wearing asbestos suits in hell before he agreed to abandon the CIO. Instead, his loyal delegates voted to withhold $48,000 in annual taxes due the parent organization and to initiate an aggressive radio campaign to push the CIO. To further demonstrate their scorn for William Green, the feisty new organization threatened to boot Green out of his position in the UMW, a move that would technically bar him from the presidency of the AFL.

Green appeared before the CIO to plead his case and urge them to abandon their folly. Under the Lewis spell, the delegates roundly booed mild Mr. Green. Lewis himself silenced this thunderous reaffirmation to expel Green. Later the delegates considered but did not pass a resolution to seek legislation to do away with the Supreme Court because of its curtailment of the New Deal.

Another speaker at the upstart convention was Edward Francis McGrady, Assistant Secretary of Labor. Once chief lobbyist for the AFL, McGrady asked the CIO if it stood with the President of the United States. Over the answering affirmative roar McGrady shouted, "Let that be the answer to the moneybags of Wall Street!"

Another New Deal cabinet member, Assistant Secretary of the Treasury Josephine Roche, addressed the gathering and was applauded. A Colorado mine owner, she had been first to bargain with the UMW.

Senator Joe Guffey rose to promise that if his coal bill was declared unconstitutional he would fight to the finish. He must have seen the handwriting on the wall—the Guffey bill was outlawed in May. At the end of the convention, the CIO pledged itself to go "forward with Roosevelt, fighting under his banner for re-election." To prove this was not mere talk, they also agreed to dip into the union war chest to support the program.

Such politicking was heresy to the traditionally nonpartisan AFL, and William Green made a strong appeal to the union not to follow Lewis' lead. It was a vain plea. Labor was already running hotter for Roosevelt in 1936 than it had for La Follette in 1924. Already Lewis, Sidney Hillman of the Amalgamated Clothing Workers, and George Berry of the Printing Pressmen's Union and official custodian of what was left of the NRA, were forming the "Non-Partisan League" to work for Roosevelt. A major aim of this group was to try to woo over the New Deal's Jim Farley so that he would not appoint Dan Tobin as the AFL official Democratic vote-getter.

Following the lead of the Non-Partisan League, other unions left previous affiliations and plumped for Roosevelt, too. David Dubinsky of the Ladies' Garment Workers and Emil Rieve of the Hosiery Workers renounced socialism to move into the New Deal camp, decrying the "black reaction" that would grip the country if FDR was not returned to the White House in November.

Lewis had done an about-face from Republicanism. As he had already said, it was well to work with those who would work with you. Roosevelt had shown that he would work with labor, and Lewis now moved to the White House where he helped write the labor plank in the Democratic platform.

The man who had vowed to create industrial unionism had seen the writing on the wall. He needed the New Deal, and he was willing to pay for it. Assessing his membership, he came up with a sizable campaign fund. Like a shrewd card player, he anted up a check for $250,000. Roosevelt was no amateur either, and he declined the offer saying he would call on Lewis as he needed him. By the time his needs were totaled, the CIO had plunked down about $500,-000 instead of the original offer.

As the internecine warfare went on, Lewis countered the continuing threats from AFL brass with bold moves that drove mild William Green to near-frustration. To a repeated order to disband the CIO, Lewis flaunted his strength by offering to put up $500,000 toward organizing the steel industry, if the AFL would put up one million dollars. It was as if a man caught swiping pennies had responded to a warning by planning to rob the biggest bank in town.

For years steel had adjoined the miners' territory, a juicy plum for the plucking by those brave enough to try. But the AFL craftsmen weren't interested. They had talked of it for years, as Lewis now accused them, but had done nothing.

Even the steel workers seemed uninterested. The Amalgamated Association of Iron, Steel and Tin Workers was an elite of some 7,000 skilled craftsmen whose leader, Michael Francis Tighe, shunned the "rubbish" as did Dan Tobin. NRA had dropped more than a hundred thousand converts into Amalgamated's lap, and Tighe hadn't rested easy until he forced them out. Now, at 78, he was a staunch friend of William Green and deplored the industrial unionism of Lewis.

But while the AFL and Tighe pretended not to hear the brash offer of Lewis, many other Amalgamated members did. At their convention at Canonsburg, led by Secretary Treasurer Shorty Leonard, they voted to go industrial though primly refusing the cash offer for the time.

A negotiating committee, hesitant about stirring up trouble in the AFL, went first to William Green. But he had neither money nor compromise for them and cautiously they sent a feeler to the CIO asking for a conference. With characteristic boldness, Lewis told them flatly not to waste their time or his. If they were ready to deal, fine; if not, forget it. Three days later Tighe's lieutenants came to Lewis, caps in hand, to sign up with CIO and to get their $500,000.

Stunned, the AFL watched the man they were threatening to expel succeed where they had never been able to. Disclaiming interest in organizing unskilled workers, Green said the AFL would watch and see what would result from this brash move on the part of the outlawed CIO. Lewis sarcastically replied that he could not conceive of his old friend watching with the women from the safety of a tent on the hillside while labor did battle in the valley below.

"They are planning to scuttle your ship and cut your throat," he warned the AFL president, advising him to join the CIO forthwith and take a place of honor at its council table.

Instead, Green persisted in his threat to oust the CIO for good and all, despite the fact that since the Lewis camp now had more than a third of the membership it thus could not be voted out by a two-thirds majority.

While the AFL Executive Council stewed, Lewis moved forcefully ahead in the campaign against steel. Shortly after he made known his intentions regarding the industry, Rexford Tugwell, late of the New Deal, counseled with him. As a result, Lee Pressman, who had also been purged from the administration, joined the steel organizing committee. At Tugwell's request, the UMW arranged the freeing of jailed Memphis sharecroppers.

Clinton Golden, late of the National Labor Relations Board, also joined the committee, along with Socialists Julius Hochman and Leo Krzycki, Mike Tighe's lieutenants Joseph Gaither and Thomas Gillis, and others. Heading up the push was UMW Secretary-Treasurer Philip Murray.

It was a formidable undertaking the CIO had embarked upon, and no one was more aware of that than Lewis himself. He could still remember his own futile attempt to crack steel in 1913, and the similar failure of Foster, the Communist, in 1919.

The symbol for the new war on steel would be the abortive Homestead Strike of 1892, when Carnegie Steel's Henry Clay Frick had called in the Pinkerton men to stand off strikers when the plant was shut down to make a wage cut stick. In a day-long battle, triggered by the union, seven strikers and three detectives were slain in the bloody Homestead massacre.

Now wreaths were placed on the graves of the strikers who had died, and Pennsylvania's Lieutenant Governor Thomas Kennedy, who was also International Secretary-Treasurer of the UMW, orated at length and promised the aid of Governor Earle.

The industry got the message, and the American Iron and Steel Institute took out full-page ads in 400 newspapers across the country to state its case. Secretary of Labor Frances Perkins reminded steel that this was not a strike, and hoped "iron and steel do not do anything foolish and against the public interest." Lewis professed peace, but warned that inasmuch as history proved to him that steel always fought the unions he was ready to return their fire.

Taking to the air with free time given by NBC, Lewis said he was taking up the cudgel for no less than forty million American workers and in ringing tones challenged those who would halt him. NBC was a subsidiary of Radio Corporation of America, at that moment fighting a strike of United Electrical and Radio Workers backed and partly financed by Lewis himself!

While Phil Murray carried the fight to steel, Lewis fought with Green and the craft AFL unions. It was time for the Executive Council to meet in Washington and the fearful watched for the dreaded open break in the powerful union.

Lewis and Green sat across the aisle from each other and wrangled while the New Deal sweated it out. Both factions made trips to the White House to seek favor, but wisely Roosevelt played both sides and Secretary McGrady fought to stave off calamity until the election day on November 3.

Lewis had been permitted to write the labor plank, but Tobin had been made the official AFL vote-getter. Delicately the administration tightrope-walked the issue to preserve labor's vote as a bloc. It looked like a vain hope when in August the AFL suspended the CIO in a shrewd move that would prevent it from voting and thus permit an ouster by the remaining members.

One of the leaders in the fight to throw out the CIO was William L. Hutcheson, boss of the carpenters' union. He had earlier made the mistake of calling Lewis a big bastard when Lewis goaded him about being small potatoes, and Lewis had clobbered him with a huge fist. Now Hutcheson

41

threatened to pull his carpenters out of the AFL unless it divested itself of the Lewis industrial taint. Disband in thirty days, the suspension said, or get out for good.

Watching the proceedings from across the street in a neighboring building, Lewis snorted that the suspension was a farce, and in reprisal said again that he would sack Green. Rumor had it that the bartenders' union would offer Green a job, and then he announced that he was an honorary member of James C. Petrillo's musicians' union.

"Just like Green," Lewis shouted, "to fiddle while Rome burns!"

The AFL was split wide down the middle now, and at Tampa even the posters advertising the convention were the victims of a prankster. The symbolically clasped hands that were part of the design were printed instead as clenched fists angrily shaking at one another.

Now, with maritime strikes paralyzing the West Coast, the New Deal was caught between the devil and the deep blue sea. Secretary Perkins could not dive into the fracas for two reasons: she was a woman, and she was also considered an outsider by labor. So Assistant McGrady was forced to jump into the breach in California at the very time he was needed to make peace within the AFL at Tampa.

Peace-loving William Green was a man being torn apart as the AFL sniped at the rival CIO. The convention asserted itself as against Communism, Fascism and Nazism, while accusing Lewis and his members of harboring Communists. It protested the firing of a left-leaning professor from Yale, but failed to express official sympathy for the embattled workers in Spain's civil war. It did not act on a bill to boycott the Hearst papers. It favored the thirty-hour week but wasn't for a Labor Party. And finally, after all the shouting was over, it had done nothing about the rift within itself. In fact, it voted to do nothing at this time.

William Green lifted the quarrel to the heights of heaven and said, "Dual movement began in heaven when Michael the Archangel rebelled against God. The Executive Council did not hesitate to act—it expelled his Satanic majesty and his dual movement from heaven."

Lewis had been called Satan before, and he permitted himself a Mephisthophelean sneer and denounced the Tampa convention as a "sitdown strike against labor," in his *Union News.*

42

There were other sitdowns to be reported around the country in the lay press, and Lewis was getting the credit for the technique whether he could actually lay claim to its origin or not. In his own defense he pointed out a precedent in the sitdown of slaves building the Cheops pyramid in 3700 B.C.!

At the Bendix plant in South Bend, Indiana, 1,100 workers sat it out for a week. In Detroit, 1,200 Midland Steel Products workers sat down on the job. Goodyear Tire and Rubber workers struck and won out for the CIO.

On land and sea union members slowed down, sat down or walked off. On the East Coast, Joe Curran led the strikers, and Harry Bridges did the job out West. In sympathy around the world, dock workers in Le Havre, France, refused to unload the U.S. Line's *S. S. Washington*. In Hawaii Anna May Wong and other travelers were forced to ride a pineapple barge from the harbor out onto the open sea to board a liner. Taxi drivers in Ensenada, Mexico, refused to drive passengers from the Grace Line landed there instead of in California. To add to the confusion, Lloyd's of London quadrupled insurance rates on all shipping plying U.S. coastal waters.

The AFL branded the strike of 20,000 maritime workers unlawful, then 1,000 of its National Organization of Masters, Mates and Pilots and Marine Engineers Beneficial Association embarrassingly joined the wildcatters. Hollywood postponed the filming of four maritime films, and California authorities panicked over the San Francisco strike and wanted Roosevelt to come steaming into the Golden Gate aboard a warship and restore order.

1936 was as confused an election year as there ever was. With the sharp break between the CIO and AFL, Republicans gleefully proclaimed, "A vote for Roosevelt is a vote for Lewis!" For his part Lewis announced that Landon, the little man from Kansas, knew just about as much as a Bulgarian goat herder as to what was wrong with the country.

He was for Roosevelt, all right, but by now the Non-Partisan League was actually considering the formation of a third party for the 1940 elections. That way the unions would not have to depend on the whim or vagary of candidates, but could trust one of its own. The candidate? Most eyes went to none other than John L. Lewis himself, and the labor leader raised no noticed objection to this tribute.

Down to the wire Lewis was confident that he had backed

43

the right man. Landslide election results proved him correct; the money his membership had contributed was well spent and the union felt it could count on continued help from Washington. It was an accomplishment to rank with his victory over the AFL.

There was no pause after the November victory for self-congratulations. The job went on. Business was down on one knee, and labor delivered it a kick *de grâce* in the form of a demand that employers pay *all* of the new Social Security tax deduction that would shortly be coming out of pay envelopes.

Phil Murray's organizing campaign against steel was paying off. Already he had signed up more than 125,000 of the 500,000 steelworkers, and gotten Carnegie Illinois Steel Corporation hailed into the National Labor Relations Board on charges of interfering with labor's right to organize.

A full-scale strike against General Motors was a threat, and already 2,400 Fisher Body and Chevrolet workers had staged a sitdown in Kansas City. When National Automotive Fibers in Detroit dismissed men who joined the United Auto Workers–CIO, 1,500 members promptly struck and got the men reinstated, plus a small raise.

Not only in steel, but everywhere the CIO went, it was meeting with success. The sitdown progressed to a "liedown" at Berkshire Knitting Mills in Reading, Pennsylvania, with more than fifty men and women arrested for blocking the sidewalk. The John B. Stetson hat plant in Philadelphia was forced to close when CIO'ers demanded a 25 percent raise and better conditions.

Labor had made many gains in the past twelve months, even though the fate of the Wagner Act hung in the balance. During the year President Roosevelt had signed into law the impressive total of twenty-three bills, and there was also a Senate resolution introduced by Senator La Follette providing for investigation of violations of labor's rights. Such evidence of a favorable government, coupled with the smashing success of bargaining and strikes, presaged an even greater effort for the coming year.

John L. Lewis could look back over a long perilous road he had negotiated during 1936. He was the power to reckon with in labor now, and he had the receipts to show that he had helped elect a president. At year's end he assessed his members to build a million-dollar war chest for the struggle ahead.

The once-parent AFL continued its threats and bluster, but it was mostly talk now. William Green seemed almost impotent. Lewis had not simply taken his place as labor's voice; he had made a new place, an important place commensurate with his bulking physical size and stentorian voice. There was only one man in the country who towered higher, and there were some who rated John L. Lewis right alongside his President. Whether or not Lewis knew what made himself tick, he was surely right on schedule and maybe a bit ahead.

BIBLIOGRAPHY

Labor Baron, a Portrait of John L. Lewis—Wechsler
John L. Lewis, an Unauthorized Biography—Alinsky

III

The Lindberghs

Nine years earlier, Charles Augustus Lindbergh's flight from New York had brought America to its feet cheering wildly. Now, in 1936, another Lindbergh flight had plunged the country into despair. With his wife and second child, the Lone Eagle had fled to the safety of England. He greeted the New Year in sad silence from an ancestral home in Wales.

Why had the Lindberghs fled? According to Walter Lippmann, yellow journalism's tyranny was the reason:

> It is no use to deplore the departure of the Lindberghs and then to turn to some keyhole columnist to find out the details of someone else's private life. Genuine respect for human privacy does not exist among us today. What with those who wish to be in the limelight at any cost, those who are afraid to stand up for their rights, and those who have an infantile curiosity to learn the inside story of the inside story of the facts of life, there has gone out of the public taste the capacity to realize and to resent the treatment of personal lives as a spectacle for the mob.

Columnist Walter Winchell, who had correctly predicted the birth of Charles A. Lindbergh, Jr., four months in advance, now publicly professed his shame in being an American. It was a shame shared by many others. U.S. lawlessness and the inability of the country to do anything about it were driving the Number One hero from his native land to seek safety abroad. Most papers proclaimed it a national disgrace and legislators stormed for new laws against kidnaping.

In Paris the newspaper *Le Jour* said that American law had proved insufficient protection against gangsters. The German press professed itself unable to conceive of such a thing happening in a civilized nation, and Madrid's *Sol*

46

said, "Nowhere have police and judicial organizations given more manifest proof of impotence."

There were also those who condemned the Lindberghs for "peculiarities" and "ridiculous actions." The Lone Eagle was called a quitter, and even Kansas City's City Manager Henry McElroy called him a coward. McElroy's own daughter had been kidnaped and *he* had stayed.

Other well-known figures before the Lindberghs had fled to England when threatened by kidnapers, however. Among these were auto manufacturers Errett Cord and Horace Dodge. The Lindberghs and the Morrows had held a serious council of war before making the decision. Their grief was not over with the death of their firstborn; constant threats, insane and otherwise, poured in to harass them. Young Jon Lindbergh might be the next victim. Someday one of the tens of thousand who scrawled demands for money might take overt action.

The "yellow journalism" that Lippmann and others deplored was no help. One day as Jon's teacher was driving him to school, curtains in a parked truck near the grounds dropped to reveal ominous steel tubes pointing at the baby. Run down by state police, the truck turned out to be loaded with movie cameras and newsmen.

Later, a speeding car forced the teacher off the road and men jumped out to race toward the baby. Mercifully it was again cameras they pointed at the frightened boy, but his picture was plastered across front pages to positively identify him for any would-be kidnapers. Despairing, the Lindberghs were forced to take Jon out of school.

So it was that just before Christmas, 1935, three unnamed passengers boarded the freighter *S.S. American Importer*. Even the ship's officers did not know in advance who their famous passengers were. With secretly arranged six-month immigration permits, Lindbergh paid a one-way fare of $293 for two adults, one child. Holed up in the cabin, they tensely waited departure.

When sailing time came and the ship remained tied up, the Lindberghs knew another agony of suspense. Checking, Lindbergh found that a strike of radiomen was threatened and they might be unable to leave. Then, just before three in the morning, the ship sailed out of the harbor in much the same direction Lindy had taken back in 1927 in a smaller craft called *The Spirit of St. Louis*.

The story of the flight broke Monday morning in the

47

New York Times. Of all the newspapers, only this one was so favored. Reporter Lauren (Deac) Lyman had befriended Colonel Lindbergh years before, and his and the *Times'* courteous treatment of Lindy were rewarded now. Lyman would get a Pulitizer prize for his smashing exclusive story.

Wires sent to the *S.S. American Importer* were returned marked *"Addressee Not Aboard."* While the freighter steamed toward the east, the three Lindberghs decorated a tiny tree thoughtfully put aboard for them. The protests and lamentations increased in the U.S. The death of young Charles had been called second in horror only to the crucifixion by Dr. "Jafsie" Condon, and now the press dredged up another Biblical reference in comparison to the new move by the Lindberghs.

And when they were departed, behold, the angel of the Lord appeareth to Joseph in a dream, saying, Arise and take the young child and his mother, and flee into Egypt, and be thou there until I bring thee word: for Herod will seek the young child to destroy him. When he arose, he took the young child and his mother by night, and departed into Egypt.

St. Matthew 2:13-14

"Egypt," unfortunately, knew of the Lindberghs' coming. London's *Sunday Observer* noted warningly: "It is worth remembering that when it comes to sensation-mongering more than one newspaper in Fleet Street can hold its own with any in the world." And the staid London *Times* did its bit by featuring a two-column photo of Jon Lindbergh on the front page of its Sunday edition. Cynics said Lindbergh should tell the British he was coming to collect the war debt and thus gain all the privacy he wanted.

The freighter was to dock at Liverpool, and the largest assemblage of reporters ever gathered there was on hand to greet the privacy-seeking family. Upwards of a hundred British newsmen converged on the Gladstone dock, bolstered by others from the continent. Among them was a woman photographer from Paris and reporters from Sweden. To guard against the wily prey tricking them, reporters had also covered Cork and Queenstown, Cobh, Belfast and Glasgow. They manned tugs and speedboats, and even racing automobiles and airplanes.

According to the *News Chronicle,* Lindbergh could have spared his family much of its tribulations. This London paper's lead story for December 31 read as follows:

> Colonel Lindbergh himself is so celebrated a person, and the flight of his family from America has been so sensational, that it was idle to suppose that his arrival in this country could fail to excite the curiosity both of the public and the Press. It is not an illegitimate curiosity. A public figure cannot claim that his movements and his intentions are of no concern to anybody but himself; and when they are of so dramatic a character as to set two continents talking, it is idle to expect the Press of the world not to seek to chronicle the development of the drama.
>
> If Colonel Lindbergh is wise, he will satisfy at once by a frank and full statement the public desire to know his immediate intentions. Mystification will merely serve to sharpen curiosity. Not nearly so much attention would have been attracted to his arrival had it been less shrouded in a mystery which has excited instead of allaying the general curiosity. That done, Colonel Lindbergh may rely upon it that he is very unlikely in this country to be pestered with a publicity which he does not desire.
>
> Responsible English opinion, in common with responsible opinion all over the world, sympathizes warmly with him in the horrible persecution to which he and his family have been so long exposed. He will suffer no such molestation here. In a week or two he may be sure of all the privacy he can desire; but the best way to assure this is to avoid the appearance of shrouding the whole affair with an air of mystery.

Lindbergh, of course, could not have changed his nature if he had wanted to. Stolidly and silently braving the clamor of questions, he strode down the gangplank bareheaded in the rain and carrying the son they sought to protect. Flash bulbs popped and Jon hid his head on his father's shoulder. Anne Lindbergh smiled wanly as the trio reached the safety of a taxi and were driven to the Adelphi Hotel.

Aubrey Morgan had sailed ahead of the Lindberghs aboard the faster *Westernland* and was making arrangements for a place for the Lindberghs to stay. He was Anne's brother-in-law, and his father's home was in Landaff, near Cardiff, Wales.

Meantime, the trio remained in the seclusion of a three-room suite at the Adelphi, guarded by a detective and un-

seen even by the waiter who brought their meals into the
living room while they kept out of sight in a bedroom.

On the fourth day, the Lindberghs bundled Jon up and
slipped out a servants' entrance to the hotel and into a waiting car. Aubrey Morgan had come to take them to Landaff.
They arrived after dark, and the only figures about were
constables, some afoot and others patrolling on bicycles. Inside the big house the Christmas tree still stood, to little
Jon's delight. For the first time in two weeks, his parents
could sigh in relief.

The reception in England must have chilled the Lindberghs more than the damp winter weather. The *News
Chronicle* ultimatum was more or less echoed by other papers, and while the *Daily Mirror* published an editorial titled
"Leave Them Alone," its front pages pried and poked at
the newcomers. But slowly the privacy they had sought returned.

The New York *Herald Tribune* editorialized as follows:

> The Lindberghs can live with some freedom in England not
> only because there has been . . . no recorded case there in
> recent times of a kidnaping for ransom, but even more, be-
> cause of the adult public sense of good taste, restraint and
> respect for individual rights and privacies which underlies the
> British freedom from crime. Now that Americans have driven
> one of their leading men to flee in secrecy from a life which
> they made intolerable for him, they would do well to meditate
> upon the value of those virtues.

Despite the *News Chronicle's* bold affirmation that a public
figure could expect no private life, its readers disagreed
loudly. One reader stated, "Your news columns pander to
the instincts of those who would make this country like
America." Another asked, "Could not, then, our national
newspapers agree to refrain from publishing any news of
their whereabouts or their plans?" No writers agreed
with the paper's thesis, and a rival paper, the *Manchester
Guardian,* hoped that the "quarry escape to enjoy in
complete quiet the hospitality of the country." It went
even further:

> But if the hunt goes on, it may be pertinent to inquire
> whether this is not a wrong for which the law provides a
> remedy. The definitions the courts have upheld of what is

50

"annoyance" or "nuisance" included many things more trifling than persistent and unwanted press attention.

By the time the Lindberghs left the Adelphi Hotel, only U.S. newsmen remained. At Landaff, finally, they began to enjoy the "peace and rest" given as their object in taking out passports for the trip to England.

Back in America the unfinished business of Bruno Richard Hauptmann, convicted kidnapper of the Lindberghs' first child, continued. For a variety of reasons Governor Hoffman had granted a thirty-day stay of execution. Hauptmann continued to protest his innocence. There was the usual flood of phony confessions from crackpots in various parts of the country. The "Committee of Witnesses," which had claimed all along to have complete evidence that the killing was an international plot against Lindy, clamored louder for action. According to them, German and Japanese interests, angry at Lindbergh for beating them out in China with airline plans, had hired Hauptmann and his partner Fisch for revenge. There was even a cryptographic symbol incorporating the Luft-Hansa aircraft symbol and the rising sun of Japan.

Other theorists thought the Russians were striking at Ambassador Dwight Morrow, Anne Lindbergh's father, for his frustration of Communist aims in Mexico. As evidence, they pointed out that one man mentioned in connection with the case was called "Red" not because of the color of his hair but because he was a member of a Communist maritime union. No lesser commentator then H. L. Mencken agreed with Governor Hoffman's delaying tactics, since "it is impossible to imagine him [Hauptmann] committing the crime alone."

Thousands of miles away the Lindberghs waited. Lindy visited Parliament, sitting in the Distinguished Visitors Gallery while members debated whether or not the divulging of shocking evidence in murder cases was adequately restricted by the Act of 1926.

It was comforting to know that England had no record of a kidnaping for ransom in recent years, the closest thing to it being the occasional stealing of a child by a band of raggle-taggle gypsies with no thought of harm or extortion in mind.

In March, Phoebe Elsie Whately died of cancer. Only 51,

51

Mrs. Whately had been the Lindberghs' cook in those terrible days when Charles, Jr., had been kidnaped.

When the Lindberghs visited the House of Commons they had been the guests of Lloyd George and Harold Nicolson, author and Member of Parliament. Nicolson and his wife, novelist Victoria Sackville-West, lived in Sissinghurst Castle, and Nicolson had an idea that the Lindberghs just might like another place he owned in the village of Weald in Kent.

Called "Long Barn," the house was some thirty miles from London and would offer complete seclusion to the visitors. There was room for a laboratory for Lindbergh to pursue his scientific work, and Anne would have privacy for writing her new book. Fittingly, the ghost of the famous printer Caxton was said to return nightly and run a hand press in the room next to Jon's nursery; such stimulation should benefit a talented writer. In March the Lindberghs moved into Long Barn, having leased it from Nicolson.

This flight to safety was no passive retirement. In his work with the famous Dr. Alexis Carrel, who had kept a chicken heart alive for a score of years, Lindbergh had begun to develop a mechanical kidney. This apparatus was needed to flush away wastes from living organs growing in Carrel's "perfusion pump." The flier's mechanical inventiveness had carried over from airplanes into other technical fields as well. An example was a navigational watch he had invented. But such a device was child's play compared with the tasks Carrel set him and Lindbergh plunged all his energies into the new problems in his laboratory at Long Barn.

Young Jon had the run of the estate, and enjoyed swinging from a tree in the garden or helping his mother with miniature digging tools he'd been given. Except for their painful memories, the time in Weald would have been idyllic for the young family.

Back in New Jersey, work went feverishly on to wring the truth from the German carpenter who still professed his innocence. The brilliant criminal lawyer Sam Leibowitz, who had gained fame in the Scottsboro Negro trials, was called in to try to crack the case. The money to pay him came from Mrs. Evalyn Walsh McLean, socialite swindled by Gaston Means in the Lindbergh kidnaping aftermath.

But even the skill and perseverance of Liebowitz could

not prevail. Hauptmann was adamant, and in the end there was no recourse but to carry out the death sentence. The Paul Wendel confession was repudiated when it was proved that *he* had been kidnaped by five men and tortured until he signed the statement! Now the kidnapers were being prosecuted. The Court of Pardons refused further petitions for clemency for Hauptmann.

At 8:44, Robert Elliott, the official executioner, threw the switch that jolted Hauptmann with 2,000 volts of electricity. Twice the procedure was repeated. At 8:47½, prison doctor Howard Wiesler put his stethoscope to the prisoner's chest and pronounced him dead. The news was cabled to England, but in accounts in the papers there no comment from the Lindberghs was mentioned. None had been solicited. The privacy that even the *News Chronicle* had predicted had come to the Lone Eagle and his family.

The world's most famous flier had not been in a plane once since coming to England for safety. Now, in April, he went to the Air Ministry in London to have his license renewed.

"My name is Lindbergh," he explained to the clerks there. "I am sorry to trouble you and hope it will not cause any difficulty."

There was the slight difficulty that more than thirty days had elapsed since Lindbergh had flown. He offered to contact Washington for his American flight records, but the Air Ministry decided that would not be necessary. Considering the flight he had made across the ocean nine years ago, and others since then, it was willing to take a chance on him and authorize him to fly private aircraft anywhere in Great Britain. The Lone Eagle had wings again.

The Lindberghs were beginning to be mentioned in the British press once more, but now the news was truly legitimate. A few weeks from the time they had landed in Liverpool, Edward VIII came to the throne after the death of King George. Lindbergh had known the new king in the days when Edward was Prince of Wales, and it was natural that the refugees from America be invited to dine with him.

Late in May they met at York House for dinner. There were four other important guests—Prime Minister and Mrs. Stanley Baldwin, and another couple, a Mr. and Mrs. Ernest Simpson. For the first time the name of Wallis Simpson, long connected romantically with that of the new ruler, appeared defiantly in the *Court Circular* in company with that of the Prime Minister. The effect on staid Britishers was to make them forget the Lindberghs completely.

In June came a grim reminder of the tragedy the Lindberghs had left behind them on the other side of the Atlantic with word that the sum of $14,665 in gold notes had been deposited to the account of Colonel Charles A. Lindbergh in a Manhattan bank. The money was what remained of the $50,000 he had paid in ransom to kidnaper Hauptmann.

The flier had met and talked with Edward's War Minister Alfred Duff Cooper, who considered air attack from Germany a real danger. He had received a letter, too, from Major Truman Smith, military attaché in the American Embassy in Berlin, suggesting that Lindbergh participate in a tour of Germany that Smith could arrange and which would be valuable to American military intelligence.

After carefully considering this "spying" proposal, Lindbergh agreed. Now Lindbergh prepared to fly with his wife to that country to make an address. In Germany there was no problem of insuring complete secrecy for the mission. Hitler granted Lindbergh's request to visit, and muzzled the German press as only that dictator could. So in the last week in July, Lindbergh borrowed a Gypsy Moth plane and took off in the morning from Penshurst in Kent.

At a little after five that afternoon the cabin plane set down gently, not on a commercial field in Germany, but at the bristling military field at Staaken. The Lindberghs climbed out to see rows of huge bombers. *Der Führer* had permitted the landing here to further safeguard their privacy and the Lone Eagle blinked in awe at the sight. His mind began to catalogue the scope as well as the details of what he was being permitted to see, sights that may have had some bearing on the address he made to the German Aero Club:

"We who are in aviation carry a heavy responsibility on our shoulders, for while we have been drawing the world closer together in peace, we have stripped the armor from every nation in war.

"It is no longer possible to shield the heart of a country with its arms. An army can no more stop an air attack than a suit of mail can stop a rifle bullet.

"Aviation has, I believe, created the most fundamental change ever made in war. It has abolished what we call general warfare. It has turned defense into attack.

"We can no longer protect our families with an army," said the man who had found that bitterly true in a different sense. "Our libraries, our museums and every one of the institutions we value most are laid bare to bombardments.

"Aviation has brought revolutionary changes to a world already staggering with changes. It is our responsibility to make sure in so doing we don't destroy the very things which we wish to protect.

"As I travel over Europe I am more than ever impressed with the seriousness of the situation which confronts us. When I see that within a day or two damage can be done which no time can ever replace, I begin to realize we must look for a new type of security, a security which is dynamic, not static—a security which rests on intelligence, not in forts. And in the fact that intelligence must be combined with aviation I find some cause for hope. It requires more intellect to operate an airplance than to dig a trench or shoot a rifle.

"Education which is required in aviation must also teach the value of civilized institutions. Our responsibility in creating a great force for destruction may be somewhat relieved by knowing that we have allied this thought with intelligence and education and that we have moved that power farther away from ignorance. I find some cause for hope in the belief that the power which must be bound to knowledge is less dangerous to civilization than that which is barbaric. It is the responsibility of aviation to further the combination of strength and intelligence."

The text of his address was printed in full in the German papers, along with the news that Lindbergh's character symbolized the heroic qualities which Hitler was seeking to impress on Germany's youth. In England the papers commended Lindbergh because his "frank, truthful and courageous words have rendered a notable service to Europe and perhaps to the entire world." The Eagle was back in the news, not as "Flying Fool" or artificial heart technician, but as a serious, authoritative thinker on a grave world problem.

"Here's to bombers, may they fly slower," Lindbergh

toasted a group of German pursuit pilots, "and here's to pursuit planes, may they fly swifter!"

Lindbergh toured Germany, visiting factories, even flying the big new bombers. Hitler did not receive him, and even at the Olympics, where they sat close, did not deign to recognize him officially.

But Air Minister Hermann Göring and his ex-movie star wife entertained the American visitors. After the Olympics, where Lindbergh chatted with American athletes and even jogged about the track, it was time for him and Anne to board their plane and fly on to Denmark.

The flier had seen and soaked up enough information about German aircraft strength to hang a spy. It was almost as if Hitler had wanted him to know all these well-guarded secrets, and to convey an impression of power to the men back in England.

There was a coincidence that must have jarred Lindbergh. Everywhere in Germany he saw the black swastika that had taken on such ominous significance. In 1927 the propeller of Lindbergh's *Spirit of St. Louis* had been decorated with just such an emblem, for good luck!

Another facet of Charles August Lindbergh was displayed at Copenhagen's Danish Biological Institute shortly after the famous flier left Germany. This was his initial appearance before a scientific body like that at the International Congress of Experimental Cytology, and he had come to help Dr. Carrel set up the robot "glass heart" Lindbergh had helped perfect.

To 250 learned scientists, the man who had recently flown Germany's newest aircraft now demonstrated the workings of the pump that spurted a red fluid through the arteries of a cat's thyroid gland. Clad in a surgical smock, Lindbergh explained the mechanical heart to the interested cytologists. Not intended to replace the human heart, of course, or even an animal's heart as such, it nonetheless functioned to keep the thyroid alive and continuously secreting its chemical substances.

For the lecture session in the great hall of Cristianborg Castle, Lindbergh and his wife sat modestly at the back while Carrel paid tribute to him in French.

"Modern technique now realizes what old-time biologists only dared dream. It is now possible to study living cells where our ancestors studied only dead tissue," Dr. Carrel told the assemblage. "The robot heart is one of the most valuable means of help, created through the ingenuity of Charles A. Lindbergh."

The scientists commented that here was a flier who might well be remembered longer for his other activities, and reporters and curious Danes milled about the Institute for a sight of the bashful flier-scientist.

Back in England, Lindbergh sought an audience with Prime Minister Baldwin and told him what he had learned of Hitler's aerial might. The minister's reaction was so apathetic that Lindbergh was shocked and humiliated. Only America's War Department seemed interested in his findings—through Major Truman Smith of the American Embassy in Berlin, who had first investigated the possibility of the Lindbergh trip.

In September word came from America that Perry Lindbergh, the flier's uncle, had died at the age of ninety on his ranch in San Luis Obispo. That month, too, the French government contacted Lindbergh regarding his participation in its proposed tenth-anniversary celebration of his historic New York-to-Paris flight.

The newspaper *Intransigeant* announced proudly that it had been decreed that Colonel Lindbergh's exploit be commemorated as an historical event. Tying in with the Paris International Exposition, a race over the same course was planned, with a prize of one million francs for the winner.

More exciting to Lindbergh was taking delivery on a new airplane built especially and secretly for him by Miles Aircraft. Called the *Mohawk,* the craft had a 200-horsepower engine that pushed it along at 200 miles per hour for a cruising range of 1,000 miles. Fitted with seats that could be converted to bunks, and a sliding canopy over the cockpits, the *Mohawk* had the latest in American blind-flying equipment. It was painted black and orange for high visibility.

No joyriding ship, the *Mohawk* carried Lindbergh to Ireland in November for a meeting with President Juan Trippe of Pan American Airways. Farflung Pan Am had almost completed its Pacific empire with the China Clipper and was now ready to blaze a trail across the Atlantic. The idea had been a pet of Lindbergh's from the time he flew his

Spirit of St. Louis over the same route, and his residence in Kent made it easy for him to do some necessary spadework for Pan Am. He was still a consultant for TWA also, the route President Jack Frye called "The Lindbergh Line."

At Baldonnel Airdrome in Dublin Lindbergh rendezvoused in the *Mohawk* with an airliner load of airline officials and the Air Chief of the Irish Free State Army. At Ryanna, on the Limerick County side of the Shannon, a big landing field was under construction.

Lindbergh paced it off and studied it with a critical eye. He drove around it in a car, and then gave it the acid test by flying the *Mohawk* in from every possible angle. One day, he knew, big passenger airliners would come in out of the west. His report must be accurate and thorough; his notes were voluminous.

Next day he took President Eamon de Valera up for his first airplane flight. That night he dined with De Valera and other top officials at Dublin Castle. There was another American in Ireland, too; Postmaster Jim Farley, who was visiting his family home and possibly talking a little airmail contract business with De Valera. Lindbergh had tangled with Farley in the airline "scandals" back home. Their paths did not cross in Ireland.

On the afternoon of the twenty-fourth, Lindbergh made his farewells and climbed into the front cockpit of the *Mohawk*. Roaring off the runway, he headed for Croydon Airport, near London.

Meeting heavy fog, he changed his destination and put down at Sealand military airfield, far short of Croydon. Instead of notifying Croydon of his change in plans, he asked officers at Sealand to keep mum and spent the night visiting with them and discussing flying exploits.

Next day headlines around the world blazed "Lindbergh Lost!" and for almost twenty-four hours the people thought he was actually missing. He had never yet accepted his position as a world figure, and was amazed at the furor made over his short disappearance.

He was the full-time flier now, and on December 14 he appeared in evening clothes at London's Innholders Hall as guest for an airmen's dinner put on by the British Empire Guild. A tablemate at the dinner was Germany's Zeppelin designer, Dr. Hugo von Eckener, who had flown in from Friedrichshafen to attend.

Christmas at Long Barn was a joyous one. The year had softened the Lindberghs' grief and young Jon played happily around the Christmas tree and the stockings hung at the big fireplace. Lindbergh was busy and enthusiastic with his artificial kidney project and the important aviation work he was doing; Anne was making progress on the book that would be called *Listen! the Wind.*

In America many people debated whether or not Lindy and his family would come home in the spring. In the village where he lived, Englishmen wondered the same thing. After all, the federal agents back home had made great strides in curbing kidnapers where local authorities had failed. Since young Charles had died, 177 kidnapers had been convicted. Hauptmann had died in April for his crime. In June a prison escapee named Arthur Gooch had made the mistake of kidnaping a guard to assist his getaway. Sentenced to hang, Gooch had appealed but President Roosevelt had refused to give executive clemency.

"Use of the executive power," he said, "would be to render nugatory a law carefully considered by the Congress and designed to meet a national need."

But if the Lindberghs indeed were considering repatriating themselves, the headlines on the paper Lindbergh bought in the village one day after the Christmas holidays drove the thought completely from their minds like the cruel lash of a whip.

"KIDNAPED!" screamed the London paper, and in sick horror Lindbergh read about a family in Tacoma, Washington, named Mattson whose son was seized from before his own Christmas tree by a lone intruder.

There was a terrible familiarity in the details. The kidnaper had thrown down a ransom note demanding $28,000, of which $10,000 was to be in old fives and the rest old fifties and hundreds. After that came the business of intermediaries who failed to recover the child, of pathetic advertisements unanswered.

A grim-faced father strode silently home to where his young son played safely about the tree. There would be no return to America now. The "Lone Eagle," who at once typified his country's ideal of youth and its prowess in the air, was still an exile from his native land. It was to take even greater tragedies to bring him home.

BIBLIOGRAPHY

The Hero, Charles A. Lindbergh and the American Dream—Davis
We—Lindbergh
The Spirit of St. Louis—Lindbergh
Kidnap—Waller

IV

Edward and Wallis

On the 16th of January, 1936, a note was delivered to Edward, Prince of Wales, as he was shooting with friends in Windsor Great Park. The note was from his mother, telling him of the illness of his father, King George. The King had caught cold, and colds were hard on the regent. "I think you ought to know that Papa is not very well," Queen Mary wrote Edward.

While she herself professed not to consider the King in immediate danger, the royal physician, Lord Dawson, was not too pleased with his condition. Perhaps it would be wise if the Prince would come to Sandringham for the weekend, though in a casual manner so that the King not suspect that he had been warned of the seriousness of the illness.

The King was in his seventies, and soberly his eldest son left his shooting and returned to Fort Belvedere. Here he handed the discouraging news to a lady friend, Mrs. Ernest Simpson, while he phoned his pilot to ready the airplane for the Sandringham trip early next morning.

On the seventeenth, the King's bronchial catarrh worsened and it was necessary to give him oxygen. In the days that followed, the news was not good. Lord Dawson's concern was well founded and Prince Edward drove to London to confer with Prime Minister Stanley Baldwin.

On the twentieth, just four days after the urgent note summoning Edward to his father's side, the royal physician issued a bulletin that admitted to the world that the King was moving peacefully toward his death. Just after midnight the Prince called Mrs. Simpson to tell her, "It's all over."

"The King is dead! Long live the King!"

In the evening of the twenty-first, the King's body was carried the slow half-mile to the Church of St. Mary Magdalene. The plain wooden coffin had been hewn from Sandringham oak. Queen Mary walked in the procession with others of the family. She was protected from the rain by an umbrella, and Edward, who did not have a suitable coat of his own, was prevailed upon by Mrs. Simpson to slip on the heavy fur coat of his dead father.

Throughout the land the music of the national anthem rang out:

> Send him victorious, happy and glorious,
> Long to reign over us.
> God save the King.

The words were neither fitting nor prophetic. The Prince who became King with his father's dying gasp did not do so especially gloriously; neither would he reign for long over the people who thus exhorted him. For years he had been the country's most democratic prince; he would prove within this year he could not be its ruler. But gamely he made a start.

On January 21 there was also the Accession Privy Council, meeting in St. James's Palace, the beginning of the reign of King Edward VIII. On the next day, the King gave some indication of his democracy at the first Proclamation of the Accession, also at St. James's.

As the Garter King of Arms, Heralds, Pursuivants, and Trumpeters in traditional medieval costume appeared on the balcony of the palace, the King himself watched from an apartment across the way. Standing with his friend, Mrs. Simpson, he explained his unusual departure from custom.

"The thought came to me," he said, "that I'd like to see myself proclaimed King!"

In deference to the mourning Queen, King Edward let her remain in Buckingham Palace and himself stayed in York House. He was not overly fond of "Buck" anyway. When he made his first radio address to his subjects he hinted again that here was a different kind of monarch.

"It now falls upon me to succeed him [King George] and carry on his work.

"I am better known to most of you as the Prince of Wales —as the man who, during the war and since, has had an opportunity of getting to know people in nearly every country of the world under all conditions and circumstances. And although I now speak to you as King I am still that same man who has had that experience and whose constant effort it will be to continue to promote the well-being of my fellow men.

"May the future bring peace and understanding throughout the world and prosperity and happiness to the British Empire and may we be worthy of the heritage that is ours."

Prince Edward Albert Christian George Andrew Patrick David had become Leige-Lord of Great Britain, Ireland, and the Bountiful Dominion beyond the seas, King, Defender of the Faith, and Emperor of India. But true to his word he still began his days by jogging about the palace, or even running the three miles from Fort Belvedere, his bachelor hideout, to Windsor Lodge in shorts and turtleneck sweater. Called a sardine in his cadet days, he was still trim and had kept his "fighting weight" to 146 pounds. Indeed, the only concern of the royal doctors was to keep him from doing too much exercising.

"Still that same man," he brought his democratic leanings to the throne. Officials in close attendance no longer had to wear the traditional and severe Prince Albert, but now were prescribed the morning coat instead.

On a trip to Glasgow to inspect the liner, *Queen Mary*, then abuilding, he also took time to go knocking on doors in the poor district and then to wonder aloud, "How do you reconcile a world that has produced this mighty ship with the slums we have just visited?"

After he had showed Lord Provost John Stewart a trick with a coin, he endeared himself by begging, "Please give me back my penny. You know I am a Scotsman!"

Penny wise did not make the new King foolish, however. He petitioned through Chancellor of the Exchequer Neville Chamberlain for money to sustain the royal family, adding, "His Majesty desires that the contingency of his marriage be taken into account."

Up jumped Labour Party member Will Thorne to ask "whether His Majesty has given any guarantee that he is going to get married." Laughter greeted this demand but the question was a big one and in the minds of most Britishers.

The young Prince had had lady friends, including even Mrs. Dudley Ward, wife of the Right Honorable William Dudley Ward who was twenty years her senior. But since Mrs. Ward was divorced from her husband in 1930 Edward had not spent any time in her company. There was some speculation on Lady Mary Cambridge, but nothing definite was known, not even by the Queen Mother herself, who tactfully reminded her son every chance she got of his duties in that direction.

Nevertheless, Parliament got around to approving a budget for the ruling Windsors. Edward was to get $2,050,000 for himself, $595,000 for his wife, and an additional $200,-000 for his first male offspring when those happy days arrived. The House of Commons had pared some of the budget, but Radicals still complained of the nearly $3 million outlay. "Bigger and better doles for the royal unemployed!" they cried.

It was hardly a fair attitude, of course. The Windsor holdings brought England some $6 million a year and the family would thus be getting only half their earnings. Still, Edward, who had demanded his penny back like any true Scotsman, was in the happy financial fix of having his worth increasing at something like $2,000 a day. In castles and palaces alone the sovereign was worth close to $50 million.

As befits a democrat, the King revived the old custom of dispensing "Maundy money" to the poor on Maundy Thursday. Traditionally the King gave to as many of the elderly poor as his age equaled. Edward was 42, but he presented bags of money to 71 oldsters, since his father would have been that age.

Further evidences of liberality showed in the King's decree that there be no mourning at Ascot, and in his display of the royal legs with garterless socks to push an elasticized British brand at the Industries Fair in February.

In one concession to his new weighty responsibilities, the young King cut down on his flying. But he wasn't strong for the pomp and circumstance usually favored by royalty. His speeches he composed himself on his own Underwood portable, submitting them then for checking by the royal speechwriters.

For his first radio address he dared to write the word "radio." Aghast, the officials changed it to "wireless" instead of the common, democratic, American term. Boldly Edward slashed a line through "wireless" and reinstated "radio." As an aid to him in making the address, all his speeches were retyped on a long roll of paper and cut apart at natural break points so that he would not have to turn a page in mid-sentence.

He also shocked the Windsors and the rest of England by

buying a Canadian-built McLaughlin-Buick rather than a British car. Like a youngster with a new toy, he spun it around in the drive before the palace and insisted that his shy brother George take the wheel and try it out.

When it came time to receive the Privileged Bodies of Great Britain, he again stunned the traditionalists by rushing these personages through in two hours rather than the accustomed two days. "He fairly had them at a dogtrot!" a horrified onlooker said. To stimulate interest in the opera, the King leased a box at Covent Garden, though he was not seen in attendance. He preferred smaller gatherings and one performance he saw was the play, *Storm in a Teacup*, given privately at the home of Lady Cunard.

The famed democracy was in evidence when he inspected the Coldstream Guards. Sticking his head in at the mess hall, he bawled out, "Any complaints?" in a tone mocking a tough sergeant. And he and Queen Mary each generously gave $5,000 toward a King George Memorial for children's play places. Together with Labour Minister Ernest Brown he visited training centers for the unemployed at Slough and Acton and applauded the work of the trainees.

June 23 was his birthday, and someone pointed out that the King, like his father before him and his brothers, was born on a Saturday. He was 42 years old. Not wanting the royal birthday turned into a florist's racket, Edward suggested that his celebrating subjects wear a daisy or buttercup, or some other flower from their own gardens, in lapels. Despite muggy summer weather, the King donned the royal uniform, including towering bearskin busby, and mounted a royal stallion.

The people thrilled to see him at saluting point for the colorful pageant of the Trooping of the Color. Edward VIII, in addition to being King, was also Admiral of the Royal Navy, Field Marshal of the Army and Air Marshal of the Royal Air Force. Beyond this he held commissions in a dozen military groups. The royal wardrobe included some eighty uniforms necessary for proper garb on all occasions!

The Coronation had been announced for May 12 of 1937, but there was still the ticklish question of whether or not there would be a queen to crown, too. This problem was giving everyone from tradesmen to high officials fits by the minute and Lloyd's of London was quoting insurance odds against there being a queen of about twenty to one. This detail was important to the makers of souvenir mugs to sell at the Coronation; should they put one or two heads on their wares? Officials concerned with the ceremony itself had equally grave considerations.

"A Queen's coronation is invariably separate from that of the King," said one statement. "If a Queen is to be crowned, the rite of having a lady-in-waiting open her robe while the Archbishop of Canterbury anoints her bosom with a cross of holy oil will doubtless be foregone as it was in the case of Queen Mary."

The King had his problems, too, beyond the one of taking a wife. Besides matters concerning his subjects were international affairs. There were foreign ministers to see in this time of tension the world over. In February, shortly after his accession, Edward gave an audience to Germany's Baron von Neurath, and surprised most people by speaking long and cordially with that envoy. The ruler, it seemed, leaned toward Hitler's Germany. The meeting with Russia's Maxim Litvinoff, on the other hand, was of a different nature, and the Foreign Minister said in an interview that he had found the new King "a mediocre young Englishman who reads one newspaper a day."

On April 20 the King congratulated Hitler on his birthday and on the thirtieth he received Prince Farouk, who had been attending school in England but had now become King of Egypt on the death of his father, Fuad. The trouble between Italy and Ethiopia was depressing, but it seemed that all England could do was lift the sanctions imposed on Mussolini. When Emperor Haile Selassie, routed from his country, came to England asking to see Edward, the King refused such an audience, though he did send Selassie greetings on his forty-fifth birthday.

During the first months of the King's reign he had managed to see much of the lady he had shown the urgent note describing his father's illness and with whom he had "watched his own accession."

With typical democratic frankness, Edward made no attempt to keep these meetings secret, but the press and official publications made no note of her. In May a dinner took place that for the first time placed the name of Mrs. Simpson in the *Court Circular*. Alongside such names as Prime Minister and Mrs. Baldwin, Lord and Lady Duff Cooper, Lord and Lady Wigram, Lady Cunard, Lord and Lady Mountbatten, and the American celebrities, Colonel and Mrs. Lindbergh, were those of Mr. and Mrs. Ernest Simpson.

The Prime Minister was "intrigued" by the dinner, his wife a little less than intrigued and sure that a commoner had stolen the Fairy Prince. From that fateful day on it was out in the open and England as a whole was surprised or even shocked. Was the King really interested in this slender, graceful woman who already had a husband? And just who, really, was Mrs. Ernest Simpson?

There seemed to be some question about when Edward and Wallis Simpson had first met. He said it was 1931, and she was positive that his memory erred and that it was 1930 that she first curtsied to the Prince of Wales and his brother George at the home of friends.

Some of the press thought they were both forgetful, and that the first encounter came years earlier, in 1920, and thousands of miles from England at Coronado, California, when Edward had visited that Navy town aboard a battleship and entertained U.S. fliers, including Lieutenant Winfield Spenser and his wife Wallis Warfield Spenser.

Wallis Warfield, named for her father, who didn't live to see his daughter, married the Navy aviator in 1916 at the age of 19. Their marriage had failed by 1923, when the Spensers were separated. A trial reconciliation also failed, and finally in 1924, Wallis divorced Winfield Spenser. He drank, she said. He was destroying himself and she didn't want him to destroy her in the process.

She tried selling elevators for a time, but sold none. Then she visited abroad and met Ernest Simpson in London. Simpson had a wife at the time, but they were separated. Mrs. Simpson later said that Wallis had "what it took" to get a man, because she took Ernest away from her while she was ill in a Paris hospital. Wallis and Ernest were married in 1928.

Simpson had been born in New York, but he grew up in England and considered it his home. He had been an officer in the Coldstream Guards, and upon leaving the service associated himself with the family's ship brokerage business. He and Wallis honeymooned on the Balearic Islands and returned to London to settle down to married life.

The new Mrs. Simpson was happy with her life in London society. She had good friends, she met interesting people.

67

Celebrated for her epigrams like that on soup—"An uninteresting liquid that gets you noplace"—she made another when friends prevailed on her to allow herself to be presented at court.

"I'll do it if it doesn't cost anything," she said, and proceeded to borrow most of the finery necessary for the occasion. On June 10, 1931, she was presented to the King and Queen. But it was the earlier meeting, the time she curtsied only to Prince Edward and Prince George, that was the turning point of her life.

In the years that followed she and the Prince saw more and more of each other. He entertained the Simpsons and they reciprocated in the modest ways they could. At length there was an invitation to vacation with him at Biarritz, and though Ernest had to go to America on business Mrs. Simpson accepted and took along her aunt Bessie as chaperone. From Biarritz she went on a yacht trip, with Aunt Bessie deciding instead to motor about Italy. After this cruise the Prince made so bold as to present Wallis with a diamond and emerald charm for her bracelet.

Returning to England, Mrs. Simpson told Ernest that the trip was like being Wallis in Wonderland; for his part he wondered if it hadn't been more a visit to Peter Pan's Never-Never land.

When the Prince invited them to go along on an Austrian skiing trip, Wallis accepted for them both. Testily Ernest said he had a New York trip that interfered, and with a choice Wallis decided to go to Austria. Her husband went to his room and slammed the door with a bang.

There were more trips, and finally Mrs. Simpson decided that Ernest must be seeing another woman. She confided in the King, who secured a lawyer for her, and Mrs. Simpson assured that gentleman she wanted a divorce. It was shortly after this that Edward planned the momentous dinner, telling Wallis, "Sooner or later my Prime Minister must meet my future wife."

Ernest Simpson was there, of course, it being hard for even a man in his position to decline what amounted to a command from his ruler. But it was the last time the Simpsons went out together socially. The solicitors Mrs. Simpson had engaged through the good offices of the King were now tailing Ernest as divorce proceedings began and he would soon move from their chilly residence to the Guard's Club.

In July something happened that might well have changed

the course of history. As the King rode his horse down Constitution Hill in a parade, a redhaired clubfoot named Jerome Bannigan tossed a loaded pistol under his horse's hooves. A vociferous radical and opponent of capital punishment, Bannigan preferred to be known as George Andrew McMahon. He was the author of such articles as *Why I Shall Not Marry, Unmoral Girls, Vacuum Cleaner Vampires,* and *Is Nudism Immoral?* and ran an herb shop.

The King saw the tossed object, and his horse shied, but he kept bravely on. Told that it was a gun and loaded as well, he exclaimed, "The damn fool!" and kept on riding. Hauled away by alert police, Bannigan was tossed into jail.

Facing a sentence of twenty years or more, he told a wild tale of being enlisted by a foreign power to murder the King for $750. The foreign power was Germany, according to the herbalist, but the Court preferred to think that Bannigan was daft and ended the case by giving him two years for "alarming the King."

Other threats against His Majesty came from Ireland, result of a mistaken rumor. Somehow the word got around that Edward was planning to force a union of England and Ireland and immediately a rash of outburst in protest flared in Belfast. "DOWN WITH THE FENIAN KING!" the banners proclaimed until the cooler heads straightened out the confusion.

For Mrs. Simpson life continued to glitter like Wonderland. She met *the* people of England, and many important personages from other countries. She had even met Von Ribbentrop, the man Edward called a "broken gramophone." Her own gatherings grew in stature, and she was now the undisputed hostess for His Majesty.

When, in August, the King planned a long junket across the continent she went along as a member of the party of fifty or so. David, the name she called the King, was constantly at her side, heedless of the attendant publicity that was beginning to anger Baldwin and many others in government.

When the King had climbed aboard one of the new "flea boats" of the Royal Navy for a trial run at 45 knots and the launching of dummy torpedoes at a destroyer, the press had reveled in the news. But this seagoing jaunt aboard the *Nahlin* chartered from Lady Yule drew reproving looks from officialdom and no photos in the press.

Mrs. Simpson's luggage was boldly labeled in big letters,

69

contrasting the discreet names on the King's. When police took cameras from sight-seers for snapping the couple, the King laughingly returned them with his best wishes.

He had suggested earlier that he would give Baldwin something to talk about, and now he was doing just that, with a vengeance. The censors were as strong-willed as he, and the harder he tried, the less news appeared in the papers of England. In fact, the Japanese wistfully asked if their Emperor could perhaps enjoy the same censorship as the American lady Mrs. Simpson did.

Starting out the junket in August, the King flew from England to France, to become the first king to fly abroad. The long trip covered many countries and was a combination of goodwill tour and vacation for him and Mrs. Simpson. They listened to Beethoven's *Fidelio* in Austria, and the King bought a Dalmatian fisherman's shirt for a souvenir.

He was also reputed to have invented a "King Edward Cocktail" made from gin, chartréuse and Dalmatian champagne. But when a bartender in Washington, D.C., tried the recipe it blew up on him as he vigorously shook the mixture in a closed shaker. A reporter who tried the drink reported it was a sickly green and tasted like an empty lard can. The King also whopped some 3,000 golf balls from the *Nahlin* into the Adriatic Sea while Mrs. Simpson and a golf pro looked on. He learned a new game of that area, called *botsche* and somewhat like lawn bowling.

Back in England the papers and the newsreels were being assailed for failing to censor the "assassination" incident on Constitution Hill, since the showing of details could possibly aid others with similar ideas. There was going to be something else named for the King, a battleship abuilding to be called the *King Edward VIII*, and it was to be hoped it wouldn't explode like the cocktail had.

Returning home after the *Nahlin* cruise, Edward tangled promptly again with his Prime Minister on the subject of women. If Baldwin didn't let up, the King threatened, he just wouldn't go "to your beastly old Coronation!" And why all the secrecy? the King demanded. He himself put Mrs. Simpson's name in the *Court Circular, by itself* this time, and there were near-coronaries all over London.

The press had a bad hour of soul-searching but finally concluded that if the King could dissolve Parliament or sell the Royal Navy, he could probably place his lady's name before the public. But still there were no pictures of Wallis, or Wally, as the boisterous American papers were beginning to call her.

There were pictures of His Royal Highness though. A new commemorative issue of stamps was just out, a highly controversial head-only picture of Edward with no identification of any kind. In case it didn't go over, there were more traditional full-figure stamps ready to be struck off. But eager subjects snapped up the new stamps by the millions and before worried postal officials could catch their breath the whole thirty million were gone. This was a reassuring measure of the popularity of the King.

Again Scotsman Edward journeyed north to dedicate a hospital in Aberdeen. There was terrible confusion on this trip when Mrs. Simpson arrived at the depot to join him and he missed the dedication, according to some, to meet her. Angrily, Scots painted signs on the streets castigating the "American harlot" but the King was blissfully unaware.

The couple visited at Balmoral Castle, where the King had his pipers play a tune called *St. Louis Woman* for his lady, and surprised his fellow huntsmen when he came upon a stag and dropped his gun to shoot it with his new German camera.

In London things were at the boil. Besides Baldwin, the Archbishops of Canterbury and York were among those flatly refusing to admit the possibility of Edward marrying the American woman. The clerics had even refused to attend any function to which she was invited. Baldwin had the temerity to refer to Mrs. Simpson as "damaged goods" and others added, "Yes, and American into the bargain!"

The divorce lawyers had had good fortune. A letter apparently intended for Ernest had by some strange chance, according to Mrs. Simpson, been addressed to her. It was the final straw, and she did the only thing a cultured and sensitive lady could do. She wrote a letter, too, and addressed it properly to her spouse.

Dear Ernest: I have just learned that while you have been away, instead of having been on business as you led me to believe, you have been staying at the Hotel Bray with a lady. I am sure you realize this is conduct which I cannot possibly overlook and must insist you do not continue to live here with

71

me. This only confirms the suspicions I have had for a long time. I am therefore instructing my solicitors to take proceedings for divorce.

This had been way back on July 23, of course, though Mrs. Simpson did not file for divorce until October 14. The pattern for the divorce was standard for British courts. As usual, the husband must be guilty, at least technically, of adultery. In this case, Ernest was accused of bedding one Mrs. E. H. "Buttercup" Kennedy at the Hotel de Paris near the resort of Maidenhead. Simpson was not contesting the divorce, and Mrs. Simpson's lawyer asked for a "decree *nisi* with costs."

To save Mrs. Simpson all embarrassment possible, the trial had been held at the Ipswich Assizes Court, His Lordship Justice Hawke presiding. Lord Hawke, as a matter of interest, had been Attorney General to Prince Edward. If he granted a divorce, the only man who could question the decision was the King's Proctor. The divorce was indeed granted, though the *nisi* qualification made it necessary for Mrs. Simpson to preserve her own good name for six months, at which time the decree would be final. If she, too, fell from goodness, she and Ernest would be marooned in what was bitterly called "Holy Deadlock" by British cynics.

With the divorce granted, Mrs. Simpson was escorted from the courtroom, which was then quickly locked to keep clamoring reporters in. Outside she was spirited into Edward's Canadian Buick, which sped her away to her new home on Cumberland Terrace. Police cars blocked those of reporters and the law smashed two cameras.

The British censorship all but clamped the lid on what had happened, but headlines in America screamed the news that Wally was divorced and pondered noisily whether or not the King would now marry her. An Irish columnist ordered news stories from an American clipping service and was buried in some 25,000 Edward-Wallis stories from America. The British press gots its remarks to the King only by having its verbal comments picked up by foreign newspapers.

The King had just appeared in Whitehall to swear to be a faithful Protestant and to read the customary speech from the Throne. It had been written by his cabinet, and about the only thing new in it was substitution of "I" and "my" for the traditional "we" and "our." Keynoting the speech was the statement reflecting Prime Minister Baldwin's belief that "the policy of the Government continues to be based on membership in the League [of Nations]."

The word was out, despite any attempts to keep it bottled up. The woman the King seemed enamored of was free of her husband, and interviews in American papers that had Ernest Simpson say he considered the sovereign's interest in Wallis platonic sounded like drivel to those in England who chuckled about the "unimportance of being Ernest."

With knowing winks they said that Simpson would get his—a knighthood, a baronetcy, a peerage or maybe a court office. Hadn't a tearful Queen Mary moved out of Buckingham Palace, either in protest or in resignation?

When those higher up went tight-lipped and uncommunicative, American reporters collared the British comman man and woman in the streets and polled them on their opinions of the Edward-Wallis situation.

A housemaid said, "I don't know what to think. Perhaps she will go back to America and he will marry the Duchess of York." But Wallis had said she would never return to the land of her birth after the vicious way she was being treated in its press.

A clerk grinned and said, "Good luck to him!"

"Gallivanting around with foreign women!" a shopgirl snorted indignantly, and a movie usherette echoed the sentiment wistfully by asking, "What's the matter with English girls?"

An ex-soldier said of fellow veteran Edward, "I don't care what he does," while a philosophical bus driver expressed a similarly broad-minded view. "If her old man don't mind, I don't think its anybody's business," he allowed.

The Queen Mother, finally prevailed upon to comment, had much the same thing to say. "The friendship is His Majesty's affair," she protested. Other less kind Britishers voiced the opinion that Mrs. Simpson was the biggest menace to England since George Washington.

In the U.S. the Washington *Daily News* printed a brief eleven-word account of the divorce: "The Court granted Mrs. Simpson, American grass widow, her divorce yesterday." The headline was "GOD SAVE THE KING!"

In San Diego, California, first husband Spencer, now a Navy commander, wished his ex-wife the best from his hunting accident sickbed.

In New York Wallis' Aunt Bessie boarded the *Queen*

Mary to rush to England in case she was again needed as chaperone. In Washington Jimmy Walker discovered "Mrs. Simpson" in the Biddle painting adorning the new Justice Department Building.

By now Mrs. Simpson was receiving letters threatening to do away with her, and warning her that her fate would be that of all kings' mistresses.

While Baldwin twisted the King's arm, Red Parliament Member William Gallacher put his approval on the marriage if the King desired it. Right away the cry was raised that the whole thing was a Communist plot. Could the King marry Mrs. Simpson, after all? Surely he could, unless she was Roman Catholic and she wasn't that. Wouldn't the marriage be bound to be "morganatic," leaving her a commoner? No, if the King took her to wife she would automatically be Queen Wallis, a possibility that made much of the upper crust shudder convulsively.

By November 13, the crisis was such that Edward's secretary, Alexander Hardinge, wrote him the following letter:

SIR,
   With my humble duty.
   As Your Majesty's Private Secretary, I feel it is my duty to bring to your notice the following facts which have come to my knowledge and which I know to be accurate:
   (1) The silence of the British Press on the subject of Your Majesty's friendship with Mrs. Simpson is not going to be maintained. It is probably only a matter of days before the outburst begins. Judging by the letters from British subjects living in foreign countries where the Press has been outspoken, the effect will be calamitous.
   (2) The Prime Minister and senior members of the Government are meeting today to discuss what action should be taken to deal with the serious situation which is developing. As Your Majesty no doubt knows, the resignation of the Government—an eventuality which can by no means be excluded—would result in Your Majesty having to find someone else capable of forming a Government which would receive the support of the present House of Commons.
   I have reason to know that, in view of the feeling prevalent among members of the House of Commons of all parties, this is hardly within the bounds of possibility. The only alternative remaining is a dissolution and a General Election, in which Your Majesty's personal affairs would be the chief issue—and I cannot help feeling that even those who would sympathise with Your Majesty as an individual would deeply

resent the damage which would inevitably be done to the Crown, the corner-stone on which the whole Empire rests

If your Majesty will permit me to say so, there is only one step which holds out any prospect of avoiding this dangerous situation, and that is for Mrs. Simpson to go abroad without further delay, and I would beg Your Majesty to give this proposal your earnest consideration before the position has become irretrievable. Owing to the changing attitude of the Press, the matter has become one of great urgency.

ALEXANDER HARDINGE

There was a P.S. that the secretary was going on a hunting trip, but could be reached. The King didn't bother, deciding to forego Hardinge's services thenceforth. Mrs. Simpson did not leave the country at that time, and Edward denounced the letter as impertinent. He tried to see Baldwin again, then had to dash off to the coal mines on an inspection tour. As if in prophecy, the Crystal Palace in London burned as December was ushered in, a month to cap the climax of a crucial year.

Friends suggested the idea of the "morganatic" marriage, and while Edward rebelled, he promised to discuss it with Baldwin. He even began a speech for a "fireside chat" à la Roosevelt and King George himself, so that he could present his side to the British people. Then came the last straw. Baldwin and the government rejected any possible marriage, even the morganatic compromise!

Angrily Edward abandoned the planned radio address, while Mrs. Simpson fled to France. In the streets crowds cried, "Flog Baldwin!" and "God Save the King!" Newspapers headlined "Grave Crisis!" and Lord Castelrosse, intimate of Lord Beaverbrook, said that Mrs. Simpson had built up Edward's inferiority complex, and that the attraction between them was not sex. Authority Havelock Ellis echoed this sentiment, suggesting that the King was actually searching for a mother and had found her in Wallis.

BBC radio had no time available for "King's Men," who included Winston Churchill in their number, yet pro-Baldwin speakers were given time to broadcast the view that Edward was erratic. On December 10, erratic Edward shocked the nation and the world by bowing to the will of his government in this renunciation:

After long and anxious consideration I have determined to renounce the throne to which I succeeded on the death of my father, and I am now communicating this, my final and irrevocable decision.

Realizing as I do the gravity of this step, I can only hope that I shall have the understanding of my peoples in the decision I have taken and the reasons which have led me to take it.

I will not enter now into my private feeling, but I would beg that it should be remembered that the burden which constantly rests upon the shoulders of a sovereign is so heavy that it can only be borne in circumstances different from those in which I now find myself.

I conceive that I am not overlooking the duty that rests on me to place in the forefront the public interest when I declare that I am conscious that I can no longer discharge this heavy task with efficiency or with satisfaction to myself.

I have accordingly this morning executed an instrument of abdication in the terms following:

I, Edward VIII of Great Britain, Ireland and the British Dominions Beyond the Seas, King, Emperor of India, do hereby declare my irrevocable determination to renounce the throne for myself and for my descendants and my desire that effect should be given to this instrument of abdication immediately.

In token whereof I have hereunto set my hand this 10th day of December, 1936, in the presence of the witnesses whose signatures are subscribed.

EDWARD R. I.

George VI was King now, and a puzzled Princess Elizabeth was asking, "But what happened to Uncle David?" Uncle David, the ex-king of England and now Duke of Windsor, would shortly speed from his home to exile on the continent, not aboard the yacht *Enchantress* as originally planned, but the Navy destroyer *Fury* since that would be more dignified, to wait for the divorce of the woman he loved to become final the following April.

It had been a momentous year for Edward and for Wallis; it had been a historic one for the English, who saw a kaleidoscopic procession of three kings in the twelve-month space. Finally, the whole world had seen a man so democratic that he would not be king if it meant losing the woman he loved.

Rightly or not, the romance was spoken of in the same breath with Abelard and Héloïse, Romeo and Juliet, and Antony and Cleopatra. Madame Tussaud's famous museum had immortalized Edward and Wallis in wax, and fittingly, Hollywood was offering the participants a million dollars to come to movieland! Another country was heard from, too, when Adolf Hitler claimed Edward was railroaded from his throne because of his pro-German leanings!

BIBLIOGRAPHY

The Heart Has Its Reasons—Windsor
Gone with the Windsors—Brody
Her Name Was Wallis Warfield—Wilson
The Woman Who Would Be Queen—Bocca
A King's Story—Windsor
King Edward VIII, an Intimate Biography—Bolitho

By 1936, President Franklin Delano Roosevelt's New Deal was in its fourth year. *(U.S. Signal Corps, The National Archives)*

FDR with New York's Governor Herbert H. Lehman and two Navy officers *(U.S. Signal Corps, The National Archives)*

Roosevelt on the campaign trail. Fellow passengers on his train are (left) John L. Lewis, president of the United Mine Workers and (right) Marvin McIntire, White House secretary. *(Wide World Photo)*

New York's Mayor Fiorello H. LaGuardia (foreground) shows Secretary of Agriculture Henry A. Wallace (right) the municipally operated Bronx terminal market. *(Wide World Photo)*

J. P. Morgan, the head of the House of Morgan, during the hearing of the Senate Munitions Committee investigating World War I financial activities *(Wide World Photo)*

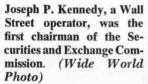

Joseph P. Kennedy, a Wall Street operator, was the first chairman of the Securities and Exchange Commission. *(Wide World Photo)*

At the convention of the National Union for Social Justice in Cleveland, The Rev. Gerald L. K. Smith, Father Charles Coughlin and Dr. Francis Townsend greeted the delegates. The convention endorsed William Lemke, the Union Party presidential nominee. *(Wide World Photo)*

Dr. Francis E. Townsend is greeted by young and old delegates at a Townsend Plan convention. *(Wide World Photo)*

Upton Sinclair, (above) author and Democratic nominee for Governor of California, visits Harry Hopkins (right). *(Wide World Photo)* Earl Browder, (below) Secretary of the Communist Party, at his party's ninth annual convention, June, 1936. *(Wide World Photo)*

A scene from a 1936 Federal Theater production, (above) *It Can't Happen Here*. *(Work Projects Administration, National Archives)* "The Sweatshop and Tenement of Yesterday Can Be the Life Planned With Justice Tomorrow"—the George Biddle mural (below) in the Department of Justice Building, Washington, D.C. *(Public Building Service, National Archives)*

Bruno Richard Hauptmann, the convicted kidnapper-slayer of the Lindbergh baby, stares out from behind bars at the state prison in Flemington, N.J. On April 3, 1936, at 8:47 P.M., he was electrocuted. *(Wide World Photo)* Col. Charles Lindbergh and Anne Morrow Lindbergh in Boulogne, France, on April 29, 1936. They were recognized on the beach and were forced to flee back to England. *(Wide World Photo)*

Col. Lindbergh worked in conjunction with Prof. Alexis Carrel and Prof. Albert Fischer (right). At the International Congress of Experimental Cytology in Copenhagen, Lindbergh explained to the assembled researchers the function of the mechanical heart he had helped to perfect. *(Wide World Photo)*

Before his abdication, King Edward VII and Mrs. Wallis Simpson strolled on the Dalmatian beach. *(Wide World Photo)*

Joseph Stalin after addressing the Soviet All-Union Congress, December, 1936. *(Wide World Photo)*

Attorney Samuel Leibowitz conferring with seven of the "Scottsboro Boys." *(Wide World Photo)*

Barcelona during the Spanish Civil War. *(Wide World Photo)*

General Francisco Franco (right) with Col. Jose Moscardo (left), commander of the Nationalist troops that had been trapped in the Alcazar. *(Wide World Photo)*

Haile Selassie, exiled emperor of Ethiopia, addressing the League of Nations at Geneva. *(Wide World Photo)*

Gen. Achille Starece, Secretary General of the Fascist Party (officer at left), leads his troops toward Gondar, in northwestern Ethiopia. Many of his troops were native soldiers. *(Wide World Photo)*

"The Black Eagle," Col. Hubert F. Julian, an American soldier of fortune, drilling Ethiopian recruits. *(Wide World Photo)*

Emperor Hailie Selassie, in England, June, 1936. *(Wide World Photo)*

Adolf Hitler on November 18, 1936. Rudolf Hess stands in front of the car. Propaganda minister Joseph Goebbels can be seen on the left side next to Hitler. *(Wide World Photo)*

V

Adolf Hitler

Hitler and his Nazis had been in power for three years now. Germany was not the same country he had taken over; everyone was agreed on that, from the fervent little man with the mustache down to the poorest peasant.

That peasant was now protected by the Hereditary Farm Law, since the *Führer* was aware that "the ruin of the German peasant will be the ruin of the German people!" The small farm now was the peasant's birthright and only death could wrest it from him. Besides that, prices for farm produce were up a healthy 20 percent. Soon, according to the *Führer*, the Reich would be self-sufficient with respect to food.

There was another problem licked, too—that of unemployment. Where there had once been six million jobless, now the number had dived almost to a mere one million. Even Communists, deprived of their trade-unionism, sheepishly admitted that at least they weren't going hungry.

A good skilled mechanic got the whopping wage of 19.5 cents an hour; unskilled laborers drew 13 cents. Of course, there were some deductions, like income tax and Labor Front dues, contributions for sickness, disability and unemployment insurance, as well as the *Winterhilfe*, or winter relief. These deductions added up to a whopping big 35 percent bite of the total, but Hans paid. If he tried to shortchange the government he could be fined heavily.

Workers noticed other changes, too. There weren't any raises any more. There weren't any strikes either. The boss ruled with an iron hand, and the only way to make more money was to work faster and hope for more money on a piecework basis, or put in more hours. A man didn't drift from job to job any more either. Nowadays he carried a government-issued workbook he had to show to get a job, and Hitler frowned on job-jumping.

But who worried about such trivial things with "Strength

Through Joy" to make life worth living? For a few dollars Germans could take a trip to Madeira and return; for even less they could spend a week in the best ski country in the world, all expenses paid.

Youngsters, too, were taken care of. As Hitler told those who opposed him, *"You* do not matter; your child is already in our camp." There was "Strength Through Joy" for the strong and healthy boys and girls who labored and played in the country. Many of them made more than hay in the bracing sunshine, and the irreverent winked and recited a parody couplet: "In the fields and on the heath, I *lose* Strength Through Joy!"

Adolf Hitler hadn't gone far in school, and now he changed education to suit himself. Heidelberg University professors ranted about such things as "German physics," and rejoiced at having given the boot to Einstein. It was officially declared that Jews were not true scientists, but corrupters of knowledge.

There was good music to listen to, and the *Führer* had gotten rid of all the degenerate and senseless modern art. Being an artist himself, he was well qualified to select what should replace the junk and what he should drive a righteous booted foot through. "We do not discuss artistic judgment," he exulted. "We make decisions!" It had been necessary to burn a few books, and set the newspaper editors straight, but things were rolling smoothly now.

Even religion was being Germanized, though some diehards like Niemöller complained. The reverend had published his autobiography *From U-Boat to Pulpit* and been highly praised by the Nazi press. In turn, he had been openly grateful for Nazism, for which he himself had fought for so long. Now he began to wonder.

Martin Luther, four hundred years earlier, had left some advice which the *Führer* was now following. Luther had advocated getting rid of the Jews, depriving them of course of all their cash and jewels in the process, and that was being done quite rapidly. The German Christian, Dr.Krause, advocated dropping the Old Testament and its "tales of cattle merchants and pimps," as well as rewriting Jesus' teachings more in line with Aryan beliefs.

Just a few months ago the Nuremberg Laws had made the Jews subjects and not citizens, and forbade them to marry or to have sexual relations with Aryans. They could not hold public office or practically any other job or profes-

79

sion. Half of them were out of work. Besides this, Jews could not employ Aryan servants under 35 years old.

Most stores carried signs that read, *Jews Not Admitted.* Hotels turned them away, as did whole towns. Road signs such as *Sharp Curve, Drive Carefully* had been expanded with the further instructions, *Jews 75 Miles an Hour!* Jewish mothers had trouble buying milk for their children, and drugstores turned them away, too.

But those were the Jews. Aryan Germans were happy. Tourists from abroad could see that when they crowded into Germany, as they were doing in 1936. Travel was generally unrestricted, except for places like military installations and concentration camps. Germans were free to travel abroad, too, if they had the inclination and the money to do it.

And how did the rest of the world see Hitler and his new Germany? American writer John Spivak, in his book, *Europe Under the Terror,* pointed out that there were tyrants preying on the German people, a people he characterized as dolts. Superefficient gangsters, Spivak called the grafters who were fleecing Germans and shipping their profits out of the country despite the watchful eye of Dr. Hjalmar Schact, Minister of Economics. Hitler's profiteering, more respectable than some, according to Spivak, consisted of his publishing firm, which put out *Mein Kampf,* textbooks and the official *Voelkischer Beobachter* party organ.

In the U.S., Porter Sargent, dean of private school promoters, found Hitler increasing the birth rate and improving the product, in contrast to a lack of such improvement in America. England's Lloyd George was well pleased with Hitler, and praised him highly as a great leader who was solving his country's problems, including the important one of unemployment. Coming from the man who in 1918 had advocated hanging the Kaiser, this was tribute aplenty.

Not everyone was fooled by Herr Schicklgruber, however. James Grover McDonald, the League of Nation's High Commissioner for Refugees, resigned his job in frustration and despair. McDonald declared that the law in Germany was no longer anything but what the Aryan man made it. He had this on pretty good authority, too, and quoted Nazi Alfred Rosenberg to back up his thesis. Soon, German Commissioner of Justice Dr. Hans Frank explained to jurists that the law could be found in the speeches of the *Führer!*

"Say to yourself at every decision, 'How would the

Führer decide in my place?' " Frank ordered. Hitler was advancing from mere lawmaker to law itself.

England was finding out from an apoplectic Hitler that his laws reached to the international scene. There would be no air pact with Germany in 1936, and Britishers who had gone along with Hitler's violation of Versailles realized that he was going to build 47,000 tons of carriers this year, plus squadrons of large torpedo-carrying seaplanes.

The *Führer* turned on German radio stations and banned all commercial advertising for that medium. There were those, even in America, who took some secret satisfaction from this edict. The cynical pointed out that Hitler, as a newspaper owner, stood to profit by such a change, particularly with the captive audience he seemed to have. Subscribers to the official party organs were now getting "lifetime" identification books in which a record of their subscription renewals could be kept. This, said Herr Hitler, would give them a feeling of closeness, a sense of security and of belonging to Germany.

It was obvious early that 1936 was going to be a year of change for Germany. Take wedding rings, for example. The *Führer* decreed that henceforth wedding rings could contain only one-third gold; the remaining two-thirds must be base metal. This idea he may have borrowed from *Il Duce,* to whom Italian women even in America had sent their gold bands, later to be replaced with iron wedding rings.

Not forgetting the Jews, Hitler's Nazis were cleaning up the hymns sung in church. Names like Jerusalem, Zion and even Jehovah were being purged. Minister of the Interior Wilhelm Frick was also cracking down on one of the last jobs open to Jews—that of traveling salesmen. This type of work gave them too much opportunity to spread lies about Aryans, Frick complained.

On the third anniversary of Hitler's rise to power, 25,000 Storm Troopers gathered to do him honor. "Welcome to Berlin," Joseph Goebbels cried. "We have purged it until it is no longer a Jewish cesspool!" A triumphant Hitler stilled the throng, and told them in all humility:

"All that I am, I am through you; all that you are, you are through me! Whoever opposes us now, my comrades, opposes us not because we are Nazis but because we have restored military independence to Germany. We are no longer defenseless Helots but citizens of the world, self-confident and erect. Germany will be as peace-loving as any

81

nation can be, provided we Germans are not touched in our honor! Comrades, fighting and sacrificing remain before us!"

Germany had a new constitution now, the *Führer* informed it. This surprise was possible because of certain enacted basic laws, and now all the Fatherland was under Adolf Hitler.

There was another surprise, kept secret until circulation of the *Official Gazette*: a new cabinet decree law signed by Hitler and War Minister General Werner von Blomberg. Among other things, this decree empowered the Army to take law and order into its own hands. It also named the Supreme Commander of the Army, Navy and Air Force. His name just happened to be Adolf Hitler.

In February there were problems. In Switzerland, a young Jew from Berne pumped five bullets into Dr. Wilhelm Gustloff, a German physicist at Davos Observatory. David Frankfurter, the assassin, surrendered immediately to the Swiss police.

"He was a Nazi agent who poisoned our atmosphere," he said in explanation. "My bullets should have hit Hitler himself."

Gustloff was truly an agent of Hitler, spreading the word in Switzerland through youth groups. He was from Schwerin in Germany, at forty-one a sharp scientist whose weak lungs had prompted the move to Switzerland. The Nazi paper *Frankische Tageszeitung* screamed:

> Another in the long series of Jewish ritual murders which began with the slaughter of the Aryans by Jews thousands of years ago and is now celebrated annually in the feast of Purim!

The Nazis demanded the death penalty, but the Swiss government sent its polite regrets instead. As a political assassin, Frankfurter drew a fifteen-year sentence. The Nazis might well have pressed the case but for the nearness of the Olympic Winter Games for which Herr Hitler was to be host.

Already the *Juden Verboten* signs were coming down temporarily for the benefit of tourists who would soon arrive, and discretion would be the better part of righteous indignation. Goebbels managed a vicious reprisal though. Henceforth there would be no meetings of Jewish theatrical groups, no concerts and no lectures.

Everything was sweetness and light in the twin towns of Garmisch-Partenkirchen, chosen for the Winter Games. The setting was perfect, and the Germans had spent a million and a quarter dollars on buildings and other facilities. Fifty thousand chilled but happy tourists were on hand to watch the athletes of all nations make their grand entrance.

Organizing Committee President Karl Ritter von Halt rose to announce Host Hitler. The great man spoke: "I hereby declare these Fourth Olympics Winter Games of the year 1936, held in Garmisch-Partenkirchen, open!"

A German athlete in the arena spoke for the contestants, the torch across the way blazed, and the games were in progress. Some said Hitler looked longingly across the snowy mountains toward Austria, not far from the scene of the games.

The games were a success. Magnanimously the Germans had even allowed a Jewish hockey player, Rudi Ball, to play on the team. He did an excellent job, and Germany took a second place. Hitler's "friend," 28-year-old actress Leni Reifenstahl, was everywhere acting as a semiofficial hostess and filming the proceedings for posterity. She was at home in the snowy mountains, too, having spent so much of her time skiing in a bathing suit that she had earned the nickname "Oily Goat" from the journalists.

Never before had there been so well organized an Olympics management, and foreigners were mightily impressed. Here was a happy people, united under its *Führer*, with glowingly healthy and rugged athletes a testimony to "Strength Through Joy" and vice versa.

In addition to Hitler and his hostess, Goebbels, Göring and Von Ribbentrop acted as goodwill ambassadors, too. One glorious "Italian Night" frolic saw a thousand guests entertained in spectacular splendor. Everybody got to know everybody and friendships blossomed, like that between Rudolf Hess, Deputy Leader of the Nazis, and England's Lord Hamilton.

America and England were generally convinced that the Olympics were a smash success. No evidence of impartiality was found, and some spokesmen began to gain more understanding of Herr Hitler.

Britain's Secretary of State for War, Alfred Duff Cooper, did a bit of reminiscing and came up with the conclusion that his country's own Nurse Edith Cavell, though a courageous woman, deserved what she got from the Germans in World War I. And the Earl of Cork, in a public speech, justified Germany's sinking of the *Lusitania*. Why, "the Lusitania might have been used to transport ten thousand American troops on a single voyage to fight Germany," he reminded his listeners tolerantly. "If women and children choose to cruise about in war zones, they must expect what they get. In sinking the *Lusitania* as an act of war, the German Admiralty was right!"

Distance, of course, lends enchantment. Belgium, hard by the Nazi soil, did not share England's faith in Hitler. She actually was afraid of imminent invasion, and said so.

"We must prepare for an invasion even more sudden and devastating than 1914," Belgian spokesmen said. They had a grim reason for their statements. "Today," one of them noted, "many experts recommend military invasion without notice or declaration of war."

"Nonsense," Hitler scoffed. "We want only peace and justice."

From Berlin, then, he set out on a sad journey by train to Schwerin and the funeral of poor Wilhelm Gustloff. The *Führer* himself delivered the oration.

"You did not die in vain, Wilhelm Gustloff!" he assured the dead martyr to Nazism, white-knuckled and close to tears. "What your Jewish murderer did not foresee was that he prepared the way for an awakening of millions and millions of Germans to a truly German way of life. In every office will hang Gustloff's picture! My dear Party Comrade, you will never be forgotten; Gustloff will be the patron saint of all Germans living abroad!"

A sample of the truly German way of life showed up in the trial of an alleged anti-Nazi named Nisselbeck. The suspect was an American citizen living in Munich, but he had made the mistake of talking against the party. A Nazi criminal selected Nisselbeck as the guilty man from photographs. Asked how many photos he was shown, the Nazi mumbled, "One or two."

There was another trial going on in Schwerin that caused some embarrassment. Adolf Seefeld, a 65-year-old suspect in the murder of perhaps as many as thirty young boys during sex orgies, was found guilty of a mere dozen of these. For his horrible crimes he got fifteen years, castration and the loss of his head; the sentence last mentioned to be carried out first. Much as the Nazis wished otherwise, the murderer was no Jew. The best they could salvage was that "Liberalism" was a major contribution to the crime.

Some French newspapers were doing their best to make progress difficult for Herr Hitler. A journalist from the powerful *Paris-Midi* came to interview the *Führer*, pointing out some pretty obvious inconsistencies between German talk and actions. Hitler charmed him right out of his doubts. Arm about the Frenchman, Adolf argued, "Isn't it obviously wiser for our two countries to get along together?"

It was *so* obvious, and so exactly what the French wanted to believe that the French cabinet was mollified. In return, it had the noisy paper, *Le Journal*, raided and seized all copies of a Sunday feature titled "Hitler's Secret Loves."

Le Journal had made the mistake of detailing some of the *Führer*'s amours. There was Jenny Hang, sister of a one-time Hitler chauffeur, and Erna Hanfstaengl, sister of Hitler's friend "Putsi." Even Winifred Wagner, widowed daughter-in-law of the composer, and Margared Slezak, daughter of the Viennese tenor, had taken Hitler's fancy. Leni Riefenstahl, a current favorite, had protested that the Leader's love could only be platonic.

The romantic tie mentioned in *Le Journal* that most ired Nazis was that with Hitler's own niece, Greta Granbald. This attachment had come in the early days. According to one version, worried Nazis had ordered the "accident" that killed the luckless girl and freed the *Führer* for the important work ahead. Another rumor had it that she'd committed suicide; still another that Hitler had shot her. Adolf himself was portrayed as still carrying the torch for the dead girl.

The League of Nations bumbled along without Germany, and England's "Eden diplomacy" seemed like a walk on a treadmill. But if the Allies didn't know what they were doing or where they were going, Hitler most assuredly did.

On March 7, German soldiers marched without opposition into the demilitarized Rhineland. Germans were ecstatic. In Cologne one old burger declared that he was going to treat the first German soldier he could find to a riproaring drunk—and he was going to get drunk with him. "Heil Hitler; thanks be to God!" he exulted. *"Deutschland Uber Alles!"*

At most there might have been 35,000 soldiers, Allied intelligence reckoned. It was a token force, a handful of men compared with French military might. German generals themselves trembled and shook in their boots. If the French had made any effort at retaliation, the Germans would have had to pull back immediately or be blown to bits. Hitler himself admitted that "A retreat on our part would have meant collapse." Only Hitler had the gall, the calculating daring, to make such a move. He had calculated well. The French did not send the Germans packing.

At noon on the fateful day the *Führer* turned the Reichstag into a frenzy with his announcement:

"Men of the German Reichstag, in this historic hour we unite in two sacred vows." Choked with emotion, the *Führer* waited for pandemonium to subside. "First, we swear to yield to no force whatever in restoration of the honor of our people. Second, we pledge that now more than ever we shall strive for an understanding between the European peoples—Germany will never break the peace!"

The Rhineland reoccupation was the turning point for the Third Reich. For two days Hitler suffered "the most nerve-racking period in my whole life." But it worked.

"After all," England's Lord Lothian remarked, "the Germans are only going into their own back garden."

Eden, though concerned, said, "We have no reason to suppose that Germany's present action threatens hostilities."

The London *Daily Express* polled 5,000 Britishers and found that 55 percent of them preferred the Germans over the French, 24 percent favored the French, and the rest held no opinion. Germans boasted loudly that now they had crossed Lord Baldwin's "British frontier," the Rhine, and the British had done nothing about it. As if Hitler needed any excuse, he claimed one in the new French-Russian alliance which, in his words, "violated Locarno." Wiseacres said the demilitarized zones stood out plainly—they were the ones full of soldiers.

"I never felt myself as dictator of my people," Adolf told the faithful, "but only as their leader. I have therefore decided to dissolve the German Reichstag so that the German people by their ballots may now pass judgment on my leadership and that of my associates. Germany has regained her honor!"

What Hitler proposed on the heels of the Rhineland coup was an election that would go down in history as perhaps the strongest mandate ever recorded. Its voters were still under the potent spell of German *soldiers* actually and firmly entrenched in the territory "stolen" from Germany at Versailles and Locarno. The international backdrop was becoming more confused, with the 550th anniversary of Heidelberg University about to be blackballed by scholars at Oxford, and Director Wilhelm Furtwängler canceling his New York Philharmonic Symphony concert because of Jewish pressure he euphemistically referred to as "politics."

As the propaganda turned furor to frenzy for the forthcoming election, the Gestapo did its best to find the instigators of a campaign against the *Ja* ballot Hitler wanted. Brave underground workers, men and women who clearly saw the bloody handwriting on the election notices and had the courage to fight against it, passed out bits of paper with the plea, "Comrades vote NO! Every NO is a vote against war, misery, famine, concentration camps and murder." Followers of the deposed and jailed Communist Ernst Thalmann also spread anti-Nazi leaflets wherever they could.

It was a new kind of ballot that the *Führer* was presenting to his people, a ballot that took all the work from voting. "Those things that are too complicated I have simplified," Hitler said. This election, ostensibly to vote in the new rubber stamp Reichstag, 661 strong, required only that the voter write *Ja* or place a mark in a circle. There was no place for a *Nein* vote; this would have to be written in across the face by anyone brave and foolish enough to risk the danger. There would be plenty of risk.

A typical manifesto posted for Berliners read: "Voting begins at 9 A.M. and ends at 6 P.M. No German Comrade dare be absent, and I urge most voters strongly to vote during the morning hours." Thus far the urging was fairly standard, even commendable. But from here on the tone changed: "By 1 o'clock in the afternoon the election must be over. During the afternoon I will have all laggards dragged to the polls. None shall escape us, the town is surrounded and shut off."

Hitler campaigned tirelessly, whipping the populace to fever heat with speeches every other day, and then once a day as Propaganda Minister Goebbels planned a fitting climax. At Essen's Krupp steel works, the faithful and the fearful gathered obediently. Goebbels shrieked over nationwide radio, "Raise the flags!" and millions of swastikas were unfurled at that instant, defiant banners from every flagpole and most windows. Triumphantly Goebbels proclaimed, "Adolf Hitler *is* Germany!"

87

As the *Führer* mounted a platform atop a half-finished Krupp locomotive, every whistle in the land shrilled a tribute for a solid, screaming minute; for the next there was as deafening a silence. Then the Great Leader was ready. Raising an arm, he launched into an hour and a half of Nazi haranguing for the Germans gathered around him and their radios elsewhere.

"Germany wants peace!" he cried angrily. "But there can be no real world peace without equality." Farther along, he told them he himself possessed neither bonds nor shares, "not even a bank account!" All Hitler possessed was Germany itself; all the faithful had to do was signify agreement by saying *Ja!*

Next day was even greater. Two million Germans heard the final speech at Cologne. Waving Nazi flags handed out by brown-shirted workers, the milling, shouting, crying, singing mob waited before the great cathedral for their leader. They were not disappointed.

"I have hurt millions," he told them solemnly, "but I had to do it to create national unity. Who can find a basis for the charge that we have not been loyal to the treaties? God's grace is once more upon us, and we sink to our knees and ask the Almighty to give us His blessings and strength to stand firm in the struggle for freedom!"

Elsewhere in Berlin, the pastor of the American Church was slapped across the face for failure to give the Nazi salute. There would be freedom—freedom for good Nazis to do as Hitler chose they should. Millions of Germans, still clutching their paper flags, echoed Hitler's sacrilegious finale by singing, "We step up before God the Just to pray." And well they might pray.

Hitler was aided by every modern technique Goebbels could think of in the campaign. The *Graf Zeppelin* and the shiny new *Hindenburg* circled over Munich broadcasting tributes to the *Führer*, urging the *Ja* vote. There were 52 *Ja*'s cast aboard the *Hindenburg*; no mean feat when Commander Ernst Lehman recalled that there were only 50 people aboard. Hitler surely seemed to be getting divine help.

Election Sunday dawned to the racket of militant Hitler Youth banging on pans, and marching bands picked up the task shortly. Those who didn't hurry to the polls were aided in that direction.

There truly was no escape from such high civic responsibility. So effective was the campaign that when the votes were tallied Adolf Hitler emerged as victorious as any man could ever hope to be. Of the 45½ million eligible voters, 99 percent scratched *Ja* on the ballot or left it blank. A pathetic handful of about half a million had spirit enough left to write in *Nein* and pray God the watchers didn't see them commit such an act of treason.

For some it was a vain hope, for Nazi election workers had written numbers on ballots with milk; invisible to the electors but detectable later on. Germany had delivered itself unanimously into Hitler's hands, for better or for worse.

The Rhineland sweep and the 99 percent election jarred the world when it finally sank in. Eden's White Paper protested dazedly:

> The demilitarized zone embodied in the Versailles Treaty was for time without limit. It was an enduring undertaking. . . . If Germany refuses to rejoin the League, other countries must organize peace without her and Britain must make it clear that Germany is to have no free hand to attack Poland, Czechoslovakia, Austria, or Russia. If Britain speaks plainly there can be no war.

There were those who wondered what amount of speaking, plain or otherwise, would do any good now. Among these was American saw-maker Alvan Simonds. "I don't see how anybody can make agreements of any kind with Germany," he told an interviewer in Singapore. "She regards agreements as scraps of paper."

Unfortunately for Simonds, he then sailed with his wife on the Hamburg-American liner *Reliance* for Manila. Before he reached that port, and the safety afforded by its armed police protection, he was cursed and jostled by German passengers, had his feet trod upon and his wife spat at. The couple spent five days in their stateroom, and a luckless German friend who sympathized was attacked and beaten by the other Germans aboard.

A joyful Hitler began to reward his underlings with new and weird military titles. Göring and Von Fritsch became "Colonel-Generals," and Fleet Commander Erich Raeder was made an "Admiral-General," a unique amphibian distinction.

Benevolently the *Führer* let it be known, "I believe we shall be able to preserve for our people—*and possibly for others*—that peace upon which so much happiness and prosperity depends."

There was time, too, for the great Leipzig Trade Fair, featuring the advances the Reich was blessing Germany with. These included the scientifically designed bomb shelter of engineer Martha Burger, graduate of Munich's Institute of Technology.

Remembering the horror of World War I, the lady engineer had come up with a boiler-like metal gadget to be buried in the ground. It had bunks and provision shelves, as well as chemical filtration of the air supply for purity, and a pressurized interior to keep out gas.

Hitler made glowing promises to the fair-goers, including that of plenty of gasoline and rubber in the not so far-off future. The *Führer* had another dream in the back of his mind, too. Only one family in a hundred had an automobile in Germany now, but Hitler would remedy that. He would have a people's car, a *Volkswagen,* designed, and make it cheap enough for all to own!

There were some doubters, of course. On the sly, German businessmen were telling foreign correspondents that Hitler would bankrupt Germany in a year; that inflation, unemployment and starvation would bring about his collapse and the return of the Hohenzollerns. For their part, the Communists predicted a revolt in *less* than a year.

Elsewhere in the Reich, Bishop Muller was laboring to Nazify the Gospel of St. Matthew, with an Aryanized Sermon on the Mount, and no more reference to Jews, Pharisees or King Solomon! One typically mutilated result of his labors read: "When your comrade in excitement strikes you in the face, it is not always correct to strike back immediately."

Sports Leader Hans von Tschammer und Osten grumbled about what he considered too much eagerness to get up groups to go see the Schmeling-Louis fight. He didn't mention that part of his concern was the embarrassing odds being quoted—ten to one in the Negro's favor. But this was a minor annoyance to Germans celebrating the *Führer's* forty-seventh birthday. The Leader passed out more presents, including a field marshal's baton for General von Blomberg—the first time such a thing was ever done in peacetime. He proffered the same honor to Ludendorff, but the old man refused.

There was a parade of the growing German Army, and the slogan, "Today we own Germany, and tomorrow the world," was on everyone's lips. Göring, caught up in the fever of excitement, referred in a speech to Hitler as Supreme War Lord. This was a bit premature, and gave poor Goebbels fits. Across the Channel, Eden timidly asked for some specific answers on specific points, and was cockily silenced by the news that Hitler had already told the world all the answers.

In the midst of joy it was once more the Führer's sad duty to bury one of his top party men. His current chauffeur and bodyguard, 32-year-old Julius Schreck who affected a Hitlerian mustache for obvious reasons, died suddenly of an inflammation of the brain. There was no preacher; a philosopher did the honors, and then Himmler told the dead man, "You will serve the *Führer* in Valhalla!" Hitler himself had reserved a rare honor for Schreck—a *Schutzstaffel* detachment would henceforth be known by his name.

In June there was an abortive *"putsch"* in Linz, with a couple of foolish Nazis getting themselves killed. A confident Schuschnigg was still in control, and pleased enough to climb into his old uniform for Old Soldiers' Day, "rejoicing in the revival of the soldierly spirit."

In 1914 the Kaiser had maneuvered his fleet in practice in the North Sea. Now in 1936, the Danes were aware that something was again rotten off Denmark. Hitler went aboard his yacht, *The Whim*, to see at firsthand how his bootlegged Navy was doing. An apologetic British intelligence had an anonymous flier circle over the area at a very high altitude, taking pictures of the illegal maneuverings of a force that should not have been in existence.

While the *Führer* was thus openly scoffing at the League and the world, Max Schmeling did his bit by trouncing Joe Louis in only twelve rounds of the championship fight. German rejoicing knew no bounds, and Tschammer und Osten kicked himself around the block for not packing boatloads of German spectators for the affair.

The Germans went wild. One paper proclaimed that "Max Schmeling has smashed the adversaries of National Socialism and saved the prestige of the white race!" There was one unfortunate sports writer by the name of Bulow who

91

had predicted that Louis would win, a conclusion held by nearly everyone. For his pains, Bulow was blacklisted for life with all German papers. Schmeling won, according to Nazis, because he had been permitted to see Herr Hitler before sailing to America.

In Paris, Anthony Eden was saying brave words about the French frontier being England's, too. Remembering that the Rhine had been called the frontier earlier by Baldwin, the Nazis jeered scornfully.

Playing footsie with the Free City of Danzig now, Hitler was promising to make it a big war base and the spearhead for a drive at Russia. So cocky did Danzig become that the Nazi Senate President, Arthur Greiser, not only laid down the law to Anthony Eden at a League meeting, but thumbed his nose at the assembly as he left. Britishers, used to such treatment figuratively, were rocked by the real thing.

Mussolini had finished the job in Ethiopia by now, and the League withdrew its sanctions. The poor Emperor Haile Selassie, who had been accorded a hero's welcome when he arrived in England, was seen off by a handful when he left. One war was over, but another was getting hotter. Franco was fighting the Loyalists in Spain, and Hitler decided to aid him with bombers. Göring was elated; here was a perfect proving ground for his fledgling *Luftwaffe!*

Austria and Germany announced a pact, and it began to look as if Germany would not bother to come back into the League of Nations. She was doing pretty well without it. Coolly the *Führer* selected Joachim von Ribbentrop as ambassador to England.

"He knows everyone," he said of the former wine salesman, "even Mrs. Simpson."

"That's just it," countered Göring, "They know him, too!"

But Hitler prevailed, and Ribbentrop's task was to work for separate agreements with the British, furthering a split with the French.

Protestant pastors had written a ten-point letter of protest to Hitler, strongly censuring just about everything he was responsible for in the Reich. Worried onlookers feared that only the upcoming Olympics kept Hitler from vicious reprisal.

German law continued to be pretty much what Nazis made it. Ludwig Hoffmann, from Chicago, made two mistakes and was trapped in that law. First, he took his wife on a visit to his birthplace in Nuremberg. Second he sounded off at a beer party to the effect that the Nazi, Julius Streicher, a fat, bald, older copy of Hitler, was also a *lump*. For his mild epithet, Hoffmann found himself in jail.

Another visiting American was tactful enough to keep out of a cell. From across the channel in England, came Colonel Charles Lindbergh and wife Anne Morrow. Flier Lindbergh addressed the German Aero Club, warning of the horrors of war and pleading for education and understanding.

Hitler and Air Force boss Göring were not present, but amazingly the German press lauded Lindbergh as the heroic type emulated by the Hitler Youth movement. The text of his talk was printed in full, and he was then taken on a tour of airfields and factories such as no other foreigner had been permitted.

The hospitality at the Olympics was a repeat of the treatment at Garmisch-Partenkirchen earlier that year. Tourist rates were a big incentive; advertisements in the U.S. had held up the bait of everything at fifty cents on the dollar. The big new Olympic Stadium in Berlin packed in more than 100,000 spectators every day, and there were more reporters on hand than in Geneva. Hitler himself missed few days, and let himself in for more than he bargained for during one of his visits.

Mrs. Carla de Vries, thousands of miles from home in Norwalk, California, with her husband, was determined to make their Olympics visit a momentous one. So, while the *Führer* sat watching the events in the Aquatic Stadium, and Mr. de Vries sighted through the finder of his camera, the lady sneaked through the cordon of S.S. men, autograph book in hand.

When she shoved it under Hitler's nose, he blinked in astonishment but nevertheless signed. Most celebrity seekers would have called that good, but not Mrs. de Vries. While loyal Nazis watched in frozen horror, an impromptu wrestling match seemed to take place. Suddenly the lady grabbed the grim-faced *Führer* and kissed him soundly!

Happily Mrs. de Vries scampered back to where hubby had preserved the whole thrilling episode on film. Doubtless there were millions of jealous *fräuleins* that day. Stunned at the lethargy of his S.S. men, Hitler dismissed the troopers who had failed him. Realizing that it could have been a bullet as well as a kiss, he doubled the guard and laid down an ultimatum.

On opening day German athletes won first places in track

and field events for the first time. But the supremacy of the Aryan race was short; Jesse Owens saw to that. The U.S. team garnered twelve firsts, and the Cleveland Negro was responsible for four of them. Sports writers in Germany who had whipped up all sorts of excuses for the expected defeat of Schmeling now had a place to use them. Owens and other Negroes who had paced the U.S. to its win over third-place Germany were dismissed as being not really people, but "black auxiliaries."

Not only the Negro was slighted at the Olympics. Captain Wolfgang Fuerstner of the German Army had been commissioned to build the Olympic Village. He worked at it, and was pleased to hear it rated a first-class job. But the reward he prayed for did not come; he was told that his threatened dismissal from service would be carried out as scheduled; Fuerstner was part Jewish. Crushed, he put his gun to his head and pulled the trigger. Hitler had killed another Jew.

With the Olympics over, the Nazis got back to more serious business. With Stalin increasing his army, Hitler decided that he had better expand his own forces to 800,000 men. Panicky Frenchmen suddenly realized that their neighbor, who was not legally entitled to any army at all, now had enough troops to start a war with no further conscription.

To further point up France's plight, the *Führer* dispatched Hjalmar Schacht to Paris, where the minister reminded the French that it had taken him only five hours to fly there.

"We are really quite close, you see!" he said, as if pleasantly surprised.

All in all, Hitler was in fine fettle for the annual party congress at Nuremberg. Four years earlier he had promised the faithful that they could nail him to the cross in 1936 if things weren't better. Now he proceeded to remind the million exuberant Germans just how much better off they were.

It took him two hours to do the job. Unemployment was down, living standards were up—Jews excepted, of course. Automobiles were being produced six times as fast, and more then 640,000 tons of ships were being built. The Krupp works was turning out products, too, and the aircraft plants were busy with further surprises to guarantee Germany's regeneration. A high point of the big shindig was the fly-over of 400 spanking-new warplanes.

Far from being a candidate for a cross-nailing, the

Führer himself was going to *do* the nailing. He had even picked out a nailee—Soviet Russia.

"We will conquer the Russian star with the German swastika!" Hitler shouted. "We cannot let the countries around us succumb to Bolshevism; we are not living on the moon!"

All it would take was a plan, and Göring borrowed his from the Red enemy. Let Russia have its Five-Year Plan; Hermann had a Four-Year Plan he had sold to the *Führer*. There were some other plans, too; some that might have irked those Germans old enough to remember World War I and the word *ersatz*. A chemist named Bergius was working on a method of making food out of wood, just in case there was ever a need for it. Right now it was fit only for animals, but a nation being weaned on "guns before butter" might get to try the tasty sawdust.

In the U.S. Franklin Roosevelt was re-elected by a whopping majority, and Germany mounted the bandwagon of well-wishers for the occasion. Roosevelt, the Nazis proclaimed, was a prime example of what they called the *"Führerprinzip"*—the policies of Herr Hitler himself.

Eminent psychologist Carl Gustav Jung, a Swiss, did not quite agree. Roosevelt, according to Jung, was the "chieftain" type of leader; Hitler a "medicine man." Medicine man Hitler was sure he had diagnosed the patient's illness properly, and was prescribing as best and as fast as he knew how. He had cast a prognosis, and would shortly come up with a timetable.

Kaiser Wilhelm, forced to content himself with being Commodore of Kaiserlicher Yacht Club since his abdication in World War I, suddenly had the last of his toys taken away. Hitler ordered the group disbanded, and its quarters turned over to a real navy.

Across the channel in England, Sir Samuel Hoare, First Lord of the Admiralty, saw the handwriting along the docks and urged ships equal in fighting power to any opposition. The Nazis had gotten rid of the yachts, and suddenly made it known that they had two 35,000-ton capital ships in the works. One of them was named the *Ersatz Hannover*.

Author Hitler's fame was spreading. The Anderson Art Galleries in New York held an auction, in time for Christmas shoppers, of rare first editions of *Mein Kampf*. The uncut version of the Hitler word was stronger than later editions. One suppressed chunk read:

95

Germany must have a peace, supported not by the palm leaves of lacrimonious hired female mourners, but founded by the victorious sword of a Master-People which brings the world into the service of a higher *Kultur*.

Perhaps it was professional jealousy that prompted Hitler's outraged cries of "insult" when the Nobel Prize for Literature was awarded Carl Ossietzky, a fellow German. Another piece of writing, critical of Nazism, had put Ossietzky in jail three years earlier. Now Hitler had him placed in a sanatorium, forbid a trip to receive his prize, and announced the Nazis would grab the $40,000 for themselves.

The *Führer* had stated that progress was being made rapidly, that "in three years, Germany will be ready!"

Now, a week before Christmas, 1936, Hermann Göring stood before a group of party officials and industry leaders and announced, "We are already on the threshold of mobilization and we are already at war. All that is lacking is the actual shooting!"

The Nazis were offering a gift of peace, German style, not necessarily with good will to men.

BIBLIOGRAPHY

Mein Kampf—Hitler
Der Fuehrer—Heiden
Secret Conversations—Cameron, Stevens
The Rise and Fall of the Third Reich—Shirer

VI

The Spanish Civil War

Eruption in 1936 of the most terrible civil war in history had been heralded by almost a hundred and fifty years of bloody struggle in Spain, and we must touch briefly on this prologue.

Hot-blooded Latins fought hot wars that killed off an old monarchy in 1808. In 1834, "liberal" reforms were sought in constitutional government, and in 1868 the Army routed the monarchy again. In the resulting vacuum the class struggle was added to the religious aspect of Spanish fighting. The Spanish-American War in 1898 was another blow at the glorious tradition of a once-powerful monarchy.

Social awareness was coming to Spain, and economists "locked up the Cid's tomb" as the first step in preparing for the new order. Nationalism, class hatred and antichurch sentiment exploded in Barcelona's riots of 1909. By 1917 general strikes had so paralyzed the country they were put down only by the Army. And in 1923 the tottering King Alfonso yielded to Dictator General Primo de Rivera.

Iron-handed De Rivera presented Alfonso with an ultimatum demanding nothing short of military dictatorship. The tired king had no choice, and ended up calling the General his "Mussolini."

From 1923 to 1930, De Rivera forbid all political parties, imprisoned his opposition, but killed no one. There were no more of the ruinous riots or strikes, and with the help of Calvo Sotelo, Minister of Finance, the dictator pushed a public works program that boomed the economy. He also ended the war in Morocco victoriously.

A colorful and courageous figure, he drank hard and consorted with gypsies. Attending the theater one night, he smoked a cigar in spite of the signs prohibiting such an act. When someone timidly pointed out his transgression, he rose grandly, waved his cigar and announced, "Tonight everybody smokes!"

In the end, economics finished off the dictatorship. Coincident with the disastrous crash of 1929 in the United States, Spain suffered a slump. This wrecked De Rivera's highway and railroad programs and now his brother officers rose against him. Liberal and professional alike joined the fray, and Finance Minister Sotelo quit. Wearily the dictator merely "retired," exiling himself to France.

Alfonso tried ineffectually to fill the breach De Rivera had left. But by now the Republicans, Socialists and Nationalists banded together and plotted a rebellion. Although the revolt was abortive, pressure on the King forced him to agree to elections on April 12, 1931.

The results of the elections indicated to Alfonso the strength of the Republicans, and he issued a final statement to the effect that "Sunday's elections have shown me that I no longer enjoy the love of my people. . . . Until the nation speaks I shall deliberately suspend the use of my Royal Prerogatives."

Claiming he could have bested his enemies, the King professed to want no part of a civil war. He exiled himself on the coast, the tail end of the Bourbon kings.

The accession of the new Republic had been remarkably smooth and free of bloodshed, but the years following were hectic. Republicans were attacked from the left by radical screams to destroy the decadent civilization of Spain, and from the Church, whose Cardinal Segura made public a letter praising the Monarchists and condemning the new government.

A few days after Segura's letter, rioting broke out, with Monarchists and Republicans killing one another. Newspaper plants were demolished and the burning of churches began. Anarchists in Spain numbered perhaps two million at this time, and middle-of-the-road Republicans were faced with the problem of dealing with these fanatics and at the same time worrying about the plotting of the Monarchists, who included many Army leaders.

When workers struck at Seville, the government called in the artillery and killed 30 and wounded 200 more. In the village of Castil-Blanco the Anarchists incited the whole population to attack the government's Civil Guard. Four were killed, their heads smashed and their eyes gouged out. One body had thirty-seven knife wounds. In the town of Sallent the CNT, as the Anarchists were known, raised a red flag over the town hall and took over the town for several hours.

The country by now was a patchwork of alphabetized factions warring on each other and the government. Opposing the CNT was the rival UGT union. There were also the POUM and PSUC, Communist unions, and FUE, a student union. On the far right were the Falangists of Don José Antonio de Rivera, son of the former dictator, the JONS, a student organization, the UME, a secret military organization, and others.

By 1932 General Sanjurjo headed a rightist "rising" against the government. Like the one in 1931, this, too, fizzled out and the Republicans rocked along until the Anarchists rebelled in 1933. The government was forced to kill many of them in the province of Cádiz, invoking the *"ley de fugas"* or "law of flight." As a result the government was accused of promoting a regime of "blood, mud and tears." Strikes continued and multiplied.

Finally came the "October Revolution" in Barcelona, Madrid and the mining region of Asturias. Between the devil and the deep, the Republican government called on General Francisco Franco-Bahamonde and the Foreign Legion to quell the miners' revolution.

With the end of the October Revolution, 30,000 political prisoners were jailed. These included all the Socialist leaders, those of the obstreperous Catalan government, and men like Manuel Azaña and Largo Caballero.

Though the fearful middle class would have welcomed a seizing of more power by the strengthened right, nothing was done in this direction. José Antonio de Rivera and his triumphant "blue shirts" wrangled with the JONS and apparently rested on their laurels. Young De Rivera did write to Franco suggesting a military coup, but the General did not answer.

There were no political executions, and though left-wingers had been sentenced to thirty years, the right weakened and let Manuel Azaña out almost immediately. The "Cortes," or Parliament, was weak and vacillating; seventy-two ministers had served it in the short space of four and a half years. Now President Alcala Zamora despaired of making something of the present Cortes and dissolved it. Elections were held in February of 1936 that would lead directly to the Civil War, a war that would exceed even the American Civil War in death and destruction.

Such had been the violence of Spain's recent past that the 1936 elections were called the most peaceful in years—there were only 8 killed and 32 wounded! 'Premier Valladares' Centrist government promised neutrality in the revolution-antirevolution question, aligning itself with the conservative right. But the left surged to a sweeping victory. Membership for this extremist group in the Cortes shot from 107 to 230, while the right, "Anti-Revolution" bloc dropped from 228 to 200. The Centrists held 65 seats, and allied with the right still outweighed the left, but in the confusion following the elections rioting swept Spain.

With the "mandate" of the "Popular Front" victory, leftists broke open the jails and freed the 30,000 political prisoners as well as many murderers and other criminals. They even tried to free lepers from the asylum at Fontilles, failing only when the lepers themselves refused to leave the institution.

Premier Valladares chose to turn over control of the Cortes to Manuel Azaña as leader of the Popular Front. Catalonia was given local autonomy. The Institute of Agrarian Reform began to move thousands of landless peasants onto their own farms, and amnesty decrees forced employers to hire back all workers while retaining those they had. Ex-convicts paraded with red flags, singing the *Internationale* and shouting, "Love Live Russia!"

The value of the Spanish peseta dropped and moneyed and titled Spaniards began to flee across the border into France. Some of them, like the Duquesa de Fernan Nunez, were forced to buy their way out with jewels left "for safekeeping" with Spanish border guards. Guitarist Andrés Segovia and his wife fled, minus her jewels and his children by a former marriage. Even political grafter Juan March, who had recently been "selling" governorships to the highest bidder, fled.

President Zamora had feared that Don Gil Robles, of the right-wing party, would try a coup and become dictator. Now the Cortes was in the hands of Azaña's Popular Front, a coalition of Socialists and Communists which was part of the *Comintern's* United Front called for by Joseph Stalin.

With this new stature the Communists in Spain began to multiply like rabbits. In the space of a month from the February elections, more than 50 people had been killed and 200 wounded in violent fighting between left and right.

100

Seventeen churches and 11 convents were burned, along with 33 rightist clubs, 10 newspaper buildings and 22 other buildings. Peasants were said to be overrunning President Zamora's estate.

The Falangists of De Rivera fought back, riding around the cities with machine guns. A bomb was placed in the home of left-wing Cortes Leader Largo Caballero, and De Rivera was jailed in reprisal. When he was tried, he pleaded his own case and lost.

Flinging off the lawyer's robe, he stamped on it in a rage. "Bastards!" he cried at his accusers. "There is no more justice in Spain. *Arriba, España!* Up, Spain!"

In the ensuing riot, a statue of justice was hurled against a wall and De Rivera was subdued by a flung inkwell. Dozens of Fascists in the courtroom were arrested and De Rivera was bustled off to jail where he would remain for the rest of his short life.

In the Cortes, Don Gil Robles protested that Russia had sent $200,000 to finance the revolution. Catalonians shouted him down with cries of "Down with Fascism!" and seceded.

In April the leftists under Azaña moved with the speed and strength their right-wing enemies had refused to use. On a technicality, President Zamora was removed from office. Shortly after that, as strife continued, Azaña himself was elected President by a vote of 238 to 5, with 30 Monarchists abstaining and 115 Catholics casting blank ballots. Santiago Quiroga was named Premier.

Now the man who short months ago had been in jail, a political prisoner, headed his country. Don Manuel Azaña at 56 was a flabby, frog-faced man whose skin had a greenish cast. Right-wing newspapers called him "The Monster" and it was common talk that he was a homosexual. He had, however, married ten years earlier. As President he received a salary of one million pesetas a year, plus a similar sum for his young wife.

Despite Azaña's protestations that Communism in Spain was impossible, his underlings loudly proclaimed such sentiments.

Margarita Nelken, a Socialist Cortes member, said, "We want a revolution, but it is not the Russian revolution which can serve us as a model, since we must have huge flames which can be seen all over the world and waves of blood which turn the seas red."

101

And Largo Caballero, who had avidly read Marx and Lenin while in prison, stated, "When the Popular Front breaks up, the triumph of the proletariat will be certain."

Back in 1934, General Francisco Franco had beaten down that proletariat. A brilliant soldier who had fought strikers in 1917 and the enemy in Morocco during the twenties, Franco was a plump professional with a rather shrill voice. He had set records as the youngest officer for his rank with each promotion, and his devotion to duty had delayed his marriage to Carmen Polo.

Something of his character is shown in a legendary story of his encounter with a burly legionnaire who was so sick of the Army fare he threw a plate of the poor food into Franco's face. Franco calmly and silently mopped his face and uniform with a handkerchief and completed his tour of inspection. Then he did three things: He ordered the food improved, he restricted the whole detachment to its post for ninety days, and he had the soldier shot for insubordination. His brother, Ramón, was a famous aviator and also a good Republican. His brother-in-law, Ramón Suner, however, was a leader of the violently right-wing CEDA.

The government chose Franco mainly because they were not sure any other officers would obey; they specified Foreign Legion troops and Moorish regulars because they feared local conscripts would be beaten by tough dynamite-tossing miners. General Franco took the towns of Oviedo and Gijón in two weeks of fighting. He used aircraft and tactics described as atrocities. Some 300 soldiers and civil guards died, and more than a thousand revolutionists, most of whom were miners. Confiscated were 90,000 rifles, 3300 pistols, 10,000 cases of dynamite, 30,000 hand grenades and 330,000 cartridges!

Now in 1936, General Franco had been shipped off to the Canary Islands in a protective banishment. Strikes were again rampant, particularly in the cities of Madrid and Barcelona, where everybody from elevator workers to bullfighters demanded more money. In Madrid alone there were 100,000 idle workers and the threat of a general tie-up of the railroads.

Minister of Labor Juan Lluhi settled the elevator strike by simply arresting and holding the owners until they met the demands of the workers! Meanwhile the Anarchists blew up so many water mains that half the buildings in Madrid were without water. Murders were common on the streets, and when Falangists shot two Socialists, the Socialists in turn caught a young Fascist, stripped him naked and lashed him to a tree where they smashed his skull with machine gun bullets. A rumor that priests and nuns had poisoned the candy of youngsters in a tenement district touched off rioting against the Church.

On July 13 came the murder that was to be the last straw. At three o'clock in the morning a police car, dispatched by Azaña's government, halted in front of the apartment of Calvo Sotelo, now Cortes leader of the rightist opposition to Azaña's government.

Led by Captain Condes of the Civil Guard, the special police went up the stairs and rapped on Sotelo's door. When he had inspected the papers of Condes and had been assured he was just wanted for questioning, Sotelo left his family, promising to let them know what the trouble was as soon as he could. "Unless," he added, "these gentlemen are going to blow my brains out!"

Minutes later they did just that as the car raced off at top speed. Two shots were fired into the back of Sotelo's neck and his bloody corpse was then delivered unceremoniously to East Cemetery in Madrid. The police told the attendant that it was a night watchman they had found in the street, and it was not until noon next day that the assassination was discovered.

Simultaneous with the killing of Sotelo, another group of police had been dispatched to kill Rightist leader Don Gil Robles. Providentially for him he was out of town for the weekend. But when the murder of Sotelo was known it was enough. To add to the crime, Azaña refused to let Sotelo's body lie in state anywhere. Thirty thousand rightists attended the funeral, a funeral held the same day as that of a Lieutenant Castillo who had been killed by Falangists.

Rioting broke out at the funeral and four more died under police fire. Chaos reigned in the city as Gil Robles addressed the Cortes in tribute to Sotelo. He blamed the government not just for Sotelo's murder, but for sixty others in the last month alone. Then he, with many others, quit the Cortes as a final protest.

At midnight on July 16, General Franco, accompanied by his wife and daughter, went aboard a boat that would take him to Las Palmas, where the military governor conveniently had just shot himself dead. Franco had started a fateful journey that over the next three years would take him from banished Army Chief of Staff to the most powerful and lasting dictator the modern world had ever known.

The military "rising" was no spontaneous, unplanned thing. Long ago General Franco and political leader Gil Robles had laid out secret gun emplacements in Spain against the day they would be needed. More recently, a fast plane had left England and made its way carefully to Las Palmas. Now it was ready to whisk Franco from the Canaries to the town of Melilla, where the first overt act of the rebellion took place.

When word of the planned revolt leaked out early in Melilla, however, it was necessary for the officers in on the plot to take command prematurely. Franco remained on Las Palmas, proclaiming himself in command of the Canaries in a manifesto broadcast on the captured radio.

While phone lines out of Spain to the north went dead, to the great alarm of other countries, the Spanish government itself was shocked each time a garrison was called and responded with a triumphant, *"Arriba España!"*

In a single day Franco's forces controlled all of Morocco and its 20,000 troops. They seized the radio station at Ceuta and began broadcasting as if they were in Seville, claiming victory there, and announced the fall of Madrid as well. Actually, the garrison at Seville, along with the Civil Guard, went over to the rebellion, while workers barricaded the suburbs, and set fire to churches and factories.

Cádiz, Jerez, La Línea, Córdoba and Algeciras quickly fell at least partly into rebel hands. Málaga soon followed. In Madrid the government wrung its hands and Premier Santiago Casares Quiroga hastily called on President Azaña and Cortes leaders to pull its fighting factions together to meet the attack.

Three thousand taxi drivers volunteered themselves and their vehicles. Threats were made to the upstart General Franco, along with hopeful compromise suggestions that would make him call off his soldiers. Radio broadcasts told of the revolt being crushed, and speakers like the woman Communist, La Pasionaria, pled with even the women to fight with knives and burning oil.

"No pasaran!" she cried, in what would become the Loyalist watchword. "They shall not pass! It is better to die on your feet than live on your knees!" Interspersed

104

with the speeches and news broadcast was recorded music, bizarrely including *The Music Goes Round and Round.*

The government-favored UGT union had previously been issued some 8,000 rifles for political police duty, but cautious Premier Quiroga refused to hand over more arms to the clamoring citizenry. Government planes were sent to bomb Morocco, but they were ineffectual. One break did come, though, when the officers of three destroyers on their way to Melilla sought to deliver the ships to the rebels. The crews refused to go along with such treason, and imprisoned the officers and sailed back to Cartagena and Loyalist control.

With the world seemingly going to pieces about him, Quiroga resigned as Premier. Azaña appointed Martínez Barrio to succeed him. A hundred thousand workers shouted "Traitors!" and renewed their demands for arms. Barrio hastened to comply, and soon truckloads of guns were in the streets and being delivered to the impassioned populace.

It was Sunday now, traditionally the day of the toreador, but there would be no bull fights then or for a long time to come. General Franco had flown to Tetuan in Africa, while ships carrying his soldiers were heading for the mainland of Spain.

Already Franco could claim Andalusia, Valencia, Burgos, Valladolid, Aragon and the Balearic Islands. In the Asturian mining sections, the same Major Aranda who had bested the miners in 1934 moved in again to take Oviedo. But Madrid and Barcelona held fast, despite troops in commandeered cars moving up from the coast. For the first time in hundreds of years bearded and burnoosed Moors were fighting stunned Spaniards on the mainland.

Most of the Navy was kept in the government's hands by the men of the ships themselves, overpowering their officers as the crews of the destroyers had done. Franco had only one gunboat, the *Dato,* which he put to good use hauling troops from Africa to the mainland. He also used aircraft to transport Foreign Legionnaires.

After the first whirlwind days of Franco's thrust from Africa, the war settled down to a long, hard grind. It soon became apparent that Franco was being aided by Mussolini. Early in August, twenty-one Savoia-Marchetti bombers took off from Sardinia and headed for Melilla in Spanish Morocco, scene of the first revolt. Eighteen of them reached their goal almost 800 miles distant, but three of them crashed embarrassingly in French Morocco. They carried crewmen who were obviously Italian Air Force regulars, plus cargoes of machine guns, grenades and ammunition. Also in evidence with Franco's troops were German steel helmets. In return, it was rumored, the General had already promised Mussolini the town of Ceuta, across from Gibraltar, as well as the Balearic Islands for a naval base.

The Loyalists, too, had help from the outside. In Moscow's Red Square a hundred thousand Communists had voted 200 million rubles to help the Spanish workers, and Russian freighters were on their way to Spanish ports. French Army men, officially neutral, went to the aid of clumsy militiamen unable to properly use artillery.

Eventually there would be thousands of German and Italian troops fighting with Franco. These countries also provided planes and pilots. One of the first aerial successes of these foreign pilots was the bombing of the government's biggest gunboat, *Jaime Primero*. Communists from Russia, meanwhile, joined the Loyalist militia, and eventually there would be the International Brigades with sympathizers from many countries, including the United States. The only group in any way comparable to the Brigaders were some 600 Irish Catholics who fought for Franco.

Bert Acosta, famous American flier who was Admiral Byrd's pilot, flew for Loyalist Spain for a salary of $1,500 a month, plus a bonus of $1,000 for each Nationalist plane he shot down. Acosta recruited more Americans, but before year's end he was back in the States protesting to the Government that he had not been paid the salary promised him and asking that Uncle Sam seize a Spanish ship then in an American port loading with American plane engines a dealer insisted it was his right to sell.

The United States officially observed a policy of nonintervention along with most major powers. Even Germany and Italy pretended nonintervention when it suited their aims. France aided the Loyalists as much as she dared while at the same time trying to force Italy to desist from helping Franco. With its gold hoard of some $400 million, the Spanish government was in a better financial position than were Franco and his Nationalists. This money was shipped to France to bolster Spanish credit.

The government maintained its hold on Madrid and Barcelona and the proletariat was having a field day. By late

August more than 200 churches had been burned, and the Communists sparked the looting of religious buildings and the killing of clerics. A fortune was confiscated from the priests, and one exceptional haul was some eight million pesetas found in the corsets of the sister of the Bishop of Jaen. About $40 million was taken from the Church.

Elsewhere Loyalist women helped themselves to sewing machines while their men drove off in newly liberated Fords and Chevrolets. An estimated $70 million in American property was confiscated despite the efforts of Embassy people pathetically posting warnings against such flagrant violations.

Premier Barrio had stepped down by now for Don José Giralt Pereira, scientist and Chancellor of Madrid University. More than forty generals had been dismissed from what was left of the Army under Republican control, and so most of the officers were recruited from the Anarchists, Socialists and Communists.

More than half a million guns had been handed out to the soldier populace, and a thousand militiamen were being trained a day. Asked about target practice for them, an officer snorted derisively. "They get their target practice at the front," he said, "on live targets!"

By now the split defining the government Loyalists and Franco's Nationalists was obvious. On the side of the government were the incensed working classes and landless peasants, plus Socialists and Communists of Spain and elsewhere in the world. For Franco were the Church, Monarchists, Fascists and landowners, plus Hitler and Mussolini. To retain the help of the Monarchists, Franco permitted the flag of ex-King Alfonso to fly over troops in the south.

There were incidents that came dangerously close to involving foreign powers in the fight. The American Ambassador to Spain, Claude Bowers, had written a letter home a few weeks earlier deprecating all the worry over the turmoil in Spain. The strikes were not nearly so bad as the New York elevator strikes, he said, and Spain was agitated by propagandists who hated democracies.

Now Bowers reconsidered, and fled San Sebastian to safety in France after briefly using the U.S. Coast Guard cutter *Cayuga* as a floating embassy. Not so fortunate was the Norwegian consul at San Sebastian whose pregnant wife was shot and killed by teen-age snipers. The yacht *Blue Shadow* was shelled in the Mediterranean by Franco's forces, killing her British skipper and injuring his wife, who was

107

the former Eloise Drake of Norwich, Connecticut. Later, the *Cayuga* put in to San Sebastian to take off refugee Americans.

A Nationalist cruiser, the *Almirante Cervera,* bore down on the tiny American vessel and warned its skipper she would fire if he dared take any Loyalists aboard. The *Cayuga's* captain answered, "Thank you!" and went on with his loading. When the *Almirante* unlimbered eight 6-inch guns, the *Cayuga* cockily swiveled its own 5-incher. Finally the cruiser steamed off without another word.

Other sea encounters were more serious. A Red warship made the mistake of halting and searching a German freighter. In a rage, Hitler dispatched three pocket battleships to patrol the waters off Spain. When a German ship was bombed with more than twenty dead, the *Führer* in retaliation had his warships shell at pointblank range a town held by the Loyalists.

The fighting dragged on in Barcelona. Signs went up proclaiming *"Private property is confiscated!"* and there were new waves of fleeing refugees. A Madrid paper declared, "The only good bondholder is a dead bondholder!" The parting greeting of *Adios* was used no more, since it meant "Go with God." In its place was *Salud,* literally "Health."

Those who escaped into Portugal or France reported that gangs of young boys and girls roved the streets with machine guns. Under pressure of the war, morals suffered. "Marriage by usage" became common, with people who lived together ten months automatically considered husband and wife. The time was cut in case the woman became pregnant.

Yet Barcelona continued a gay spot for troops on leave, with movies like Shirley Temple's *The Little Colonel* and the Marx Brothers' *Duck Soup* to study for military tactics as well as for fun, and traveling theatrical groups were "conscripted" to give five shows a day for salaries of a dollar a day and a meal ticket.

The atrocities committed were among the worst ever recorded, with little edge to either side. One writer decided that he could excuse the Loyalists because their acts seemed dictated by sheer animal spirit, while those of the Nationalists were carried out in a cold and calculated manner. Militiawomen were raped and their breasts cut off by the invading soldiers, and the warning, "Do you want to be raped by the Moors?" was a strong goad to a grim defense.

Priests and nuns alike were murdered and mutilated. Nuns were brutally raped; one was murdered because she refused to marry a militiaman. A priest was set upon by an Anarchist mob and beaten unmercifully while they reviled him.

"Blaspheme and we will forgive you!" the tormentors cried.

"It is I who will forgive you," the priest insisted. He was loaded down with a cross when he said he wanted to be like Jesus, and finally shot in the head. His last request was to face his captors so he could bless them. Rosaries were thrust into the ears of churchmen until their eardrums burst, and the mother of two Jesuits had a cross rammed down her throat.

When there was time for such luxury each side presented the goals it was working toward. Though he stood for dictatorship, Franco pledged some social reforms. For its part, the government stood for collective farms, nationalized banks, railroads and so on, with a dictatorship of another kind—one of the proletariat. By now its Communists were in the ascendancy, louder and wilder than the once middle-of-the-road Republicans who had expediently taken them in.

Foreign nationals had been moved out of Madrid and other cities, though some continued to stay. Sosthenes Benes, manager of I.T. & T's fourteen-story skyscraper in Madrid was one of these. It was suggested half-jokingly that actually he had built the workers to the strength they now enjoyed, since most of them could not read or write but the telephone gave them the communication medium that was all they needed.

Outside of Germany and Italy, sentiment seemed mostly with the Loyalists. This was particularly true among sensitive intellectuals in Britain and the United States, as well as labor unions which sent money to aid the embattled workers in Spain.

Poets like T. S. Eliot, W. H. Auden and Stephen Spender saw in the Spanish workers the true spirit of democracy, and wrote lyric tributes in their names. Scientists like the Britisher, Haldane, came to Spain with his wife to be near their son who had joined the International Brigade. Writer George Orwell, of *1984* fame, fought alongside the Loyalists though he was later disillusioned, as were many others who did not find in Spain the idealism they had read into its Civil War.

The idea that the Loyalists were fighting the great Fascist

dictators caught the sympathy of men who had seen Mussolini overrun Ethiopia. When it was suggested that Loyalist Spain lay its case before the League of Nations, Ethiopia was recalled sarcastically.

Indeed, all the impotent League could muster was the halfhearted suggestion of a plebiscite to find which side the mass of Spaniards actually favored. Cynics said even the *Literary Digest* could do that much. Late in 1936, Britain and France, and supposedly Germany and Italy as well, put a *cordon sanitaire* about the war-torn country and proposed to let her stew in her own juice.

This was, of course, sham. Hitler and Mussolini were finding Spain a fine proving ground for men and equipment, including their latest aircraft. Russia sent tanks, and it was pointed out that for the first time Fascist soldiers were defeated when Loyalists routed an Italian contingent. It was a deadly proving ground. In the first two months of the Civil War, an estimated 85,000 had been killed, and 300,000 more wounded.

There were heroics on both sides. Miners trying to retake the town of Oviedo catapulted dynamite charges against strong points and swore to capture Major Aranda if they had to do it "over the dead bodies of our children." San Sebastian fell to the Nationalists.

In Toledo, the Alcazar fortress was defended by some 1,900 Nationalist soldiers, women and children who holed up inside at the outbreak of hostilities. On July 23, the Loyalist militia leader in Madrid telephoned Colonel Moscardo, in command of the Alcazar, to tell him if he did not surrender the militia would kill his son, Luis. As proof that Luis was indeed a hostage, he was allowed to speak.

"What is happening, my boy?" asked Moscardo.

"Nothing, Papa," Luis answered. "They say they will shoot me if the Alcazar does not surrender.

"If it be true, commend your soul to God, shout *Viva España*, and die like a hero," Moscardo said. "Good-bye my son, a last kiss."

"Good-bye, Father," Luis answered, "A very big kiss."

Moscardo added only, "The Alcazar will never surrender", and hung up. He was correct. For seventy-one days, while the Loyalists blasted the rock walls with 10,000 rounds of pointblank artillery fire and tons of dynamite, and sprayed it with gasoline from fire hoses so it could be set afire, the stubborn garrison held out. Dances were held inside; babies

110

were born. All the while the trained cadets kept up a fire that took heavy toll of the militiamen outside. When Franco's troops arrived and took Toledo, nearly all inside burst out in good physical condition and excellent spirits. Only 80 had died, and 500 were wounded.

As if to point up the impotence of the exiled King in relation to Spain, his son Don Juan was rejected when he offered his services to Franco's army. He returned to Paris. His brother, Prince Alfonso, pretender to the throne, lay in a hospital in New York near death from hemophilia.

The atrocities continued. At Bilbao, militiawomen attacked a prison ship and killed 210 victims, including 30 priests, with guns, bayonets and knives. Far to the north, Franco was moving toward what he smilingly hoped would be a quick end to hostilities.

At the Nationalist provisional capital of Burgos, General Miguel Cabanelles touched his sword to Franco's shoulder and appointed him President of Spain. Immediately the new ruler promised cordial relations with all countries save one—Soviet Russia.

Then began the drive south to Madrid in October. With an exuberant Franco and his army almost at the gates of the city, President Azaña, who had pledged never to leave the capital alive, fled south to the relative safety of Barcelona. By now, Largo Caballero was the Premier and the government was to all intents Communist-controlled. So vociferous was Caballero that he succeeded in alienating the British to the point where they recognized the Franco government.

As Madrid braced itself, the Loyalists were hard hit on the coast as well. A Russian freighter unloading at Cartagena was bombed by Nationalist planes and burned. At about the same time, the Franco destroyer *Velasco* engaged and sank the Loyalist sub B-6. But the defenders of Madrid had other things to think of.

By early November Franco's Moorish Silver Falcons of Death were within the city limits and had killed 125 of the defenders. Some of the Red militia actually fled across the lines to join the Nationalists. The Moors, clad in sweaters against the unaccustomed cold, were a sight to strike terror into the militia and perhaps this stiffened the resistance. The city did not fall.

By the end of November Franco was subjecting it to air raids, and the tall I. T. & T. building was hit repeatedly by the allegedly deadly thermite bombs but refused to be seriously damaged. Inside, Manager Benes served food to frightened mothers and children using the skyscraper as an air raid shelter.

In Barcelona Falangist Leader José Antonio de Rivera, long a prisoner, was executed because of the bombing. Franco announced the killing of Largo Caballero's son in reprisal. At about the same time, both Germany and Italy officially recognized the Franco government, and France withdrew its Popular Front support to make the Loyalists' future seem blacker. One-time boxer Paulino Uzcudun had left the United States and now piloted a speedboat in the Mediterranean picking up Nationalist survivors.

The siege went into its second month. Franco had optimistically promised bread and heat in Spanish homes this winter, but winter was here with a vengeance and he had still not taken Madrid. A shocked Red Cross calculated that half a million had died in the war thus far, and it was apparent now that there would be no sudden end, either way. Premier Largo Caballero appealed to the League of Nations against intervention by Germany and Italy, apparently forgetting that Russia and Mexico were then helping him.

A story in the *New York Times* claimed that 25,000 had been put to death by the Loyalists in Madrid for political and religious reasons. Perhaps it was as well that the bloody participants did not know the war would drag itself on for two more agonizing years before the smiling and confident Franco would in truth be dictator, *El Caudillo*, of the country of his birth.

BIBLIOGRAPHY

The Spanish Civil War—Thomas
The Yoke and the Arrows—Matthews
Falange—Payne

VII

Selassie's Ethiopia

Emperor Haile Selassie in 1936 well knew the meaning of the old saw, "Uneasy lies the head that wears the crown." With the Italians hammering at his very door he knew the year would be one of decision for his country and himself. Even the crown itself that he wore on occasion as Haile Selassie I, *Negusa Negast* (King of Kings), the Power of Trinity, and the Conquering Lion of Judah, was a talisman of the danger lurking for the ruler of the land many men still called Abyssinia.

The Ethiopian Emperor Theodore in 1868 made so bold as to imprison and torture some Englishmen in his anger that his proposal of marriage to England's Queen Victoria had gone unanswered. When word of this retaliation reached England, where the marriage offer had been pigeonholed and never delivered to the Queen, there was only one thing to do.

An expeditionary force under command of General Napier set out to rescue the British prisoners and to chastise Theodore for his wrongdoing. With baggage elephants in the van, and help from some of the Ethiopians themselves, Napier moved across the country in three months and accomplished his mission. The despairing Theodore blew out his own brains at Magdala, poetically using the beautiful pearl-handled pistol that Queen Victoria herself had sent him.

Justice done, and the prisoners rescued, Napier withdrew. As Prime Minister Disraeli pointed out to the world, England had no other aims in Ethiopia and left the country solely to the Ethiopians. In the confusion though, two British soldiers stole the crown and later traded it to a German trader for two bottles of rum. The trader gave the crown to his Kaiser who in turn presented it to Queen Victoria. After a long stay in the Victoria and Albert Museum, the Ethiopian crown was returned in 1925 by King George to

113

the man who wore it now. Each time Selassie looked at it he was reminded of his shaky heritage.

Despite Disraeli's noble declaration in 1868 there were countries who coveted the Ethiopian territory. Among them was Italy, whose Somaliland bordered it. The Italians went to war in 1896, seeking to subdue the African nation, but were beaten badly at Aduwa by Emperor Menelik and forced to sue for peace. When Menelik abdicated because of ill health and his nephew was deposed, Menelik's daughter became Empress in 1916, with Ras Taffari as regent. The Ras would later be known as Haile Selassie I.

A shrewd administrator and far-seeing diplomat, Taffari applied for membership in the League of Nations after the war, hoping to protect his country without the need for fighting. France and Italy, enjoying favorable economic relations with Ethiopia at the time, pushed for its membership and in 1923 the country was admitted. That same year, seeing the handwriting on the wall perhaps, Taffari signed the edict that provided for the gradual emancipation of slaves in his land.

In 1928 Ras Taffari was crowned King and when the Empress died two years later he became Emperor Haile Selassie I. His foresight in joining the League had paid dividends in 1926 when he complained of British and Italian agreements to honor each other's "spheres of influence" in Ethiopia. The resulting moral pressure brought about the dropping of a deal concerning Lake Tana. But in the thirties his luck ran out when Italy began menacing the border again.

Even Selassie's soldiers protested that their leader was too much the "businessman." Surely he was no fool on the score on international dealings. Some accused him of playing for suckers his one-time friends and seconders, the Italians, by letting Japan move in and take Ethiopia's cotton goods import business during the depression years. He compounded the insult by waiting until Italy's electrical firm of Ansaldo Lorenz had built him a powerful radio station at below-cost rates, and then booting the technicians out and operating it himself.

At any rate, by 1934 there was pitched fighting between Italians and native soldiers in the mud village of Ualual and each side protested to the League of Nations. Investigation by that body disclosed that apparently both sides were at fault and a compromise was suggested.

Italy was in no mood for such a settlement, however, and belatedly she cried that Ethiopia was in the League falsely, since slavery still existed despite the edict of 1923. This was incontrovertibly true, but surely not the real reason for Italy's invasion.

Erroneously called the "Hell-Hole of Creation," Ethiopia is actually mostly high plateau averaging some 8,000 feet in altitude and Italy considered it a fairly desirable addition to its imperial land area. Coffee is grown extensively, and other products include hides, ivory, tobacco, bananas and civet—used in perfume. Gold, platinum and potash are mined commercially and there are also large deposits of coal, sulphur, phosphate, copper and rock salt, with some lead, iron, mercury, tin, mica and petroleum.

Some parts of the country were reportedly so remote and backward that inhabitants had never heard of Selassie. Of the ten million people the majority were Mohammedan or pagan. The Emperor and his family were Semitic, Coptic Christians. Although in George White's *Scandals* Negro performers were stopping the show as Selassie and his crew, the Emperor was not a Negro. Nor was he, as legend would have it, descended from King Solomon's seduction of the virgin Queen of Sheba.

Haile Selassie, a small and birdlike bearded aesthete, numbered among his royal family the Empress Menen, two daughters, Crown Prince Afsa Aswan, and Prince Makonnen, his favorite. Selassie was 44, and his sons were 19 and 12, respectively.

For almost a year after the flare-up at Ualual things rocked along precariously. A possible settlement proposed by Britain's Samuel Hoare and France's Pierre Laval was scuttled, principally by Stanley Baldwin. Selassie gave hints that maybe it was Italy's terms and not her aims that he rebelled against when he sanctioned an oil deal that promoter Francis William Rickett worked up with Standard Oil. This lucrative arrangement for Ethiopia would also have involved the United States. It, like the Hoare-Laval Deal, was torpedoed. And in October of 1935 Mussolini had moved with force into Ethiopia, financed in part by gold wedding rings from Italian women even in New York.

Before the Italian drive of General Graziani, "The Scourge of Tripolitania," bogged down in rain and mud after two months, it had taken some 30,000 square miles of Ethiopia and Selassie had become the symbol of an oppressed small country. He cried aggression to the League loudly, and played his cards with the skill of long diplomatic practice. When the press moved in he ingratiated himself with them to the extent that they endearingly called him "Little Charlie" and became his best public relations. No slouch in the matter of publicity, Selassie hired an expert from Al Smith's staff to keep the world informed of Italy's bestiality.

Although Little Charlie was sick much of the time he amazed reporters with his vitality and the control he seemed to maintain despite his almost martyr-like mien. With the foreign press mostly in the palm of one hand, Selassie gripped the media of his own country with the other like the tightest-fisted dictator. He controlled the newspapers and the Italian-built radio station, as well as riding herd on movies and editing his own official paper.

While the Emperor bravely assured reporters that he wouldn't part with an inch of his precious Ethiopia, it was nevertheless rumored that he was willing to negotiate with European diplomats toward concessions, treaties or deals favorable to his country.

Indeed, it was thought that *Il Duce's* own troops were largely hamstrung in their invasion while their leader dickered politically. Either that or the Italian troops were even poorer than some detractors painted them, not to be able to quickly vanquish a scraggly band of "burnt-face" natives with spears.

Mussolini started off the New Year as if trying to live up to Selassie's tales of unwarranted aggression. In angry headlines the Swedish papers announced that Italian planes had bombed and strafed Red Cross workers with Ras Desta Dentu, Selassie's son-in-law. The attack took place near the village of Dolo on the Italian Somaliland border, against tents plainly marked as noncombatant. According to the boiling mad Swedes, 9 of their doctors had been killed and 23 Ethiopians perished with them. In addition, all the Red Cross supplies and equipment were demolished by bombs and bullets.

An accurate check later revealed emotional exaggeration on the part of the press, though the attack on the Red Cross apparently had occurred. One doctor was struck by a bullet, and at least one assistant had died. Prince Carl, President of the Swedish Red Cross, protested bitterly to the League of Nations and crowds screamed, "Down with Mussolini!"

116

Further damning evidence of the atrocity was the report in Italian papers some time before the incident that the Swedish unit had been spotted from the air and that Red Cross and Swedish flags were identified. And the strafing planes had dropped leaflets that said:

You have killed one of our aviators who was made a prisoner. You have cut off his head in violation of human and international law. You will get for it what you deserve.

This ultimatum was purportedly signed by General Graziani, the commander of Italian forces in Ethiopia. Far from cringing, the Italians lashed back at the Swedes and others who accused them.

"Members of the Swedish ambulance unit in Ethiopia cannot expect to be as safe as if they were walking down the streets of Stockholm," the Italian Minister in that city informed the Swedes.

The beheaded Italian flier who had touched off the trouble was identified as Sub-Lieutenant Tito Minitti and his grieving father was interviewed and quoted as saying he had lost a son in World War I and now Tito. He had four left, though, and now courageously offered them all in the fight against Ethiopia. It was not reported whether Tito's brothers shared the old man's enthusiasm.

In Stockholm, Eric Dahlberg recalled that he had warned his government against just such an occurrence as the Red Cross bombing. In 1925 Emperor Selassie had come calling in Sweden and was such a good salesman he had convinced General Virgin and other officers to resign from the army and come to Ethiopia to train the soldiers there. Dahlberg had predicted that Italy would now be gunning for the ex-Swedes or at least the volunteer Swedish Red Cross units.

The Italian press became noisier in scoffing at the charges of Red Cross murders. "We would like to know," one of them demanded, "whether it is really expected that Italy should order her soldiers to put corks on their bayonets and her aviators to fill their bombs with cologne water. Stockholm should say whether it desires our aviators before proceeding with a bombardment to release a couple of comrades in a parachute to ascertain whether there is a Swedish physician in the neighborhood."

World-wide sentiment was strongly anti-Italian, with critics wishing the Italians could have settled for another grand opera. France and the Netherlands were among those who saw another *Lusitania* in the incident, a *Lusitania* which could again draw the United States into the fray. Italy's unconcern was reflected in what happened five days later. A United States Red Cross hospital was bombed at Daggah Bur, the place where Dr. Robert Hockmann had died a month earlier when a dud bomb went off. Fortunately there were no casualties this time.

For his part, Mussolini was bragging to reporter Anne O'Hare McCormick about the capture of Aduwa and how the backward natives had fled when Italians showed movies in that town.

Other reporters were finding it tough going in Ethiopia, with hearts affected by the altitude, plus the rigors of dysentery and malaria. Redoubtable veterans like Floyd Gibbons were cracking up with nervous breakdowns. Will Barber of the Chicago *Tribune* died, and would later receive a posthumous Pulitzer Prize for his war reporting. Where once there had been 120 correspondents, the number had shrunk to a dozen or so, the ranks being literally decimated as reporters gave it up and returned home.

In February the Italian drive, that seemed to have stalled in the mud of the rainy season, began to move again. Graziani had a new boss in Marshal Pietro Bagdolio and along with him the support he needed to wage a real war. Graziani claimed to have captured a Swedish Red Cross outfit whose equipment included twenty-seven cases of ammunition, and an American movie man recalled taking a picture of Red Cross flags flying over the Prince's palace though it was not used for that purpose.

Graziani also reported the defeat of Ras Mulegheta on the northern front. This success, tied with a long-awaited statement from the Papal Secretary of State, Cardinal Pacelli, hailing Mussolini as "a most cultured Restorer of Imperial Rome" sat well with *Il Duce*. He and his ministers talked loudly against the sanctions being imposed dutifully by the League of Nations, and Bagdolio poured more men and equipment into Ethiopia.

After Aduwa, where the defeat of Italy in 1896 was avenged, Graziani had pushed on to the Holy City of Aksum and now the drive was moving up out of the coastal plains and onto the plateau itself with the scaling of 11,000-foot

Mount Alaji. There were now 300,000 Italian soldiers in Ethiopia, driving to sure victory with only the poor roads holding them back.

The timid League, with a tiger by the tail, issued an ultimatum to Mussolini in March. It was rumored that Adolf Hitler hurried to Rome for secret meetings with *Il Duce*, and then a confident Mussolini announced to the League that he was prepared "in principle" to negotiate along lines suggested by the League.

Into this faintly hopeful situation Hitler tossed a bombshell by moving boldly into the Rhineland. The League of Nations now had far more to worry about than a mild, bearded Ethiopian and his ten million dark-skinned followers. Cynics said that the Conquering Lion of Judah had indeed been thrown to the Christians.

In April the war in Ethiopia reached to the capital itself. Ten planes made a token raid on Addis Ababa, strafing two ancient planes at the airport and killing a servant at the British Legation and a dog. In April, too, the once-denounced Rickett Concession for petroleum came back in the news with the shocking rumor that the promoter had secured a five-year contract to Ethiopian subsoil rights and was in the process of selling them to Mussolini! Rickett was said to be holding out for a commission of $5 million, plus an additional $1.5 million for delivery of 75-year rights.

Mussolini's army gave no indication that he was going to do any negotiating when he had the prize already in his grasp, however. Amid growing cries from Ethiopia deploring the use of gas, Graziani drove rapidly ahead. In command of one column was the Secretary General of the Fascist Party in Italy, leading 5,000 loyal Black Shirts, as Graziani combined politics with war.

At Lake Tana the victorious Italians paused only long enough to assure England that she could have the water rights. All that stood between the invaders and total victory was Emperor Selassie and some 45,000 troops. With little choice, the defending Ethiopians made an abortive counter-attack on the Italian position at Mao Cio in the Lake Ashangi region.

As the fighting raged, 16-year-old Princess Sekai, Selassie's daughter, protested to the British House of Lords against the continuing use of gas against her father's people.

119

Backing up her claim, the Red Cross reported 3,000 cases of gassing, with some 60 dead of its effects. The Italians were reportedly using mustard gas.

Selassie had withheld condemnation of the Italians earlier for the use of dumdum bullets and now the Italians claimed that the reason was that the Ethiopians themselves were the guilty parties. Papers were advanced showing that emissaries from Selassie had purchased the soft-nosed bullets for use against the "leopards" in his country. The upshot was an uneasy stalemate.

There were atrocities on both sides. Emasculation was a favorite form of Ethiopian mutilation, and even the news correspondents were half-serious when they joked about the danger. Mussolini tried in vain to exploit the savage slashing of his soldiers; the photographs were horribly and obscenely unpublishable.

As the Italians pressed on and around the natives, it was rumored that the Emperor had shaved off his beard to disguise himself and was fleeing in disgrace on a mule. A clean-shaven Ethiopian would have stood out like a Bikini in a prim boardingschool, of course, and when Selassie turned up again in Addis Ababa after the routing of his Imperial Guard he still wore his famed beard, though it was turning gray by now. He also had an arm bandaged as a result of gassing.

Mussolini was now boldly telling the League it could go fly a kite and that he would entertain an armistice with Ethiopia on his own terms rather than theirs. In return, the tottering League salved itself by claiming that Italy's imports and exports had been cut in half by the "stiff" sanctions its members had imposed. With the anniversary of the founding of Rome in 753 B.C. coming up on April 21, Mussolini was exhorting Bagdolio and Graziani to deliver complete victory to the Italian state by that date.

Except for the miserable roads and communications, General Graziani might have succeeded. As it was, he had to pause for breath and road repairs, and at Sassa Baneh fierce tribesmen beat back the Italian-American volunteer regiment of General Frusci, inflicting heavy losses on many starry-eyed young Italians from New York, Chicago and San Francisco.

The gaunt little Emperor was finished, his tribal warriors the victims of modern weapons despite Swedish General Virgin's proud claim that the Ethiopian's warlike heritage

120

would prevail. Of Selassie's original 300,000 soldiers, matching Bagdolio's force in number, only about one in twenty was armed with a rifle. His air force, supposedly headed by cocky Hubert Fauntleroy Julian, the American "Black Eagle" from Harlem, was nonexistent as a military weapon. At Magdala, Selassie barely escaped dying in the very place the Emperor Theodore had succumbed, almost seventy years before. No candidate for suicide, the Emperor Selassie was fired on from outside by natives and his porter and chamberlain both were shot dead.

Now back in his capital, he pled with the French for asylum for the royal family in Djibouti in French Somaliland. Still claiming 5,000 loyal warriors, the Emperor proclaimed that "Ethiopia will fight until the last soldier and the last inch!"

Then he went on to call on Sir Sydney Barton, head of the British Legation to beg for aid from England. It was Selassie himself who had permitted Sir Sydney to import 150 Sikhs to protect the Legation, and the elderly English soldier wished heartily that Baldwin could have been there to hear the plea. But it was no use, and Selassie turned away in grim despair.

It was the end of the road, and Emperor Selassie, whom one correspondent romantically described as manning a chattering machine gun at the Italian strafers and driving off savage lions who menaced his children, saw no point in dying a martyr's death. With as many of his possessions as he could get packed, he, too, fled for Djibouti and safety, leaving his skeleton guard to face the oncoming Italians and the fury of the mob when it learned of the country's defeat.

Addis Ababa was a scene of rioting in its last hours before the arrival of the Italian Army. The palace that had been the Emperor's pride and joy was looted thoroughly, and in the confusion U.P. correspondent Ben Ames was slashed severely. Loyal guards at the Treasury manned their machine guns against would-be robbers of the gold Selassie could not carry with him, until sword-wielding looters lopped their hands off.

At the U.S. Legation, Minister Cornelius Van H. Engert and his staff prayed for the arrival of the Italians in a practical reversal of sentiment. Engert contacted Sir Sydney at the British Legation by radioing back to Arlington in the United States and having that station contact the British Legation, since all local Ethiopian communication had failed.

With his protective Sikh guards, Barton was in better position and Engert was advised to evacuate to that post
rather than try to hold out.

The successful reign of Ethiopia's most revered ruler had
come to a tragic end, and now the crown that once before
journeyed to England by devious ways was on its way there
again for safekeeping. So, too, was the royal family.

Embarking on the British warship *Enterprise* at Djibouti,
Selassie and his entourage sailed for Haifa in Palestine.
Also aboard were 6 royal automobiles, 10 tons of trunks,
100 cases of coin and bullion worth some $5 million, a pet
python and the Emperor's dog, Papillon (Butterfly).

At Suez an Italian steamer crammed with jeering tourists
struck up a Fascist anthem at sight of Selassie, and a British paper offered $25,000 for an interview with the Em-
peror, who paid no attention to either happening. At the
next League of Nations meeting in Geneva Italian delegate
Aloisi walked out in protest when Ethiopia's Wolde Mariam
was permitted to remain. There was no Ethiopia now, Aloisi
claimed, except as part of Italy.

In his room at the King David Hotel, Emperor Selassie
listened sadly to Mussolini's speech annexing the country
he had lost. He could stand only half of the diatribe and
flicked *Il Duce* off. Elsewhere, cynics were suggesting that
the League continue to function, but as an amicable de-
bating society, publishing valuable works on the extent of
white slavery, opium traffic and the migration of whales.
Or perhaps that its buildings be taken over by the Geneva
yacht club.

In Addis Ababa the thinned ranks of the correspondents
were made fewer by one when New York and London
Times correspondent George Steer was unceremoniously
kicked out for stories not complimentary to the new rulers
of Ethiopia. Another reporter, H. L. Matthews, was more
fortunate and even received the Italian Medal for Valor
for his "more objective" reporting of the war. In Addis
Ababa, too, the Italians executed giant, 7 foot 5 inch
Balahu, Selassie's former umbrella carrier. The charge was
espionage, and to his death by firing squad went the biggest
man in Ethiopia.

By now the ex-Emperor was sailing toward England by
way of Gibraltar. He had been transferred from the battleship that took him to Haifa to the cruiser *Capetown,* and

en route the British saw fit to further downgrade his status to incognito passage aboard a British commercial liner.

Nevertheless, there were sympathetic crowds waiting in London. There was a partisan tone to the reception, with Labor and Liberals proclaiming, "Welcome Emperor!" and the Conservatives in Parliament pretty much ignoring him. The anti-Baldwin press said:

> Haile Selassie is a welcome visitor for he belongs to that band of men with the courage to stand up against tyranny and stand by what is right at the risk of death in order that justice might live.

Official England was less cordial. When Selassie decided to lay a wreath on a patriot's grave and asked the Foreign Office for "protection," Anthony Eden referred the request to Scotland Yard. Selassie's fans waited vainly in the rain at tombside. And when the Emperor asked for an audience with the new and democratic King Edward he was informed that such a meeting would be impossible. Eden and Baldwin were swallowing a bitter pill, and apparently they wanted as few reminders as possible. There was also another crisis brewing—an internal crisis that would soon make Selassie and everybody else forgotten men.

Anthony Eden was walking a diplomatic tightrope now between the high ideals his country had stood for and the pressing practicality of dealing with strong men like Benito Mussolini and Adolf Hitler. About all that could be hoped for in these trying times, he said, was to keep the League in existence. Meantime, pressure was started to encourage the embarrassing visitor to leave England.

Part of the freeze included the boycotting of a pathetic "Imperial Garden Party" that Selassie planned. Besides England, others declining to attend included the United States, Russia, France, Germany, Japan, the Little Entente, the Scandinavian countries and the Balkans. It must have been puzzling to the little man who had stood up against tyranny in order that justice might live, but he was beginning to get the picture. Perhaps he might move to Switzerland where he owned a villa, if the Italians would permit him to be such a close neighbor.

There were some feeble gestures, of course. Sympathizers began to publish a paper known as the *New Times & Ethio-*

pian News. Some of the Ethiopian news was that the harried Negus had gone to Scotland. Other news was that the business about Italian use of poison gas was being brought up again. The Italians matched this with dumdum bullets and other atrocity stories and the news that Marshal Bagdolio, far from being lukewarm on Fascism, had been given his membership card, along with the appointment as Viceroy of Ethiopia and Duke of Addis Ababa.

The gas stories were quashed quickly in Parliament and Eden proclaimed that there was surely no more need for sanctions against Italy. There were some cries of "Sabotage!" and "Shame!" and "Resign!" and Sir Samuel Hoare, co-author of the scuttled Hoare-Laval Settlement, called Eden's plan a surrender to Italy without a shot being fired.

Counseled Prime Minister Baldwin, hand in glove with the Foreign Secretary, "We ought to remember that if there be war in this country they [the British] will pay for it on the first night with their lives. The first blow may come on the day that sanctions are first applied against an aggressor."

The League of Nations seemed to have failed, and might was the only right the world knew in 1936. But though the League had failed, said Canada's Premier William Mackenzie King, "It is not a failure. We must not despair of the League!"

Haile Selassie was among those who had not yet completely despaired. Back from a sojourn to Scotland, he boarded the train for the trip to Geneva. In the time since his triumphant entry into England, the popular ardor for justice had apparently cooled somewhat. Scarcely fifty people were on hand to see him off.

Ironically Anthony Eden was aboard the same train from Paris to Geneva with the Emperor. In the Swiss capital a Fascist prankster was masquerading as Selassie in full regalia. He laid wreaths on various memorials, and even accosted the Italian delegate to the League, Bova Doppa. But by and large the Swiss citizens seemed to be on Selassie's side, loudly cheering him and turning their backs on Eden at the train.

As Selassie made plans to address the League in behalf of his vanquished country, Eden implored him not to. It had never been done, he protested. It was pointless and dangerous. Disagreeing violently was Ireland's Eamon de

Valera, whose impassioned appeal won the right for the Emperor to address the Assembly.

Despite Eden's efforts, then, the slight figure in full costume mounted the platform and prepared to read his speech. As he began in his native Amharic tongue, Italian journalists leaped to their feet and shouted *"Viva Il Duce!"* Not once, but in continuous angry shouting, they kept it up until they were ejected bodily by League police, expelled from further service and jailed. It was the first such demonstration in the history of the League of Nations.

When order was restored, Selassie again began his seventeen-page speech. He had come, he said, to claim the justice promised him eight months ago by the fifty member nations of the League. Were the states, instead, going to set up the terrible precedent of bowing to force? In the babble that followed, it was evident that that was the intent, if not the wish, of those assembled in the body so idealistically conceived after an earlier war. Lacking the strength to do anything about aggressors, what point was there left in branding nations as such?

Only Eamon de Valera spoke out loud and clear and prophetically when he said, "If the great powers of Europe would only meet *now* in that peace conference which will have to be held after Europe has again been drenched in blood . . . the terrible menace which threatens us all today could be warded off."

The congratulations that came from England's King Edward to Emperor Selassie for his forty-fifth birthday gave. no joy to the little man on that anniversary. It had been a year of unbroken tragedy and defeat for Ethiopia. And now that his country had been raped by the aggressor Mussolini, Selassie was told that the world was surely sorry, but guessed it better not try to do more than slap the guilty party's wrists for fear he would turn on them, too. About the only offer of any kind came from Hollywood, but Selassie was not interested.

The Emperor went back to England, where he tried, with the help of press agentry and the remnants of his followers in Ethiopia, to give the idea of continuing resistance to the rule of the new Duke of Addis Ababa and his paunchy boss in Italy. But encouraging reports emanating from "Gore, West Ethiopia," turned out to be fictitious. The pitiful shreds of a pitiful army could do nothing against the might of conquering Italy.

125

In the fall, Britain and France spearheaded a final humiliation for Selassie when they tried to pack the Credential Committee and thus bar the Emperor even from attending the League, as he was on his way to Geneva again. Other members either did not have such strong stomachs or did not harbor the guilt feelings to prevent them from permitting Selassie in their sight. He retained his seat in spite of the machinations of Britain ànd France, that were enough, as one paper in the United States put it, to make a Tammany Hall politician blush.

It was a ringside seat that Haile Selassie had, a close-up view of the death of the wonderful dream that had been the League of Nations. For now he was listening to noble Anthony Eden, the proud Englishman who had fought in the trenches against the Kaiser twenty years before, seconding Germany's demands that the Covenant of the League of Nations be divorced from the Treaty of Versailles!

"Human life is not static," pronounced the flexible Mr. Eden, "but is rather a changing thing."

The years ahead would prove Eden right in a terrible way he could not yet foresee in 1936, but the little dusky man listening to what must have seemed to him a complete renunciation of justice continued to cling to one human trait that does not change. Where there is still life, there is hope. The Emperor would live to see his hope rewarded.

BIBLIOGRAPHY

Ethiopia, a Pawn in European Diplomacy—Work
John Hoy of Ethiopia—McLean
Ethiopia and Italy—Burns
Black Shirt, Brown Skin—Carter

Jesse Owens with the Wreath of Victory after he defeated Germany's Lutz Long (right) in the long jump at the 1936 Olympics held in Germany. *(Wide World Photo)*

Eleanor Holm Jarrett, America's best bet in the Olympic women's backstroke competition, was sacked from the team for "frequenting the bar" of the ship bearing the American team to Germany. *(Wide World Photo)*

A steel bridge at Harpers Ferry, West Virginia, swept away by the flooding Potomac in the spring of 1936. *(Wide World Photo)*

Millionaire sportsman Howard Hughes, before he took off on his breakfast to luncheon hop to Los Angeles in May, 1936. *(Wide World Photo)*

Donald Douglas's DC-2, which could hurtle across the sky at three miles a minute. *(Smithsonian Institution)*

The first Joe Louis-Max Schmeling fight, 1936. Schmeling gets over a right in one of the early rounds.

Referee Arthur Donavan holds Schmeling away from Louis as the eighth round ends.

Joe Louis lies on the canvas after being knocked down by Schmeling in the twelfth round. *(Wide World Photo)*

First baseman Lou Gehrig, left, and outfielder Joe DiMaggio in front of the Yankee Stadium dugout, August 31, 1936. *(Wide World Photo)*

Walter Johnson, former pitching star, tosses a silver dollar across the Rappahannock as a test of the legend that George Washington threw a dollar across the river when he was eleven years old. Johnson threw two dollars across the 272-foot channel out of three tries. *(Wide World Photo)*

Carl Hubbell warms up at the N.Y. Giants' spring camp in Havana, Cuba. *(Wide World Photo)*

President Roosevelt prepares to toss out the first ball at the Polo Grounds, opening the second game of the 1936 World Series. Standing at FDR's right is his son, Franklin, Jr. In front of the Presidential Box are Bill Terry (left), manager of the Giants, and Joe McCarthy, manager of the Yankees. *(Wide World Photo)*

G. K. Chesterton, the English author, died in 1936. *(Wide World Photo)*

Margaret Mitchell, author of *Gone With The Wind.* *(Wide World Photo)*

Marilyn Miller, musical comedy star, died at the age of 38. *(Wide World Photo)*

Marian Anderson makes her singing debut in New York. *(Wide World Photo)*

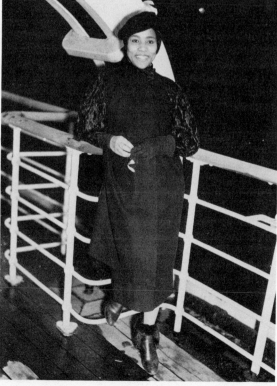

Nobel Prize laureate, Rudyard Kipling, died in 1936. *(Wide World Photo)*

At 37, Irving Thalberg, MGM's production head, died of pneumonia. *(Wide World Photo)*

Figure skater Sonja Henie turned professional after her 1936 Olympics triumph. *(Wide World Photo)*

The voice of Charlie Chaplin was first heard in his *Modern Times.* *(Wide World Photo)*

Gary Cooper and Jean Arthur appeared in *Mr. Deeds Goes to Town*. (*Wide World Photo*)

Babe Ruth appeared with Kate Smith on the singer's radio show. (*Wide World Photo*)

(Above)
Eight-year-old Shirley Temple was one of Hollywood's biggest stars. (*Wide World Photo*)

(Center). Singer Rudy Vallee (left) revived "The Whiffenpoof Song." (*Wide World Photo*). Paul Muni (right) won the Oscar for his title role in *The Story of Louis Pasteur*. (*Wide World Photo*)

(Below) Sultry Jean Harlow's private life matched her movie image. (*Wide World Photo*)

Victim of sound, John Gilbert, once a movie giant, died at the age of 38. He is seen here with film actress Rene Torres. *(Wide World Photo)*

The 1936 Ford Roadster *(Courtesy of the Ford Archives, Dearborn, Mich.)*

The 1936 Ford Club Cabriolet. *(Courtesy of the Ford Archives, Dearborn, Mich.)*

The 1936 V-8 Fordor Ford. *(Courtesy of the Ford Archives, Dearborn, Mich.)*

1936 Ford Phaeton. *(Courtesy of the Ford Archives, Dearborn, Mich.)*

1936 Plymouth (top); 1936 Willys Pickup (center); 1936 Chevrolet (below). *Courtesy Motor Vehicle Mfrs. Assn.)*

VIII

The Scottsboro Boys

On January 20, 1936, Haywood Patterson went on trial for his life in Decatur, Alabama, for the fourth time. Patterson, 23-year-old Negro who had become the symbol of the "Scottsboro Boys," was charged, along with eight others, with raping a white woman on a moving freight train.

It had been almost five years since the alleged crime took place; five years of imprisonment for the accused and five years of turmoil that reached around the world and resulted in the deaths of a number of people. Justice as dispensed in the state of Alabama had come under attack not only from Yankee newspapers, Communists and the National Association for the Advancement of Colored People, but from the Supreme Court itself.

In January of 1936, then, the whole sordid story was retold in court for the fourth time. By now, Patterson knew both sides of it by heart.

On March 25, 1931, he was riding a freight train from Chattanooga—the Alabama Great Southern. The 18-year-old Negro was bumming his way from his home town, heading for Alabama and maybe points north looking for work and excitement. Times were tough, and several trips before had proved profitable. There were three other colored boys from Chattanooga and a dozen or more others they didn't know scattered along the length of the train. There were some white boys, too—seven of them.

As Patterson sat on an oil tank car, some of the white boys clambered onto it from their car. In passing Patterson, one of them stepped on his hand. Going back, according to the Negro, the boy "liked to have pushed me off the car." And then Patterson made the gravest mistake of his life, a mistake that would put his life in jeopardy from that day on. He had words with the white boy.

"I don't argue with people," Patterson said in explaining his philosophy. "I show them."

127

When the white boys took exception to his remarks by hopping off the freight as it slowed and "chunking" rocks from the roadbed at the Negroes, Patterson and the others began to show them. A wild fracas took place in a freight car, and the seven white boys, outnumbered two to one, were beaten up and thrown off the train. All but one, that is.

With the train picking up speed so that it might have seriously injured anyone falling from it, Patterson and another Negro named Roy Wright hauled Orville Gilley to safety by his belt. Then the Chattanooga Negroes returned to their oil tanker and rode it into the town of Paint Rock. This was the version of what happened on the train as told by the Negroes, reiterated at each trial.

The six boys who had been tossed off the train went back to the depot at Stevenson and complained to the agent. He called ahead to Paint Rock, and when the train stopped there a mob of some fifty farmers armed with shotguns and pistols were waiting.

Hustled off to jail at Scottsboro, the Jackson County seat, the Negroes were told they were being held for assault and attempted murder. Their number had shrunk to nine; some of them must have anticipated trouble after the fight. Also herded into the jail were the white boys and two white girls. The girls were dressed in overalls and the Negroes claimed not to have seen them until now. In the jail, however, the Negroes were confronted with the two girls and accused of raping them.

It had been midafternoon when the boys were taken from the train at Paint Rock. By dusk there were hundreds of white people outside the jail and as night wore on lynch threats carried into the cells. High Sheriff Warren decided to play it safe and sent for the National Guard. At four o'clock in the morning the Guardsmen came in trucks and took the Negroes to Gadsden, Alabama.

By then the papers were filled with stories of "nine fiends who had perpetrated the most horrible crime in the United States" and who must pay with their lives. By March 30, the grand jury indicted all nine boys. Conviction on that charge carried a maximum penalty of death, a maximum usually reserved for Negroes who raped white women.

Besides Haywood Patterson, who was 18, there were Andy and Roy Wright, 19 and 14, and Eugene Williams,

128

13, all from Chattanooga. The others, some of them from Georgia, were Charlie Weems, 20, Clarence Norris, 19, Ozie Powell, 14, Willie Roberson, 16, and Olen Montgomery, 17.' Roberson had syphilis, and could barely walk. Montgomery had only one good eye and could barely get around unaided.

The girls who had accused them of rape were Mrs. Victoria Price, a 21-year-old divorcée, and Ruby Bates, 19. Orville Gilley was supposedly a witness to the crime. The victims had been examined by two doctors and indeed there was evidence of intercourse, although the victims did not seem greatly upset or in a weakened physical condition as a result of their ordeal.

According to Victoria Price, she and Ruby Bates were in a gondola of the freight train, a car without a top. This car was almost filled with crushed rock called "chert."

Seven white boys had ridden with them until the Negroes jumped over their heads from a boxcar and attacked them. All but two of the Negroes had knives; those two had pistols. After pitching all but Gilley off the train, the Negroes then proceeded to rape the girls, first threatening to throw Victoria from the train, striking her with a pistol on the head, and finally attacking her at knife point. Six Negroes had attacked each girl. Ruby Bates concurred during the first trial. By 1936 she had long since changed her story.

Victoria Price grew up in Huntsville, Alabama, a medium-sized mill town. The working hours were long and the wages poor. Victoria served time for vagrancy and for violating the Volstead Act. Mixed up with a married man named Jack Tiller, she went to the workhouse on an adultery charge. In March she was out of jail but restless.

Tiller quarreled with his wife, and came to see Victoria in her home. While Tiller and Victoria visited on the bed in the front room, her mother visited with a friend of Tiller, Lester Carter, who had just gotten off the chain gang for stealing laundry. Carter was called the Knoxville Kid.

Next night Carter, Tiller and Victoria were on the town. Victoria looked up her friend Ruby Bates for Carter and the four of them ended up in a hobo jungle near a lake. Paired off, they indulged in intimate love-making until it began to rain.

There was a freight train handy and they piled into it to spend the rest of the night. Things were dull in Ala-

129

bama, and the freight train gave them an idea. Why not take off somewhere for excitement? Out West they could hustle the towns and make some money. Ruby was all for it. One of nine children, she had known nothing but poverty and was sick of it.

There was only one hitch. Jack Tiller decided that much as he'd like to go, he was afraid of the Mann Act. Better if the girls and Carter went on ahead, and he would join them after they had crossed the state line.

The girls were ready to go. Both of them had on overalls over dresses. Victoria had on three dresses and they both wore coats. That way they weren't leaving much wardrobe behind. With Carter, then, they bummed their way to Chattanooga.

In Chattanooga Victoria said they stayed at a boardinghouse on Seventh Street, run by Callie Broochie. But it was evident that they spent the night in another hobo jungle. Here the girls picked up another boy, Orville Gilley, alias Carolina Slim. The boys made a shelter out of tree branches, scrounged up some chili and some tin cans to heat coffee in. That night they slept together and in the morning they caught another freight. Fatefully it was the same train that Haywood Patterson and the other Negroes had also boarded in Chattanooga.

After the nine were indicted, the court lost no time in setting a date for the trial. April 6, 1931, was selected, the date of the annual horse-trading fair at the County Seat. Coincidental or not, the choice guaranteed a large and prejudiced audience.

The population of Scottsboro was about 1,000, but now 10,000 people jammed around the courthouse. The National Guard was on hand, and there was a brass band too. The band played numbers like *The Star Spangled Banner* and *Dixie,* and according to some reports other selections including *There'll Be a Hot Time in the Old Town Tonight.* All in all it was about the biggest "First Monday" in local history.

In the jail there had been some squabbling among the two girls and their traveling companions. Carolina Slim and the Knoxville Kid would not testify about the alleged attacks, and Ruby Bates decided she could not identify her assailants. But Victoria Price stuck to her story. She was positive that all nine of the Negroes in the courtroom were

130

the ones who invaded the freight car and committed the crime they were now charged with.

Charlie Weems and Clarence Norris were tried first, the defendants being broken into three groups. The trial took a day, and the jury required only an hour and a half to reach its verdict: *Guilty*.

Quickly the band struck up the National Anthem, and those outside went wild. Only men were permitted in the courtroom audience; women and children had to get the news secondhand. The Chattanooga *Times* described the first verdict:

> Thunderous applause late this afternoon greeted a Jackson County grand jury's verdict of guilty for Charlie Weems and Clarence Norris, Negro hobos, who were convicted of attacking a white girl. . . . Hardly had the echoes of the trial died away until the trial of Haywood Patterson, Chattanooga Negro, charged with the same offense, was resumed.

It was not, of course, a grand jury that handed down the verdict. But the rest of the description was correct. The storm of noise outside came loud and clear to the jurors as they began to hear the next case.

A lawyer from Chattanooga, Stephen Roddy, had been asked by the Interdenominational Ministers Alliance, acting for the National Association for the Advancement of Colored People, to defend the nine defendants. Roddy's actions in court could hardly be interpreted as a strong defense; he merely told Judge E. A. Hawkins that he had been asked to sort of help out any lawyers appointed to defend them. Not knowing the details of Alabama law he wouldn't presume by making an actual defense.

Judge Hawkins had asked the seven available lawyers if they would defend the Negroes, and one, Milo Moody, agreed. Roddy said he would go along with Moody. To his credit, he did have put into the record the noisy demonstration outside that might have influenced the jury.

Patterson was tried on April 7. He, too, was found guilty and the following day all but Roy Wright were accorded the same treatment.

Roy, younger of the two Wrights and the boy who had helped drag Gilley to safety, was 14 and a mistrial was therefore declared because of his extreme youth. The state

131

wanted life imprisonment for Roy Wright, but seven jurors held out for the death sentence, thus affording the technicality of a mistrial. Death by electrocution was the sentence handed down by Judge Hawkins on April 9, sentence to be carried out at Kilby Prison on July 19, 1931.

The Scottsboro trial was a whirlwind and must have set something of a record. Nine defendants were tried and sentenced within five days, eight of them receiving the death penalty. Solicitor H. G. Bailey prosecuted the state's case and accused the Negroes of ravishing the two girls. The defendants admitted only to having engaged in a fight with white boys. The girls testified to multiple rape.

The prosecutor instructed the jury to get rid of "these niggers." There was no defense as such. Milo Moody made statements from time to time; Roddy, the lawyer from Chattanooga who was "just sort of watching," noted the disturbance outside when the first verdict was read. And that was all.

As his fourth trial proceeded in 1936, Patterson could recall with some satisfaction that, still protesting his innocence, he had told the prosecutor in 1931 that despite the sentence he would not die. He would die, he insisted, only when Bailey and the two girls had died for lying about him and the others. And all of them were indeed still alive.

As far as the court in Scottsboro was concerned, the law had taken its course and justice had been done at the first trial. The nine prisoners, including Roy Wright who had not been sentenced, were taken back to the jail in Gadsden and would soon be moved to the deathhouse at Kilby.

There were other people who saw in the proceedings at Scottsboro a travesty of justice. On April 9, 1931, only a few hours after the death sentence was handed down, the Communist International Labor Defense sent a telegram to Alabama's Governor Miller:

WE DEMAND A STAY OF EXECUTION AND OPPORTUNITY TO INVESTIGATE AND PREPARE FOR NEW TRIAL OR APPEAL. WE DEMAND RIGHT FOR OUR ATTORNEY TO INTERVIEW DEFENDANTS AND TO OBTAIN FORMAL APPROVAL OF DEFENSE COUNSEL, AND, ABOVE ALL, WE DEMAND ABSOLUTE SAFETY FOR THE DEFENDANTS AGAINST LYNCHING.

132

The ILD's Chief Counsel, Joseph R. Brodsky, traveled from New York to Alabama to interview the defendants. News of the case traveled around the world almost immediately and one of the first protests came from Local 10 of the Transport Workers Union in Berlin, Germany. The ILD's tack was that the Negroes were members of the oppressed working class and world-wide publicity and attendant propaganda were set in motion.

The National Association for the Advancement of Colored People retained lawyers Clarence Darrow, Arthur Garfield Hayes and Roderick Beddow. There were protest marches in Harlem, and on May Day hundreds of thousands of workers marched in protest, demanding the release of the Negroes. The All-Southern Scottsboro United Front Defense Conference was formed in Chattanooga. In Dresden, Germany, workers demonstrated in front of the U.S. Consulate.

Albert Einstein and Thomas Mann were among those who raised their voices, and Theodore Dreiser called the Scottsboro proceedings a "national emergency in justice."

As a result of the indignant furor a hearing was set for a new trial and this automatically postponed the July 10 execution, which was now denounced as "wholesale slaughter," "mass electrocution" and "legal lynching" almost everywhere except in the South.

On July 17, a week after the original death date, there were riots near Camp Hill, Alabama, in which Negroes and white men alike were shot and killed. A church was burned and shotguns and rifles blazed across the countryside in a welter of emotional outpouring. A rift was opened between the NAACP, which accused Communists of touching off the trouble, and the ILD, which denied any complicity.

The Secretary of the ILD refused to admit that his organization was proselyting Negro sharecroppers, or that the riots had anything to do with Scottsboro, stating that the trouble grew out of the long and continuing oppression of the South's tenant farmers.

The split widened, and finally the great Clarence Darrow and the other lawyers retained by the NAACP dropped the case when the ILD refused to stop propagandizing the Scottsboro case to its own advantage. The ILD denied these charges and accused Darrow of running out on the Negroes. Both sides claimed that affidavits signed by the

133

defendants entitled them to speak in their behalf. The upshot was that Darrow definitely withdrew.

There was sentiment on both sides. The ILD admittedly operated by public pressure from workers and other sympathetic groups, citing help from as far away as Russia in the person of Lenin in the celebrated Mooney bombing case. The NAACP and many others thought such tactics would only antagonize the South and guarantee failure. The fact remained that the Communist group moved the fastest and succeeded in staying the execution.

In January of 1932 the ILD lawyers, Brodsky, Chamlee and Schwab, appealed the convictions before the Alabama Supreme Court. That body upheld the convictions of seven of the Negroes, but did reverse the decision on Eugene Williams, the 13-year-old. By now the angry Southerners were denouncing the "nigger-loving Jews" for sticking their meddling noses into Alabama's affairs.

Mrs. Ada Wright, mother of Roy and Andrew, traveled to Europe with J. Louis Engdahl, the ILD secretary, and addressed groups of sympathizers in twenty-six countries. Included was a gathering of some 150,000 workers at Germany's Lustgarden. There were protests to U.S. Embassies in Latvia and France. These were added to by demonstrations in this country, including Birmingham, Alabama, and Washington, D.C.

In November the United States Supreme Court reversed the Alabama court's decision, citing the Fourteenth Amendment to the Constitution and pointing out that inadequate counsel had been provided the defendants in Scottsboro. Justice Sutherland delivered the opinion, with Justices Butler and McReynolds dissenting.

On the heels of this development, a letter written by Ruby Bates to a boy friend fell into the hands of the police. The girl gave the letter to another boy for delivery, but he got into a fight en route and was hauled into jail where the letter was found. When the defense learned of the letter, it demanded photostats to be introduced in court as evidence.

Text of the letter as printed in the book, *Trial by Prejudice,* by Arthur Garfield Hayes, one of the three lawyers originally retained by the NAACP, follows:

Dearest Earl,

I want to make a statement too you Mary Sanders is a goddam lie about those Negroes jazzing me those policemen made me tell a lie that is my statement because I want to clear myself that is all too if you want to believe me OK. If not that is okay. You will be sorry some day if you had to stay in jail with eight Negroes you would tell a lie two those Negroes did not touch me or those white boys I hope you will believe me the law dont, I love you better than Mary does or anybody else in the world that is why I am telling you of this thing. i was drunk at the time and did not know what i was doing i know it was wrong too let those Negroes die on account of me i hope you will believe my statement because it is the gods truth i hope you will believe me i was jazzed but those white boys jazzed me i wish those Negroes are not Burnt on account of me it is those white boys fault that is my statement, and that is all I know i hope you tell the law hope you will answer

Ruby Bates

P.S. This is one time that I might tell a lie But it is the truth so God help me.

Ruby Bates went to New York, where she saw Dr. Henry Emerson Fosdick and told him she had lied in the Scottsboro trial. He advised her to return South and testify for the defense. Later she went to Washington to see President Roosevelt but Vice President Garner met the group instead.

Despite the Bates girl's testimony, Victoria Price stuck to her original story. By now the ILD had recruited the services of lawyer Samuel S. Leibowitz, famous criminal specialist, and he defended the Negroes for the second trial.

Leibowitz was the man who convinced Al Capone to plead guilty to income tax evasion, and he would figure in the Lindbergh kidnaping case, too. A clever lawyer, he once had a client named Romano whose alibi was that he worked in a fishmarket. The prosecution brought in a variety of fish for the suspect to identify and thus prove himself. After Romano had flunked miserably on all the specimens shown him, Leibowitz leaped to his feet and cried, "This man worked in a *Kosher* fish market; they're trying to convict him on Christian fish!"

In Alabama Leibowitz was hated intensely by the Southerners as a meddling Northern Jew whose biggest victory, they said, would be to get safely back to New York. The

135

lawyer said he never knew when someone was going to shoot him with a six-gun, and a guard was necessary for his protection. A master at swaying juries in the North, Leibowitz plunged into the case courageously despite the hostility of the Southerners.

Leibowitz embarrassingly proved that Negroes were not permitted to serve on juries in the Alabama court, and then ripped the testimony of Victoria Price to shreds and introduced Ruby Bates as a defense witness. Despite this yeoman performance, however; or perhaps because of it, the trial seemed a repetition of the first one. About the only concession the defense had succeeded in getting for the second trial was a change of venue, to Decatur, Alabama. Here, on April 9, almost exactly a year after his first trial, Haywood Patterson was again found guilty.

However, Judge James E. Horton, who tried the second round, was of a different stripe than Judge Hawkins, and Leibowitz' strong defense did not go unnoticed. First, he ordered Roy Wright and Eugene Williams transferred to Juvenile Court because of their age. Next, he set aside the decision convicting Patterson in a long and searching review of the case. In nearly every detail, he said, Victoria Price's testimony was contradictory. Ruby Bates had recanted, and even appeared for the defense. There was little if any corroboration of the Price story by testimony of other witnesses. He summed it up in the following conclusion:

> History, sacred and profane, and the common experience of mankind teach us that women of the character shown in this case are prone for selfish reasons to make false accusations both of rape and insult upon the slightest provocation, or even without provocation for ulterior purposes.
>
> These women are shown, by the great weight of evidence on this very day before leaving Chattanooga, to have falsely accused two negroes of insulting them, and of almost precipitating a fight between one of the white boys they were in company with and those two negroes. This tendency on the part of the women shows that they are predisposed to make false accusations upon any occasion whereby their selfish ends may be gained.
>
> The Court will not pursue the evidence any further.
>
> As heretofore stated, the law declares that a defendant should not be convicted without corroboration where the testimony of the prosecutrix bears on its face indications of unreliability or improbability and particularly when it is contradicted by other evidence.

136

The testimony of the prosecutrix in this case is not only un-corroborated, but it also bears on its face indications of im-probability and is contradicted by other evidence, and in addi-tion thereto the evidence greatly preponderates in favor of the defendant. It therefore becomes the duty of the Court under the law to grant the motion made in this case.

It is therefore ordered and adjudged by the Court that the motion be granted; that the verdict of the jury in this case and the judgment of the Court in sentencing this defendant to death be, and the same hereby, set aside and that a new trial be and the same is hereby ordered.

JAMES E. HORTON
Circuit Judge

This honest act took great courage on the part of Judge Horton, for in so doing he was signing his own death war-rant as far as holding office in the State of Alabama was concerned. His was an elective job, and the next polls vin-dictively swept him out of the office he had nobly served.

Most Alabamans were hopping mad now. Ruby Bates, they said, and Lester Carter, too, had been bought by the Communists, Jews and Yanks in New York to lie in their teeth. This was why they could come back to Ala-bama and parade around all dressed up in clothes their blood money had bought.

Attorney Leibowitz got short shrift, too. He had caused a big commotion by contending that no Negroes were per-mitted on the juries of the state. To scotch this charge, a Jackson County clerk forged seven names on the 1931 jury roll. The ILD sent in a handwriting expert to expose the fake and this added to the hostilities. Leibowitz wisely tele-graphed Roosevelt asking protection as he headed south.

The judge sent in for the third trial was nothing like Horton. Judge W. W. Callahan was for conviction from the word go, and he gave Leibowitz a rough time. The prosecu-tion had free reign. When it was all over, the judge's charge to the jury left no doubt in their minds as to what they were counted on to do:

The law would authorize conviction on the testimony of Victoria Price alone, if, from that evidence, taken into con-sideration with all the evidence in the case, both for the State and for the defendant, convinced you beyond a reasonable doubt that she had been ravished. The law does not require corroboration.

On December 1, Patterson was convicted a third time and again given the death sentence. Clarence Norris was

137

convicted next. Judge Callahan denied the motion for a new trial. The condemned Patterson noted that this time the judge sentencing him hadn't even bothered to ask the Lord to have mercy on his soul. He and Norris were then sent back to Kilby Prison to await execution.

The defense was still convinced that they had strong arguments in the forging of names on the jury rolls, even though Judge Callahan felt this evidence "insufficient to impugn the honor of sworn jury officials," and in the actions of Callahan himself during the trial. He had refused to permit an adjournment which would have allowed the defense to introduce Ruby Bates' letter in time for Patterson's defense, instead of only that of Norris; he had refused to allow evidence used in the Horton trial, which discredited Victoria Price; he forgot to instruct the jury how they could find the defendant not guilty; and he used the color line by stating:

> When a woman charged to have been raped is white there is a very strong presumption under the law that she did not yield voluntarily to the defendant, a Negro, and this is true whatever station in life the prosecutrix may occupy. Whether she is the most despised, ignorant and abandoned woman of the community or a spotless virgin and daughter of a house of luxury and learning.

The court took advantage of several technicalities, however, in ruling against the defense time after time. Fate, too, conspired against Leibowitz and his aides, in a plane crash that prevented filing a required bill ahead of an arbitrarily set deadline. However, a stay of execution was finally obtained from the state court. The next move was to argue before the Supreme Court once more that a fair trial had not yet been afforded the Negroes.

In April of 1935, the Supreme Court reversed the decision of the Alabama court on the ground that Negroes had been excluded from juries. Leibowitz' skill had again saved the lives of the defendants. Now the prosecution had to start all over and it was necessary for Victoria Price to again swear out a warrant. When, in November, the Alabama grand jury returned indictments on all nine of the accused, a Negro was in the jury box and history had been made. However, it was a victory in principle only, since a two-thirds vote was all that was required to return an indictment.

Meantime, Governor Bibb Graves sent an important letter to all solicitors and circuit judges throughout the state as a result of the reversal handed down by the U.S. Supreme Court:

> Holdings of the United States Supreme Court are the supreme law of the land. Whether we like the decision or not, it is the patriotic duty of every citizen and the sworn duty of every public official to accept them and uphold them in letter and in spirit.
>
> I have received the Supreme Court's decision in the Scottsboro case, holding in effect that when there is systematic exclusion of Negroes from juries, it is discrimination against race in violation of the U.S. Constitution.
>
> This decision means that we must put the names of Negroes in jury boxes in every county in the State.
>
> Alabama is going to observe the supreme law of America.

It was, of course, one thing to put the names of Negroes in jury boxes and another to have them actually serve on those juries. At the outset of the trial in Decatur, a dozen Negroes were on the list. When one of them blundered into the jury box, Judge Callahan set him straight right away and pointed to chairs set up outside for the colored people. Then the attrition began.

Two of the potential precedent-makers decided they were past the 65-year age limit. Another allowed that his ailing boss needed him back right away and took off. Those that had no excuses of their own were eliminated with little difficulty by the prosecution. In principle, however, Leibowitz had won a major victory.

It had been apparent to many people that the Communist group working for the Negroes were grinding the ax in their own behalf. By now it must have seemed to Leibowitz that the tactics of the ILD were not in the best interests of the Scottsboro defendants, and he sought their permission to handle the case himself. He was finally successful, and in another move calculated to remove any stigma from being attached to the defense also hired an Alabaman to actually plead the case. Leibowitz, of course, remained as counsel. Now, for no pay, and meeting his own expenses, he prepared for his third defense of the Negroes.

139

On January 20, 1936, Haywood Patterson, the Number One "Scottsboro Boy," again found himself in court fighting for his life. He was a veteran of four trials, and most of the other principals were old hands, too. Victoria Price had told her tale of ordeal many times and knew it almost verbatim even without the backing up of Ruby Bates.

Judge Callahan hadn't changed his mind since he last sentenced Patterson and he let it be known that he was in a hurry to have justice done. The prosecutor, Thomas Edmund Knight, had been prosecuting the Negroes since 1933 and about the only difference now was that he was no longer Attorney General, but Lieutenant Governor of Alabama.

The question of the constitutionality of a man holding down these two jobs at once was speedily dispensed with and Knight got to work. It took him most of the day to present the state's case, and although it was by then five o'clock and the defense had no witnesses ready for the stand the court ordered that the trial must continue and that Patterson take the stand.

The defense was rushed through by Judge Callahan with the announcement that "it won't help anyone to see anything. It will just delay things."

In his advice to the jury the assistant prosecutor said, "Don't quibble over the evidence. Say to yourselves that we're tired of this job and get it behind you. Get it done quick and protect fair womanhood in this great state!"

About all Leibowitz could add was for the jury to protect the innocent, too, and then it was in the hands of twelve white men. It took the jury about as long as it had taken Prosecutor Knight, and the only thing different about this verdict was the sentence. Instead of death in the electric chair, Patterson was to get only seventy-five years in jail.

Sam Leibowitz thought that was a break, and relatively speaking it was. But Haywood Patterson had already spent five years in prison. In seventy-five more he would be ninety-eight! Bitterly he said he'd rather die.

As Leibowitz proceeded with the next defendant, the evidence of the examining doctors' testimony was challenged by the prosecution. One doctor was too sick to come to court and substantiate his statement in person; Judge Callahan announced an indefinite postponement. The nine Ne-

140

groes were hustled out to police cars for the ride back to the prison in Birmingham, and one of them almost didn't make it alive.

Before leaving Birmingham for the trial in Decatur, the prisoners had bought knives from the jail trusties against the need to defend themselves or possibly an escape try.

Riding in the middle car, Ozie Powell suddenly slipped his knife from its hiding place in the lining of his trousers' fly. Leaning forward he slashed Deputy Sheriff Edgar Blalock's throat.

What prompted the knifing was never definitely established, and lawyer Leibowitz snorted at the idea that Powell was trying to escape while handcuffed to two other prisoners, with guards in his car and other cars in front and behind. Whatever the reason, Blalock was stabbed and Sheriff J. Street Sandlin pulled out his gun and shot Powell in the head.

A portion of the Negro's forehead was shot away. Still conscious and still chained to the other prisoners, Powell was rushed to the town of Cullman and patched up. Then he was driven the rest of the way to Birmingham, some seventy miles, where the slug was extracted from his brain. It was a violent climax and it signaled the end of formal action by the law.

By now the state of Alabama was sick to death of the Scottsboro boys. Not long after the fourth trial, a truckload of Negro convicts being taken out to work on the road accidentally set fire to a five-gallon gasoline container while trying to warm themselves in the freezing weather. A larger drum of gasoline also exploded, and before guards could unlock the truck doors all but two of the twenty-two men inside perished.

Many people thought surely it was the end of the Scottsboro boys, but they were still safe in prison. There would be no more trials, the state was through with them.

The case was still a *cause célébre* to match that of Dreyfus. Maxim Gorky, Madame Sun Yat-sen and Romain Rolland were among those who appealed in behalf of the Negroes. Money was pouring into them and Patterson was getting $25 a month from Nancy Cunard of the steamship family alone. With the money these benefactors sent to them, the Scottsboro boys could command better treat-

141

ment. They bought whatever they needed, from clothes to meals, and even women; in Birmingham the guards were cooperative, for a price.

By the middle of 1937 Sam Leibowitz would succeed in freeing four of the Negroes, and a gentlemen's agreement was in the works for paroles for the rest. Eventually all would be freed except Haywood Patterson, against whom bitter Southern hatred seemed to focus. While the others got out—and back in, some of them, for parole violations— Patterson would remain in prison. It was a hellish existence that could hardly be called human, and finally he would escape in 1948 after seventeen years' imprisonment for a crime few people think he committed.

It all happened, as Patterson himself said, with a white foot on his black hand.

BIBLIOGRAPHY

Scottsboro Boy—Patterson, Conrad
Trial by Prejudice—Arthur Garfield Hayes

IX

The Olympic Games

The year 1936 saw the holding of the Eleventh Modern Olympiad in Berlin, Germany. This sports spectacle had a fantastically ancient heritage, the Olympics having begun in Greece perhaps as early as 1200 B.C. It was known for certain that between 776 B.C. and 394 A.D., when Theodosius suspended the games, Olympiads were held as regularly as clockwork each four years.

After the centuries-long lapse of time, the modern Olympics were originated through the inspired and dedicated efforts of a Frenchman, Baron Pierre de Coubertin.

Pondering the overrunning of his homeland in 1890 by Germany, De Coubertin sought to improve the caliber of his countrymen to something approaching that of the British, whose victorious empire spanned the world. From his original idea of rigorous sports training for Frenchmen, De Coubertin extended his thinking to a *world-wide* betterment of physical and moral man—the rebirth of the Olympics. It was not an easy task he set himself, but in 1896 his dream was at last realized with the First Modern Olympiad, held fittingly in Athens.

In addition to the Greek athletes participating were sportsmen from the United States, England, France, Germany, Russia, Sweden, Hungary, Australia, Denmark and Switzerland. The competent Americans dominated the contest, and indeed there was disappointment in many camps until the day of the marathon. Then Spiridion Loues won the 42-kilometer grind in a time of 2 hours 55 minutes and 20 seconds. Greece won second and third places, also, and the jealousy of "professional" athletes from America was forgotten in wild celebration. Runner Loues was a hero instantly, showered with gifts ranging from jewels to the promise from a young bootblack of free shines for life! More importantly, the success of the modern Olympics was assured.

143

Paris, St. Louis, London, Stockholm, Antwerp, Amsterdam and Los Angeles had been awarded the Olympic Games that followed the first in historic Greece. Paris was host on two occasions, fittingly enough since De Coubertin had done so much toward establishing the Olympics. Although the 1936 affair scheduled for Berlin was called the eleventh, there had actually been only nine preceding it. The sixth, planned for Berlin in 1916, had been canceled because of World War I. But now the Germans had another chance and they were determined to make the most of it.

Even before the very successful games in Los Angeles in 1932 the Eleventh Olympiad had been awarded to Berlin. In 1931, of course, Hitler was a power only in the Nazi Party and Germany was still a weak country building back from the defeat of the war. Dr. Theodore Lewald, long an Olympic committee official, was the logical choice as president of the organizing committee. First rumblings of the controversy that would cloud the 1936 games came with the denunciation by Germany's anti-Semitic Julius Streicher of the Olympics as an infamous festival dominated by Jews.

Just after the organizing committee met in Berlin in January of 1933, Hitler became Chancellor of the Reich. President von Hindenburg was named patron of the forthcoming Olympiad, but Dr. Lewald realistically went to Hitler for support for the games. The chancellor, with his vision of an Aryan superrace, and perhaps not realizing that Germany would not control the Olympics, promised the support needed.

Unfortunately, Lewald was also part Jewish, and a long struggle ensued to oust him from his position and give it to Reich Sportsleader, Von Tschammer und Osten. President Baillet Latour of the International Olympic Committee stood by his guns and told Hitler that Lewald would remain, and that the organizing committee itself and not the Nazis would run the Olympiad, or there would be none.

As the Nazis rose in power, there was growing opposition in the United States and elsewhere to sending athletes to Berlin because of the oppression of Jews and the fear that Jewish contestants would be discriminated against.

In January, 3,500 delegates of the American League Against War and Fascism met in Cleveland to urge the U.S. to boycott the German Olympics. Despite such opposition, tentative plans were made for participation. Twice the Americans demanded, and received, guarantees of fair

144

play. Plans went ahead to attend the Eleventh Olympiad despite financial difficulties along the way.

A fund goal of $350,000 was set to send a full complement of athletes to Berlin but because of the Jewish problem and also perhaps because of the depressed economic condition of the country, the full sum was not raised. Some of the athletes had to finance their own trips, but a large team of more than 400 did represent the United States.

The Olympic Games were held in two sections, widely separated in time and distance. For the winter games in January, Germany had selected the twin villages of Garmisch-Partenkirchen, some sixty miles south of Munich in the Bavarian Alps. It was evident here that the Germans had spared no expense to make the games the finest yet held, at least as far as the physical surroundings were concerned. Facilities for the athletes were superb, the plush buildings later to be used as a swank officer's club.

With the boom in winter sports in the United States, particularly in skiing, a large team of seventy boarded the *S.S. Manhattan* for the voyage across the Atlantic. The Americans, however, were not to star in this part of the Olympics. In practice the skiers did not shine in comparison with the Scandinavians, and bobsledders complained of the quality of the run, which they thought was unsound and harmful to the new-type runners of American sleds.

The winter games opened to a full house in a raging snowstorm. Some 1,600 athletes from 28 countries paraded before Hitler's reviewing stand and all of them, except the American contingent, lifted their arms in the traditional Olympic salute. Because that greeting might be taken as the Nazi salute, the Americans did not use it, and some correspondents said their reception was cooler than could be blamed simply on the weather. But the ceremonies went on.

Hitler made a brief speech opening the games, a huge torch was lighted, the Olympic bell rang, a cannon boomed, and the huge white flag with its five interlocked circles representing the continents fluttered over the 15,000 spectators who jammed the stands. Outside more thousands milled about.

There was a huge swastika at the foot of the ski jump, but for the Olmpyics the Germans had eased the fierce militarism and the vicious anti-Jewish attitude. Police wore

145

more informal garb and signs discriminating against the Jews were temporarily taken down.

Visitors were pleased and surprised at the pleasant surroundings, and linguistic waiters in restaurants wore miniature flags to indicate the tongues they spoke. Unofficial host for the American athletes was smiling Karl Schluter, who had lived until recently in Brooklyn. Schluter left the U.S. during the depression and was now working as a Storm Trooper. He entertained the Americans in his barracks.

It was a holiday attitude and one of Olympian goodwill with few exceptions. The Germans had bent over backwards and even permitted Rudi Ball, a Jew, to play on the hockey team. He repaid this great privilege by playing so furiously that Germany was barely nosed out by the U.S. in their game and then only by a technicality. There was another Jew at the winter games—Anton Lang, the Christ of Passion Play fame. Oberammergau was not far from Garmisch-Partenkirchen, and the Christus came to watch the Germans shine.

As usual there was some bickering among the contestants. Canada protested that two members of an English team were actually Canadians. In a hockey battle with Italy, America's Gordon Smith complained that his glasses were knocked off intentionally and was roundly booed by Italian partisans. Taking his game more seriously, a French hockey player bit a Hungarian opponent. But the winter Olympics, officially called the Fourth Winter Olympics, were generally thrilling and set new marks.

Norway's Ivan Ballangrud swept the speed skating events, winning three and placing second in a fourth. And his sister Norwegian, Sonja Henie, triumphed again in figure skating. She would turn professional after this victory, going to the United States and well-paying fame in ice shows and movies. The ski events were dominated by the Scandinavians also, with Birger Rudd adding to Norway's laurels in winning the jumping event.

To win the skating championship for "pairs," German Ernst Baier and his beautiful 16-year-old partner Maxi Herber had themselves photographed by a movie camera during their routines. A composer then wrote a musical score to match their skating.

When the affair closed, Norway had scored a total of 121 points to assure itself of unofficial victory as a country, though the Olympics are traditionally individual events.

146

Germany placed second with 57 points and Sweden was third at 49. The United States had to content itself with a lone first place, winning that in the two-man bobsled event. It had won the 1932 games at Lake Placid; now it placed a weak fifth.

The winter games were of course only a prologue to the main show to be held in Berlin in August. Los Angeles had been excellent, but it was evident that Berlin would outdo even that triumph. Despite some complaints of anti-Semitic and political overtones, an authority like Avery Brundage, president of the American Olympic Committee, could compliment the Germans on the winter games which 800,000 spectators attended. With respect to the lack of applause for the Americans at Garmisch-Partenkirchen, he pointed out that after all the contingent had resembled a bunch of streetcar conductors in their uninspired uniforms. Reporter Paul Gallico had found the winter games idyllic, and columnist Westbrook Pegler said that at least the winter games had prevented, for the time being, a brutal raid on the Jews.

In America the Olympic Committee was scurrying around worriedly up to a few days before the *S.S. Manhattan* sailed, trying to scrounge up the wherewithal for fares. Apathetic or economically unable, Los Angeles, which had kept the official flag since 1932, did not provide the $2,000 requested of it to send an official with the flag to Berlin. Feminine contestants waited nervously in hotel rooms in New York, subsisting on a meager 75-cents-a-day allowance from the committee and wondering if they would even get on the boat, or would have to swim for it.

Runner Gene Venzke had sold an article to the *Saturday Evening* Post and wanted permission to accept $400 in payment. He was told he could not, without losing his amateur standing, but a compromise was reached when the money was paid to a charity. The charity was the American Olympic Committee, which used it to send author Venzke to Berlin!

Even the tryouts for berths on the Olympic team were not without their difficulties. At newly opened Randalls Island the track and field competition seemed badly mishandled. Three national champs somehow managed to miss qualifying, though there was one notable exception.

Jesse Owens won three events, the 100-meter, 200-meter,

and broad jump in fine style, but it must have shaken Gordon Dunn, who won his discus event with a toss of 157 feet 7½ inches, to learn that Fraulein Gisela Mauermeyer threw an equally heavy discus a foot further that same day in Berlin tryouts!

Over at Astoria the aquatic contestants found themselves indignantly standing in line with a holiday crowd at the newly opened municipal pool. Inside, the practice "diving board" turned out to be just a wooden plank, and the pool was only three feet deep so that powerfully stroking crawlers dragged their fingernails on the bottom!

At the last moment, a tempting offer of $100,000 from a cereal manufacturer was turned down so that no taint of commercialism would mar the amateur status of the contestants. Purchases of food, including 9 tons of milk and 1,600 pounds of peanut brittle, were loaded aboard the *Manhattan* along with 334 athletes. Five of the women raised the Olympic flag to flutter over the big liner, and they were on their way. It was to be a hectic trip.

Some of the team complained about the food. There was agitation for permission to smoke and drink, and this was granted, provided the beverage be limited to beer. Curfew was changed from ten to midnight, and the athletes went on an honor system.

Breaking the monotony of the trip was the appendicitis attack that laid low Harold Smallwood, the 400-meter champ; and a more pleasant event—a beauty and popularity contest. Two Glenns shone in this affair. Glenn Hardin was voted most handsome man, and Glenn Cunningham the most popular. Among the fair sex, fencer Joanna de Tuscan was rated most beautiful, with Katherine Rawls, a swimmer, the most popular. There was another swimmer aboard who would win recognition she wasn't looking for. Her name was Eleanor Holm Jarrett.

Mrs. Jarrett was a beauty herself, and must have placed high in the competition in that category. Wife of a singer she had been in the movies and was something of a celebrity. Avery Brundage, responsible for the morals of his charges, was sworn to keep them above reproach. When Mrs. Jarrett persisted in frequenting the ship's bar and imbibing champagne, Brundage sacked her from the team for such obvious breaking of training.

Despite her pleas and those of hundreds of her team members he made the dismissal stick, and the U.S. lost its main hope in the backstroke competition. "Roistering in the bar," President Brundage said, was not in keeping with the necessarily high Olympic standards, particularly for the female members of the team.

According to the press, Mrs. Jarrett consoled herself by meeting a crown prince, and her husband Art was said to be on the way to join her and threatening to sue somebody for the defamation of his wife's character. The other American athletes were accorded a royal welcome in Germany and, far from being castigated, Brundage was elected to fill a vacancy on the International Committee. The only further casualties were two boxers, one a Negro, whom Brundage found guilty of "infectious" homesickness and dismissed from the team.

If the United States had been chary about supporting its Olympians, the Germans had gone all out to make the Berlin affair the most impressive in history. The *Reichssportfeld* had been built to include not just one stadium, but four. The main stadium seated 110,000, and total capacity at the Olympics site was nearly 500,000. With an area of more than 300 acres, the site for the games was magnificent.

The most advanced timing devices were provided, and communications and other technical arrangements were well nigh flawless. Tunnels were dug beneath the clay tracks of the stadia and windows in the bottom of the swimming pool permitted visitors an unusual view of the contestants.

It was estimated that Hitler had spent $30 million on the show. Olympic village in Los Angeles had been thought superb, but one of the bungalows that served to accommodate athletes there was on display in Germany's Olympic Village at Doberitz and looked sharecropperish by comparison. Covering more than a hundred scenic acres, the village consisted of 140 permanent buildings constructed of stone, and containing facilities for 16 to 24 athletes. A British official decided the only thing lacking were storks to perch on the roofs, and obliging Germans even provided these!

Berlin itself was arrayed in festive trimmings, and even the Jews, who were not permitted to fly the German colors, joined in as best they could by decorating their stores with Olympic flags. Although the Nazi swastika was still not officially the national emblem, it was displayed prominently in the Olympic stadia. This had been brought about in part by a riot in America by Jews who protested the goings-on in Germany by tearing down a swastika on a ship. Retaliat-

149

ing, the Nazis now flaunted their party emblem for the Olympiad.

Despite such attempts at propaganda, the pageantry attending the Olympics was spectacular. The Germans provided two religious services before the opening, one for Protestants and another for Catholics. There was a military parade, an exhibition by 30,000 blond girls and boys of the Hitler Youth. On the eve of the great day a festival play, *Olympic Youth,* especially written for the occasion, was presented by a cast of 10,000. The finale was Beethoven's Ninth Symphony and Schiller's "Ode to Joy" sung by a chorus of 1,500, as requested by the founder of the modern Olympics, Baron de Coubertin.

Prior to the opening of the games, the traditional torch had been lighted at the Temple of Zeus in Olympia. Fourteen Grecian maidens, in flowing ancient costumes, had symbolically focused the sun's rays to ignite the sacred fire. This they carried through the sacred grove to where a runner lit from it a magnesium torch and began an 1,800-mile run toward Berlin.

The relay had begun on July 20, and 3,300 runners would carry the torch in half-mile spurts to the Olympic Stadium in Berlin. The run was not without its problems. At Paracin, Yugoslavia, the flame embarrassingly flickered out and the carrier tactfully climbed into a car rather than carry a dead torch for his distance. Relit, the sacred flame again moved north, and at noon on August 1, the last runner of this great torch relay appeared dramatically at the top of the stairs of the east gate of the stadium.

The big Olympic flag was raised and guns boomed from outside the stadium as the runner trotted down the steps, across the arena, and up the steps opposite. At the top he touched his torch to the Olympic fire and the symbolic chain was complete. As the Olympic bell tolled, the first of the more than four thousand athletes began to march into the ring. Fifty-one nations were represented, the only one conspicuous by its absence was Spain, whose contestants had arrived for the Olympiad but had been recalled when the tragic Civil War broke out in their country.

As the athletes paraded past the reviewing stand some of them gave the Nazi salute. The Austrians goose-stepped in the bargain, and France was among those nations whose colors dipped to the German swastika. As the American contingent moved past, they repeated the procedure they had adopted at Garmisch-Partenkirchen. There was no fist-upraised salute; instead they clapped their straw hats to their chests.

Despite a downpour of rain, 100,000 jammed the stadium and most of them were soaked by the time Chancellor Hitler arrived in his brown uniform. As he entered, the rain had miraculously stopped and the loyal delightedly cried, "See! Our *Führer* can do anything!"

In front of this vast assemblage, the athletes took the Olympic Oath. Then no less a veteran than old Spiridion Loues himself, the man who had won the marathon for Greece way back in the First Modern Olympiad in Athens, came forward with an olive branch for Adolf Hitler. By comparison, some said, the splendid show at Los Angeles was as tame as two trained fleas racing around the brim of a hat.

With the singing of Handel's *Hallelujah Chorus* by a German choir, the athletes marched out, and the Eleventh Olympiad was officially under way. If Hitler himself had written the script for what was about to happen he could have done no better. For, where no German athlete in all the history of the Olympics had ever won a championship in the track and field events, Hans Woelke proceeded to do just that with his second toss in the shot-put! Not only did he place first, but he smashed the old record. And to make the joy supreme, another German, Gerhard Stoek, placed third in the same event. When the victory flags were raised, two of them bore the huge black swastika and Germans in the stadium went wild.

In an unofficial gesture, the two German athletes were swept up to Hitler's personal loge, where the *Führer* greeted them and added his own congratulations. He repeated this award to the three Finns who made a clean sweep of the 10,000-meter race, and then, miracle of miracles twice on opening day, two German *fräuleins*, Tilly Fleischer and Luise Kruger, outdid their male teammates by placing one-two in the javelin throw! They, too, were whisked to the *Führer* for his tribute, though this procedure had no official sanction.

By then it was getting on in the day. Only one other final competition, the high jump, was in progress and Hitler departed before it was finished at about sundown. The United States took all three first places, and Johnson and Albritton, placing first and second, were two of the ten

151

Negroes on the American team. They were not, of course, called to Hitler's box, and the idea of a snub began to circulate.

Before the next day, Count Henri de Baillet Latour, the President of the International Committee, sent word to Hitler that his congratulatory actions had been out of line, since he was officially only guest of honor, as patron. Unless he was prepared to personally congratulate all winners, then, he should refrain from appearing to make a partisan gesture.

Thus warned, Hitler explained that his action stemmed from the excitement of the splendid showing made by the Germans, and the thrill of at long last having scored in the Olympics. He promised not to repeat the procedure, and apparently kept his word.

The legend that still persists concerning Hitler's snub of Jesse Owens is just that. If anyone was snubbed, it would seem to have been the high-jump winners, and Hitler had a good excuse for that omission since he was not even in the stadium. It is, of course, open to conjecture whether he would have so honored Negroes, or if they would have accepted such plaudits knowing the Nazi feeling toward their race.

The performance in the Eleventh Olympiad was as impressive as were the surroundings. In the track and field events alone new records were set in more than half of the twenty-nine events. Generally a tone of good sportsmanship prevailed, although the soccer event precipitated a battle between the Austrians and Peruvians that ended with rioting all the way back to Lima in protest.

Avery Brundage, concerned by reports that two European female runners had recently been operated on and turned into males, had urged a physical examination of all the women entrants. He should not have been surprised, as a result, that Miss Helen Stephens from Missouri was suspect when she won the 100-meter dash in faster time than Tom Burke had won it with at the First Olympiad, and anchored the winning 400-meter relay team as well. She was examined and pronounced a bona fide girl by the Olympic physicians.

In addition to Owens' feats, Americans won the 400- and 800-meter runs, the 110-meter and 400-meter hurdles, the discus throw and the pole vault. The marathon was won by Japan's Kitel Son. The United States took first in the decathlon when Glenn Morris amassed a record 7,900 points. Germany's Hundrich won the pentathlon. Americans took two swimming firsts and won all the top places in diving competition.

Over-all, the Germans were unofficial high scorers with some 580 points total. The United States scored second with 470, then Italy—186, Sweden—167, Hungary—158, Japan—153, France—152, Finland—145, Holland—136, Great Britain—115, Austria—99, and Canada—55. But in the track and field, the mainstay of the Olympics, the Americans were the winners with over 200 points. Finland was next with about 80, and Germany third at 70 points. Exhibitions of basketball and baseball were played, with the latter sport sweeping the Olympics audience for popularity.

Played in the main stadium, the exhibition drew the largest crowds ever to witness baseball, including the World Series. An introductory lecture to the game was immediately translated into several languages and printed in quantity for distribution. The German announcer, a newcomer to the game, did his best with the following description:

> Both teams appeared with nine players. The team with the red stockings attacked first. The thrower throws the ball at a certain height toward the catcher of his team. The catcher must catch the ball if it is not captured by the wooden baton of the hitter.
>
> The defending team also had four men who guarded the rhombus [diamond] and tackled runners, as well as three people who guarded the outlying section of the rhombus in order to capture the ball for their own team. After three invalid throws, a player is out, and the same is true if the ball is caught and also if the ball is thrown into the rhombus before he finishes his run.

If one man stood out among the nearly 5,000 who journeyed to Berlin, it was Jesse Owens from Ohio. The slight Negro succeeded as no athlete had ever succeeded before, bettering the three wins of Finnish Paavo Nurmi in 1924, and his feat must have been galling to the Germans who were his hosts for the games.

Earlier in the year the Nazis conjured up an excuse for the defeat they were sure that Max Schmeling was going to get at the hands of Joe Louis in their world championship bout in New York. Negroes, after all, weren't really *human*, said Hitler and his flunkies. Thus the Aryans need not be ashamed of defeat at their hands. When Schmeling upset

Louis, and all the experts as well, they didn't need the alibi. It was resurrected now, and German writers deplored the sad state to which the Americans had sunk that they must bring their "black auxiliaries" with them.

Johnson and Albritton had already won a first and second, with Johnson setting a new high-jump record of 6 feet, 7 and 15/16 inches. So even before Jesse Owens began his string of miracles the Negro race had already acquitted itself well. But the best was yet to come.

Back in Los Angeles in 1932 a Detroit Negro named Eddie Tolan had belied his chunky bespectacled appearance by winning the 100-meter and 200-meter races. It was a fantastic performance, but over in Ohio there was a versatile Negro athlete who would shortly begin to steal Tolan's thunder.

Jesse had been born James Cleveland Owens down in Alabama, but his initials J.C. naturally led to his being called Jesse. There were seven youngsters in the family and they moved to Ohio to try to better their financial condition. At high school in Cleveland a coach encouraged skinny Jesse to go out for track to build himself up a little. Amazingly he started right off running the 100-yard dash in near-record time and before long he was unbeatable. Not just a sprinter, he ran the hurdles, too, and even tackled the broad jump.

By 1935 Jesse was a solid, 160-pound package of potential records. A sophomore at Ohio State he was ready for the Big Ten Conference track meet at Ann Arbor, Michigan. On May 25, 10,000 fans would see so much history made they would be several days believing it.

At a quarter past three, Jesse drove out of his crouch and flew a hundred yards in 9.4 seconds. He was five yards ahead of the Number Two man, but the thing that was even more important was that he had tied the world record for the distance. Scarcely breathing hard, he gauged his stride toward the broad-jump pit ten minutes later and made one jump. It was all he needed to win the Big Ten event and also to break the record held then by Japan's Nambu, the man who had been third at the 1932 Olympics. Owens had leaped 26 feet, 8½ inches.

At quarter to four, Jesse ran the 220-yard dash. He won it, too, ten yards out in front and going away, in 20.3 seconds. The word record was 20.6.

One first place in the Big Ten was a feat, against the top

154

Midwest competition. Two was outstanding. Here was a man who had won *three* firsts! Not only that, he had also tied one world mark and broken two others. But Jesse Owens wasn't quite finished. It was just about four when he completed one of the busiest and most momentous forty-five minutes in track and field history. Legs flashing like smooth pistons, he screamed over the 220-yard hurdles like the Buckeye Bullet that he was. There was nobody close, because not many runners can chop 4/10 of a second from a record time. The new mark was 22.6.

This was the Jesse Owens who had won himself a place on the 1936 Olympic team with his sweep of the 100-meter, 200-meter and broad jump at the tryouts at Randalls Island. But what would the Tan Cyclone from America do here in Berlin where the black man wasn't considered really a man? It took him longer, but when he was through his performance was a faithful carbon copy of that day at Ann Arbor.

The first victory came in the 100-meter dash. Owens exploded down the red clay track like a bullet for sure. His only competition was the timing clock, and that caught him in 10.3 seconds, a new world and Olympic record but for the slight following wind that disqualified the mark.

The broad jump was next. Until this day, no one had ever jumped 26 feet in Olympic competition. Ed Gordon had won for the United States in 1932 with 25 feet, 3/4 inch. In the shadow of Berlin's swastikas Jesse Owens catapulted through the air for 26 feet, 5 and 5/16 inches!

At Berlin, the 200-meter dash was run around a curving track. Separate marks had been set for this as opposed to the dash over a straight track, and the world record stood at 21.2 seconds. As the contestants lined up there was a cold blustery wind blowing, quartering the direction they would be running.

It began to rain just before the gun fired. But Owens paid no heed to the weather, his competition or the existing record. He tore into the tape a good five yards ahead of teammate Matt Robinson in the unbelievable time of 20.7. Running around the curve no one had ever negotiated in less than 21 seconds, Jesse almost equaled the old mark for the straight distance. He had broken the old record by half a second!

Three first places in an Olympics, and three records smashed, but the Tan Cyclone wasn't yet finished. Teaming

155

with Metcalfe, Draper and Wykoff, Owens helped take another first place: the time—39.8 seconds for the 400-meter relay. With the runners averaging less than ten seconds each, the time was a new Olympic record, of course.

It was over now, and Jesse Owens had walked four times to the victory pedestal and watched Old Glory hoisted behind him as the *Star-Spangled Banner* boomed out across the stadium. Four times the German girls crowned him with laurel, and four times he took a gold medal telling him that he was the best on the huge field for that event. There were four small potted oak trees, too, living symbols of his wonderful speed and stamina.

Back home, Ohio's governor proclaimed a "Jesse Owens Day." No need for the Nazi leader to shake his hand; that was not important. Long after the *Führer* was dead and disgraced, Jesse Owen's name, set in bronze in the proud Marathon Gate of Berlin's stadium, would continue to attest the lasting truth of that victory. In 1951, 75,000 Germans would turn out in that same stadium to cheer Owens when he returned to visit Berlin.

Long before it was over the world knew this was the biggest Olympics ever. With more than four and a half million paid admissions, gate receipts totaled almost three million dollars. There had been 110,000 in the main stadium for the opening ceremonies, and there were 110,000 there on Sunday, August 16, when the Eleventh Olympiad wound up in triumph. It was long after dark when the Olympic flame that had been carried all the way from the Temple of Zeus was finally extinguished. The games were over and, according to the humorists, American winners could return home and give their medals to Secretary of the Treasury Morgantheau since it was illegal to hoard gold.

There was the more serious worry in the minds of the Olympics people then that, despite the wonderful spectacle in Berlin, the Olympics had outgrown the thing they were intended to do. Save for Jesse Owens, the individual athletes were far overshadowed by the show itself, and this was not the way it should be. Perhaps there should be some changes made before the next Olympiad.

Greater forces than those pondered by the committee were at work, of course. The man who had designed the wonderful Olympic Village that housed the athletes had been a Jew. When Hitler refused to rescind the order barring him from the Army career that was his life, Captain Wolfgang Fuerstner killed himself. Millions more Jews would die in the years ahead. Olympic Village became barracks for men based at bristling Staaken Airport, an airport sheltering more and more war planes.

Later on in 1936, a Philadelphian named Samuel Stewart Fleisher proposed another kind of Olympics than that which had been held in Berlin: a cultural Olympics.

"In Europe," Fleisher said, "the dictators are leading children to hate and here we will be teaching ours to love beauty." It was an idealistic dream, but it came late.

Baron Pierre de Coubertin had envisioned the modern Olympiad and worked to see it flourish. The twelfth was his last, and his death within a year was strangely prophetic. The Olympic flame had gone out at Berlin: it would not be rekindled at Tokyo, as was now planned for 1940. There would be no Olympics for twelve years, during most of which death and destruction would rage around the world. President Latour would die in his native Belgium while that tiny country was under German occupation. But after the long darkness, the same sort of spirit that gave the Olympiad to mankind at Athens prevailed again in 1948.

BIBLIOGRAPHY

An Approved History of the Olympic Games—Henry
The Story of the Olympic Games—Kieran
Dr. Paul Wolff's Leica Sports Shots (1936 Olympics)—Wolff

X

Japan and China

By 1936 it was painfully apparent to the world that there were several countries bent on building themselves up at the expense of others. In his State of the Union address, Franklin Roosevelt pointed this out courageously:

> A point has been reached where the peoples of America must take cognizance of the growing ill-will and marked trends toward aggression, increasing armaments, and shortening tempers—a situation which has in it many elements leading to the tragedy of war.

There were no names named, but the description left little to the imagination concerning whom the President meant.

> Nations seeking expansion, seeking rectification of injustices springing from former wars, and seeking outlets for trade, population, and even their own peaceful contributions to the progress of civilization fail to demonstrate the patience necessary to attain reasonable and legitimate objectives by peaceful negotiations and by appeal to the finer instincts of world justice.
>
> They have hitherto impatiently reverted to the old belief in the law of the sword or to the fantastic conception that they alone are chosen to fulfill a mission and that all others must and shall learn from and be subject to them. I recognize that these words, which I have chosen with deliberation, will not be popular among any nation that chooses to fit this shoe to its foot.
>
> I emphasize on you the gravity of the situation confronting the people of the world. Peace is jeopardized by the few, not the many, and is threatened by those who are seeking selfish power.

Coming as it did at the time of the long and energetic celebration of the New Year in Japan, Roosevelt's challenge of the shoe was not answered there as soon as it was in Italy and Germany, the other obvious wearers of the size and style of footgear in question.

Eiju Aimu of the Japanese Foreign Office professed not to have read the message, although it had appeared in the newspapers in his country in summary form with some direct quotations. However, later in January, Foreign Minister Koki Hirota answered Roosevelt in a speech he made before the Japanese Diet. Replying in kind, Hirota mentioned no names either, but the hint was that someone had his foot in his mouth, rather than in a shoe. As Roosevelt's speech had stirred Americans, so that of Japan's Minister warmed the hearts of his countrymen.

It is to be regretted that there are abroad statesmen of repute who seem determined to impose upon others their private convictions as to how the world should be ordered, and who are apt to denounce those who oppose their dictates as if they were disturbers of the peace. No one is qualified to talk world peace unless he not only knows the national aspirations and obligations of his country but also understands and appreciates the standpoints of other countries.

The understanding and appreciation of another country's standpoint is often attainable through the understanding and appreciation of that country's culture and civilization. We have succeeded in building up our national strength and prestige by adding and adapting to our civilization Occidental art and science, which we have imported during the past years. Now it is time for us, I believe, to try to introduce our arts and culture to other lands, and thus contribute toward international good understanding and to the enrichment of world civilization and the promotion of the peace and happiness of mankind.

These were lofty words indeed, calculated to thrill the Japanese and to blind unwary foreigners. The Japanese regretted the unfortunate fact that King George's death had more or less pushed Hirota's Diet speech from the front pages of the British papers.

China wasn't blinded, because she was close enough to have already benefited from the introduction of Japanese "arts and culture," along with guns and troops needed to make them stick. In addition to the slap at Roosevelt, Hirota's address contained the three main points of obligation on the part of China in return for the enrichment Japan was bringing her:

159

1. Recognition by China that Manchukuo was a fact of life, even if she would not give *de jure* recognition at this time.
2. Suppression of Communist activities.
3. More extensive collaboration between China and Japan.

Not in Hirota's speech, but currently in the Japanese press, appeared suggestions that Japan push the occupation of Britain's Far East territories while that country was up to its ears in its difficulties with Italy and Egypt.

Pacing the aggressive generals in Japan were admirals who also saw the Rising Sun as needed far beyond the ocean's horizon. In 1933 Japan had dropped out of the League of Nations, and now at the London Naval Conference she rebelled at the pact that called for a 5-5-3 ratio for British, U.S. and Japanese naval power.

Firmly but politely, Japan told the Conference to go to hell and announced that she would henceforth build up her navy as she saw fit. Besides that, Admiral Takahashi cockily announced, "We have tactics to defeat the combined fleets of Great Britain and the United States!"

Of course, Japan had no aggressive motives in expansion of its sea power, just as its aims in China were not aggressive. The Navy must grow because of the growth of trade, that was all. As 1936 got under way, the Japanese Trade Council was exulting at its success in America. Even the condemnation of Japanese goods as "cheap and shoddy" in the press—particularly the Hearst publications—seemed to help Jap salesmen peddling their wares. "Americans obviously *want* cheap and shoddy goods!" exclaimed one of them as he furiously wrote orders for such merchandise.

So Admiral Takahashi announced, "Japan's economic advance means that the Navy must expand its cruising radius to reach New Guinea, Borneo and the Celebes." Among those included in that magnanimous radius were the Dutch and they were not much impressed by Japan's peaceful proclamations.

Indeed, the Dutch Minister in Japan had earlier warned Americans of the possibility of a Japanese takeover of Guam. Eiju Aimu of the Japanese Foreign Office at the same time deplored the U.S. Navy and suggested a reduction in the size of its battleships. After all, he said, it would be helpful for the crabs to lose their large claws. "The better for eating!" he joked to a British diplomat.

160

There were those in the United States who were concerned over the growing might of Japan. Senator Key Pittmann, Chairman of the Senate Foreign Relations Committee, attacked Japan by name in a speech that was given out prematurely to the Japanese correspondents in Washington and circulated widely in Japan. Branded inflammatory and jingoistic by much of the press and not agreed with by Secretary of State Hull, the speech hit hard at the harm Japan was doing to China.

Unfortunately, Pittmann's own "Silver Bloc" had done much to undermine the Chinese financially. This Silver Bloc in Congress had pressured Roosevelt to raise the price of silver, and this "free silver" forced China's dollar off the silver standard. However, no less a diplomat than the U.S. Ambassador to Japan saw a possible salutary effect in the Pittmann diatribe. Joseph Grew felt that the Japanese were getting too cocky and needed just such a reminder to the effect that the United States was not really a pacifist collection of feminine peace organizations but a strong, idealistic country that could strike fast and hard when it was aroused as it had been by the *Maine* incident in Cuba.

In his State of the Union speech, Roosevelt had referred to those who reverted to "the old belief in the law of the sword." In late 1935 just such a thing had happened in Japan's internal struggle for power. The growing feeling of freedom and strong nationalism was about ready to explode under the thumbs of the old-line Japanese bureaucrats. The situation was described as paralleling that in Germany, with a rebellion the only means of young radicals letting off steam.

One such hothead was Lieutenant Colonel Sabura Aizawa, the son of an old Samurai family. When he was passed for promotion, he saw in the action a widespread plot by his superiors to keep the extremists from power, and in angry reprisal he took up his Samurai sword and did away with his superior, General Nagata.

There had been a rebellion in 1931 in which a number of officials had been assassinated; now Aizawa claimed his act was similar and was intended to support the throne. He was nevertheless tried and convicted of murder, and although political killings were generally not so punished, he was sentenced to death at the court-martial despite pleas for clemency written in schoolgirls' blood.

Aizawa's act was a mere prologue to what would happen

161

this February 25. On that night, a thousand young Army rebels moved swiftly in a wave of terror. These were hot-headed fanatics with Fascist leanings, stirred up by recent gains of the liberals in the elections, and the conviction and sentencing of Aizawa, who was one of their kind. Called the "Ginger Group," the rebels simultaneously attacked a number of officials whose policies they disagreed with.

The former Premier, Admiral Saito, was surprised in his home by soldiers carrying machine guns. His brave wife begged that her life be taken instead of his, and actually tried to block the bullets with her hands on the muzzles of the guns. The sacrifice was in vain, and Saito died in a hail of bullets. So determined to kill him were the attackers that there were thirty-six wounds in his body.

The Inspector General of Military Education, Watanabe, was also marked for death. His wife, too, tried to save her husband, shielding his body so that the killers had to pry their weapons under her body to shoot Watanabe.

Finance Minister Takahashi was shot to death and then carved up with an officer's sword. Home Minister Goto and the former War Minister Hayashi also perished in the blood bath. There were two men marked for death who were miraculously spared.

Count Makino, who had once been Lord Keeper of the Privy Seal, was vacationing in a health resort at a hot spring. In the middle of the night Army assassins came for him, but met opposition in the Count's guard. The officer leading the rebels was killed in the fray, as was the guard who shot him.

Next the assassins set fire to the hotel in a successful attempt to drive the old man out into the open. Led by a nurse and his granddaughter, Makino was climbing up a steep cliff behind the hotel when the light from the flames illuminated him like a spotlight. Bravely the granddaughter shielded the Count, and the soldiers withheld their fire long enough for the intended victim to reach safety.

The Grand Chamberlain, Admiral Suzuki, was cornered by one of the leaders of the insurrection, Captain Ando. At gunpoint, Ando argued with Suzuki, trying to persuade him of the correctness of the Ginger Group's action.

Adamant, Suzuki finally said, "If you've got nothing further to say you might as well go ahead and shoot me." At close range Ando fired three shots, striking Suzuki in the head, the chest and the leg. With blood transfusions, and by a miracle, the Admiral lived.

It took a greater miracle to save Premier Okada, a prime target of the assassins' guns. Early in the morning of the twenty-sixth, alarm gongs sounded in his official residence. Okada roused from sleep and correctly guessed what was up.

"My last hour may have come," he told his brother-in-law and secretary, Matsuo, "but I'm not going to die in my pajamas!"

"You are too valuable to Japan to die," Secretary Matsuo told him as he struggled into his clothes to meet death with dignity.

Matsuo raced from the bedroom and down the stairs, with soldiers in hot pursuit he fled into the garden crying "*Banzai!*" It was still dark, and the trick worked. He was killed by bullets intended for the Premier. Also dead were half a dozen guards. Those who survived realized what had happened and unceremoniously shoved Okada into a closet in the servant's quarters.

All the rest of that day and into the night, Okada stayed in the safety of the closet. Matsuo's corpse continued to act the part and was made ready for the funeral, and Okada himself had the eerie experience of attending his own funeral carefully disguised against possible detection.

Concurrent with the assassinations, the Ginger Group seized control of key buildings in Tokyo, including Police Headquarters and Headquarters of the General Staff. Mimeographed statements were delivered by soldiers to the newspapers, explaining the reasons behind the revolt and its aims.

Signed by Captain Ando, who had personally shot Admiral Suzuki, and Captain Nonaka, the statement claimed that the present government of Japan was drifting away from the true spirit of the empire. The uprising was believed to be an attempt to bring the "Shogun Restoration" favored by the Fascist elements in the Army, triggered by the January elections in which liberal candidates were returned to office, and also by the Aizawa trial.

The revolution lasted only four days. It had been thought that the rebels held the Emperor himself as hostage, but soon it was evident that they controlled only the residence of the Premier and the Sanno Hotel. The government began military preparations to kill or capture the Ginger Group by force, but such action was not necessary. By means of propaganda on the radio, a barrage of leaflets, and even the sending aloft of balloons with messages promising amnesty, the government succeeded in ending the revolt peacefully.

When the last of the soldiers had surrendered, the officers who had led the revolt were given two hours to take the honorable way out through hara-kiri. It was rumored that Ando and Nonaka had blown their own brains out but it became apparent that the rest of the Ginger Group would use the trial court as a springboard for another drive against the old government.

There was indeed much sentiment favoring the revolt. Corruption existed in the government and it was apparent that Japan needed a "new deal" of its own if further uprisings were to be prevented. But the government could not see its way clear to grant the usual amnesty to the guilty parties.

As a test, it put to death Lieutenant Colonel Aizawa, the man who had chopped up General Nagata with his Samurai sword "to support the throne." When there was no loud outcry from the people following this departure from custom, the government proceeded to stun the Ginger Group with stiff sentences for the revolt.

Of 19 officers tried, 13 were sentenced to death, 5 to life imprisonment, and 1 to a lesser term. Of 10 civilians accused, 4 were sentenced to death. Such reprisals was unprecedented in Japanese history, except of course for Aizawa, who was hardly cold in his grave.

To make the government's position embarrassing, even if understandable, it had admitted to many of the revolutionists' charges by getting rid of the old Premier and appointing Foreign Minister Hirota to that position. And if there were wholesale "resignations" in the military, the same was true among the old-line government officials. Hirota was ordered to form a new cabinet, one that would play ball with the Army. Hirota made the error of trying to appoint a son-in-law of Count Makino, the man who escaped execution, to the post of Foreign Minister, but backed down in a hurry.

U.S. Ambassador Grew met with the new Premier for a discussion of the effect his policies would have on Japanese-American relationships. Hirota professed that there would be no "tampering" with the "Open Door" in China and promised to see what could be done about the worrisome flow of cheap goods into America. Good relations between the two great countries were the cornerstone of his policy, he assured Grew, just as they had always been.

Indicative of the seriousness of the sitution was the declaration of martial law for a period of time following the uprising, and the wearing of a uniform by Emperor Hirohito, the "Son of Heaven" himself. But the government weathered the storm and seemed to have things once more under control. The press was unanimous in its backing of the old guard, despite the fact that the executed men had obviously become martyrs in the eyes of many.

Expressing confidence in Japan's stability, Ambassador Grew did not share the concern of the Dutch Ambassador, who feared a Japanese thrust at Borneo, New Guinea or the Netherlands Indies. Grew could not see such an attempt by the Japanese in the near future.

Japan, of course, had plenty of trouble nearer to home with China and Russia in regard to the Mongolian territories. Inner Mongolia had reverted pretty much to Japanese control, with Outer Mongolia going to the Russians. Japanese-Russian tension was growing almost daily, and among the suspects hauled in for questioning about the recent uprising was a Russian. He was tortured extensively, including having kerosene forced down his throat, but he steadfastly denied any complicity and was finally released.

Fanned by dozens of incidents along the border, enmity flared into actual fighting as early in the year as February, and the Japs were jolted when Mongolian troops *and planes* attacked them. There were skirmishes in the Lake Bor region, and near Vladivostok, which the Japs entertained notions of isolating much as Port Arthur had been.

Sentiment against the Russians ran high and even led to demonstrations of the fanatic Kenkokukai patriotic society against Tass newsmen in Tokyo. But the Japanese had run into a tough opponent in the Red general, Marshal Vasily Blucher, and he warned Premier Hirota in no uncertain terms about violating Russian Territory.

To add to Japan's troubles were rumors of a secret alliance between Russia and China, fantastic though such an agreement seemed. Chiang Kai-shek had built his strength largely on his fighting of the Communists in China; now it was whispered that he was making a deal with Stalin that would get the Reds off his back so that he could oppose the Japanese more forcefully. This was a direct slap at Japan since she was at that moment insisting on more action by the Chinese against the Communists.

In retaliation Japan made agreements with Hitler's Germany—agreements thought to contain secret military understandings. Angrily the Russians accused Japan of linking with Hitler in planning to share British holdings in the Far East in the event of war.

Meanwhile, Japan denied that it had made any agreements with Mussolini's Italy except that there was a possibility that Italy would open a foreign office in Manchukuo and Japan in turn would open one in the newly acquired Ethiopian territory of Italy.

Military relations between Japan and the United States were becoming a bit strained, with each side refusing entry to some of its ports by visitng ships. In one instance, Japan sought permission for the training ship *Shintoku Maru* to put into a Hawaiian port. Similarly the United States wanted its destroyer, the *Alden,* to visit Pacific Islands under Japanese mandate. Neither of these requests was granted.

Britain's Anthony Eden was accusing Japan of smuggling all sorts of goods into North China to evade customs. Such cheating was injurious to legitimate trade, and Britain angrily refused to see any parallel in the smuggling of British goods from Hong Kong into Canton. Another knock at Japan's economy was delivered by President Roosevent when he raised the tariff on imports of Japanese cloth by a big 42 percent, and American soybeans were underselling the Japanese product in Manchukuo.

In a maneuver that made their alleged smuggling look like child's play, Japan armed and urged Chinese General Pai to move against the "Japanese." There were no Japanese where he marched—only Chiang Kai-shek himself. But the maneuver provoked South Chinese to bait Japanese locally and gave Japan an excuse to rush gunboats to Amoy and threaten to take over in Canton.

There was a brief and peaceful diversion as the Olympic Games got under way in Berlin. Tokyo was awarded the games to be held in 1940 and there was much proud rejoicing in Japan. The government immediately announced plans for building a three-million-dollar plant. Where the main stadium in Berlin seated 110,000, that in Tokyo would hold 120,000. The Stock Exchange in Tokyo rose immediately with this good news. In another gesture to international culture, Japan sent an impressive art collection to Boston's Museum of Fine Arts.

While Germany and Japan might be bound to one another by secret treaties, German correspondents in Japan did all they could to provoke increased hostility between Japan and the Russians. Meanwhile the French reporters in Moscow were trying to counter this propaganda and promote Russian-Japanese good will in order to keep Stalin strong in case he was needed to fight against Germany.

In September the pace quickened a bit. England announced that it had seen fit to make sure of the "escalator clause" in the naval treaty, and would begin building up its fleet. Immediately Japan told the world she was doing the same. Shortly, she said, she would have a bigger navy than either England or the United States could boast. As if to permit her Navy to flex its muscles in practice, Japan was now threatening to use it to back up the "mild principles" she was insisting on in China.

For some time there had been attacks made on Japanese sailors in China, particularly in Shanghai. Cynics claimed these were the work of *agents provocateurs*; whatever the truth of the matter, one sailor had been killed and two others wounded. If the attackers were Reds, as the Japanese admitted was quite possible, it was still China's fault for failing to police against such happenings.

Late in September trouble flared again when a Shanghai heckler pitched a pear core and clobbered a Japanese sailor. The marine garrison at Shanghai was immediately reinforced by the Japanese and an intensive search begun for the pear-thrower. Overzealous Japanese marines flagrantly invaded Chinese privacy, claiming all the while to be searching for "pear peelings."

While the military policed China, the Japanese government did a bit of policing at home. The Diet passed a bill setting up twenty-two Thought Control Offices in major cities, and fifteen Thought Control Substations in other areas. This step was necessary because some 60,000 citizens had been arrested in recent years for thinking dangerous thoughts. The police had previously been charged with correcting these mistaken Japanese, but now specialists would indoctrinate those who erred in their thinking.

Shortly after the pear incident, which engendered much hostility from the Chinese against the arrogant Japanese

Navy that was now policing them, three British sailors ran afoul of the Japanese in Tokyo. Hauled into a police station on charges of having cheated a cab driver of his fare, the men were tortured until they signed confessions for their crime.

The police used ingeniously brutal methods in exacting the admissions of guilt, one of them driving a fountain pen under a victim's nails and repeatedly forcing ink into the punctures by working the plunger.

When the sailors' commanding officer arrived to demand their release as innocent victims of a frame-up, he was accused of being drunk and chased out of the jail. The affair was said to have so angered England's Vice Admiral Colebrooke Little, in charge of His Majesty's Navy in Eastern waters, that he postponed a planned trip to Japan.

China had at last been given a "nonpermanent" seat on the League of Nations, but this vantage point from which to decry aggression seemed not to worry the Japanese. Looking for another point of entry to push their "mild principles" argument, the Japanese found it when workers struck the factory at Tsingtao in China.

Marines rushed ashore to protect Japanese interests in the plant and manhandled the Chinese so badly that the authorities demanded that the marines desist. This may have been the last straw that provoked a fantastic attempt by a drug-crazed Chinese to push his country into all-out war with the Japanese enemy.

Marshal Chang Hsueh-liang, who had recently been treated in a hospital for opium addiction, chose December to kidnap Premier Chiang Kai-shek. Chiang was not being held for ransom, though his wealthy wife and millionaire President Chang Sun could easily have raised just about any amount demanded. Instead, kidnaper Chang wanted the Chinese government to do something about the treatment that Japan was according her, and to reorganize the Kuomintang with the inclusion of the Communists, whose Mao Tse-tung Chiang had driven far up into Yenan on the northwestern frontier.

While Madame Chiang was reported to have fainted away with concern for her hostage husband, rumor had it that Chiang had been murdered by his captors. Premier Kung nervously cautioned against letting concern for one man— even such a man as the Premier—cause such a thing as all-out war with the historic enemy, Japan.

Japan felt much the same way and added the weight of its argument to that of China's cautious President. To increase Tokyo's woes, a would-be assassin of the Emperor was apprehended carrying a supply of dynamite, a spear, and—apparently for use if all else failed—a stack of petitions!

The Emperor was spared and fortunately it turned out that the Chinese Premier wasn't dead either. Before year's end he was released in good condition, much to the relief of all concerned. The threat of China suddenly rising up in anger had a salutary effect on the Japanese, however, and they began immediately to re-evaluate their China policy.

As 1936 faded into history, Japan found her over-all position much weaker internationally than it had been back in January. Only with the Dutch had she somehow mended fences. Relations with the United States were generally satisfactory, though the influx of cheap goods into that country remained a bone of contention and the Philippines a possible threat to peace. Elsewhere, the Japanese were plagued with serious difficulties.

With 1936, too, went the naval treaties. With these down the drain Japan faced the likelihood of an arms race with the major powers. The treaty with Germany had gotten her into hot water with the Russians. Even at home the government had its hands full. On the one hand, the people were dissatisfied with the domestic scene of high prices and lack of opportunity, and counter to centuries-old tradition they were now taking an active voice in government. Hirota's Diet was still in control, since it had the backing of the military, but any time the Army thought it could scrape up another Diet it liked better, the jig would be up.

While the Army had put down the revolt, the seeds of radical militarism had been sown, and the road ahead seemed to lead nowhere but to the aggrandizement of Japan. If this could not be done in China, expansion must come in the Pacific islands, and Japan had given tacit warning of this fact of life early in the year.

The military budget being proposed for 1937 called for expenditures of more then 700 million yen for the Army alone, some 200 million more than in 1936 and the biggest in the country's history. Naval expansion was obviously to be large unless Japan was going to back down from her bold proclamation of a fleet second to none. Such loss of face could not be imagined.

The Land of the Rising Sun could not turn back now. She had made her choice, and the years ahead would tell whether or not she had been right. Good or bad, 1936 had been a momentous year for the Japanese.

BIBLIOGRAPHY

Ten Years in Japan—Grew
Japan, Past and Present—Reichsauer
Report from Tokyo—Grew
The Japanese Enemy—Byas
Honorable Enemy—Hauser

XI

Stalin's Russia

Religion being "the opiate of the people," there were, of course, no decadent Christmas trees in enlightened Russia to observe the Savior's birthday in 1935. But as the New Year came in, the word was out that the banned evergreens were suddenly permissible again.

In a furor of activity, peasants chopped and hacked; Christmas trees went up all over Moscow and other cities. Without formal decorations, resourceful Russians cut stars and other paraphernalia from discarded tin cans and festooned the trees with substitutes for tinsel. About large trees erected in parks, skaters zipped back and forth and good cheer was rampant. There were even banners hung with Stalin's picture that joyously proclaimed, "Life is getting better! Life is growing merrier!"

After the long crackdown there were many who harbored guilty thoughts as they cavorted about their tree. Militant party members feared the sky must be falling down. But the word had come right from the top. At one Young Communist party gaily proceeding about a tree, with bewhiskered "Grandfather Frost," the Russian counterpart of Saint Nick, and the beauteous "Snow Maiden" peculiar to Russian lore, a conscience-stricken official leaped to his feet and halted the festivities.

"Comrades, I order you to desist!" he cried in alarm. "You are making a terrible ideological mistake. Stop, Grandfather Frost, or I shall denounce you to the Party Secretary himself!"

"Shut up, you fool!" answered Grandfather Frost, tugging aside his beard of white, "I *am* the Party Secretary!"

Maybe there was a Santa Claus after all, hopeful Russians prayed. Joseph Stalin had no white beard, but it was known that he had attended Tiflis Theological Seminary in

171

his youth. Perhaps he was beginning a swing away from the godless state he had helped to create.

Born in the Georgian village of Gori, Stalin had gotten himself arrested as a Bolshevik as early as 1902. Exiled to Siberia, he managed an escape and was back in Transcaucasia for the 1905 revolution.

Ingratiating himself with Lenin, Stalin became a member of the Bolshevik Central Committee and from 1908 to 1917 he was in and out of Siberia, freed finally in the big revolution that threw out the czars. He edited the party organ, *Pravda* (*Truth*), and in 1922, when arteriosclerosis laid Lenin low, Stalin was made general secretary.

Lenin died in 1924 and precipitated a long and bloody battle between Stalin, the right-wing Bolshevik, and Trotsky and his leftist opposition. The main point of contention between the factions was the scope needed to insure the success of socialism, Stalin believing it was best to concentrate on a single country, Russia; while Trotsky favored world revolution.

In 1926 and 1927 Stalin ousted Trotsky and deported him and tens of thousands of his leftist followers. The next two years he devoted to ridding himself of the right-wingers who had helped him to power. When the shooting died down, Joseph Stalin emerged victoriously as head of the Communist Internationale and began the push for world domination of Communists by the Soviet while Trotsky did a slow burn in exile.

Stalin was father of the Five-Year Plans inaugurated in 1928, of collectivization forced on the peasants beginning in the 1930's, of slave-labor camps, and the police state in which the secret police of the OGPU took the place of civil liberty. An estimated five million people were liquidated in bloody purges by the early thirties.

Undisputed dictator of the millions his glowering pictures looked down on, Stalin attended the January meeting of the Central Executive Committee as spectator, nonetheless, sitting with arms folded in the back row while Premier Vyacheslav Molotov gave the State of the Union address. The oration took some 3½ hours and so hoarsened Molotov that Dictator Stalin was forced to move to the front row to hear.

In the middle of Five-Year Plan Number Two, Molotov told the Congress, Russia was now triumphantly on a socialist basis despite remnants of speculators and parasites. In fact, industrial plans had been "overfulfilled" in 1935, and 1936 was going to be an even more prosperous year. There were problems, of course, but these were outside of Russia itself, where reason and intelligence did not yet prevail. Patting France and Czechoslovakia on the back as "bulwarks of peace," Molotov moved on to the less happy side of the picture.

"The Nazis," he proclaimed direly, "are ready to strike!" Germany under Hitler was violently aggressive, and Japan had the same low ambitions. Poland was casting furtively hungry eyes about as she contemplated expansion, and Italy was definitely imperialistic. Russia, on the other hand, was a model of patience and fairness in its international dealings. Take the trouble with Uruguay, for example, he pointed out. "One would think that all Russia has to do is meddle in the affairs of others!" Molotov scoffed in righteous indignation.

Premier Molotov was not the only member of his family working for the good of greater Russia. In the spring, his wife, Paulina Semionova Zhemchuzhina—using her professional pseudonym of Olga Karpovskaya—visited Mrs. Eleanor Roosevelt at the White House in Washington, D.C. Feminine pleasantries aside, Olga got down to brass tacks. As head of *Tezhe,* the cosmetics trust controlled by the State, she had turned back a whopping big profit of $85 million in 1935.

"Russian women can afford to pay as much for their cosmetics as can your American women," Olga announced proudly. "And our men are beginning to shave more regularly, and to use toilet water."

This last was, of course, a bombshell to cartoonists for whom beards and Bolsheviks were synonymous. Mrs. Molotov was not in the United States shopping for cosmetics, she let it be known. She had brought along a sufficient supply of "pure" Russian products. But she did have her eye on $100,000 worth of production equipment with which to turn out even more rouge and powder for Russian ladies and cologne for men.

There were many in Russia who had not helped build the $85-million kitty because they would rather eat than smell pretty. While the top brass proudly announced that by the end of the third Five-Year Plan Russia would be the equal of advanced European countries and approaching the U.S. by 1948, there was yet a little difficulty in 1936.

Comrade Lubinov complained at the Moscow congress of Soviet factory managers about wholesale truancy and vacations that were wrecking programs of production. And International Trade Commissar L. Y. Veitzer had to take action against a number of arrogant Communist factory managers, including shutting down a chair factory which had been answering complaints about its poor products with the advice, "If you don't like our chairs, don't buy them!"

There were a growing number of heroes in Soviet Russia, among them the aviator Chkalov, who had made a daring flight across the North Pole, and the Russian people applauded such evidence of Russian capability. In August of 1935, a miner in the Donbas Steppe named Aleksei Stakhanov performed the superhuman feat of mining 102 tons of coal in a six-hour day. The norm was about seven tons and eager Communist Party officials went delirious. Here was a means of instrumenting the Five-Year Plans with a vengeance. By October, miner Andrei Gorbatiuk made even Stakhonov look like he was sitting on his hands by producing 405 tons in a day!

The technique spread like wildfire to other industries as the Stakhanovite movement. Bricklayers laid up walls at such a rate that a visiting British unionist called the procedure "not bricklaying but brick murder!" Farmers and tractor drivers joined the movement, and two women pioneered for their sex in this field, Praskovia Angelina and Maria Demchenko. Another female, Dusia Vinogradova of the Soviet Textile Trust, became an object of worship by tending a multitude of looms by herself.

There was now a new hero on the scene, and an order was created called "Hero of Soviet Toil" to reward Stakhanov and his followers. More tangible reward came in the payment of bonuses for "above-norm" output. In February of 1936 Stakhanov came to greater glory when he was awarded a lifelong pension and twice-yearly free rides on all Soviet transportation.

But the glorified piecework system hit snags almost immediately. The new movement was superimposed on the traditional troika or "three-horse carriage" system of Lenin. This trade union control consisted of factory managers, Communist cell secretary and union representative. Stak-

174

hanovism angered the old-line Communists, who claimed the Stakhanovites were pampered too much. They cited the case of a young carburetor mechanic who was feted so lavishly that he worked at his job only sixteen days in December, nine in January, and seven in February. Textile worker Dusia Vinogradova they accused of temperamental bourgeois primping and cinema aspirations.

In Stakhanov's own section, coal production sagged after an initial increase, probably because the state raised the norm after initial pay boosts so that workers ended up working harder for the same pay. Moscow angrily wired, "YOU MUST WIPE OUT YOUR DISGRACE," and the miner who started the whole business opined that in America the workers would probably beat him up!

But despite increased production and even though wages had gone up, a peasant or worker in 1936 could buy only an eighth as much sugar, a third as much soap, a twelfth as much cloth and a seventh as much oil with his money as he could in 1913. In 1913 the grain harvest was just over 94 million tons. In 1936 it had "risen" to less than 83 million.

The ruble had been "scientifically stabilized" by Stalin at a value of five to the dollar, and Americans living in Russia were paying $4 a pound for coffee and $2 a pound for butter. Bread was selling for 40 cents a loaf and sugar for 35 cents a pound. Smokers could buy cigarettes as cheap as one dollar a pack.

The taxes were pretty steep on "luxuries" like sugar, salt, soap, cigarettes, hosiery, underwear, shoes and so on. For example, sugar was taxed 85 percent, cigarettes as high as 90 percent, and shaving cream 68 percent. The tax on sewing machines was quite low, only 39 percent, but there weren't many who could afford them.

In the city many workers made less than 200 rubles and lived a hand-to-mouth existence. Food was generally limited to bread and vegetables. You could buy a meal in a restaurant featuring a meat dish if you craved such sumptuousness, but it would cost about 25 rubles.

Of course, some high-paid officials with salaries as much as thirty times those of their underlings could afford to live fairly well, but American tourists, many of them Russian-born and returning to their native land out of curiosity, made such uncomplimentary remarks as, "What a dump!" They complained that the top restaurants were apt to

175

give menu options like "With the dinner you can have your choice of caviar, a vegetable, or ice cream."

Even such austerity was not dreamed of by people like a porter earning 120 rubles a month and with five to feed. Bread alone to keep the family alive cost more than that, so the porter worked nights mending shoes and his wife worked, too, for perhaps 90 rubles. In general, the price of foodstuffs had risen some fifteen times since before the Revolution, while wages went up only about fourfold. The answer, of course, was to be a commissar. These gentlemen were rumored to be getting in the neighborhood of 7,000 rubles a month.

Although few Russians would dare to say so aloud, there was much wistful gazing at the decadent capitalists in countries like America. One story described two women who had always known hard times in Russia meeting after several years. One asked the other how she managed to survive, though a widow and unemployed. "My son takes care of me," the widow said brightly.

"You mean your engineer son, Boris? The one earning five hundred rubles?"

"No, Boris has a family to support and he can't send his mother a kopek."

"It must be Ivan. I've heard he makes a fine salary working for the state."

"No, Ivan can afford to send me nothing either. It is my youngest son who helps me. He is unemployed in America!"

Morals, too, had suffered under the new regime. Sexual promiscuity was generally condoned, even professed as a right, as one of the new freedoms—that of the body. Lenin had conferred another right on Russian women, that of legal abortion. This measure was considered necessary because of overcrowding and the need for women to work to build the great new Russia forecast in the Five-Year Plans.

The term "kulak," originally applied to the peasants who refused to go along with collectivization because they could farm more efficiently on their own, had gradually come to mean anyone who opposed the new regime. These "wreckers" of Communism were fair game for the secret police. So, too, were children twelve years old or older who were caught stealing. Even if the theft was of bread, death was the punishment. The police could also dispose of children their parents could not provide for.

Life was better, some cynics said, simply because it was

176

a crime to remember anything to the contrary. Even the Stakhanovites were beginning to wonder if something hadn't happened to the bold new scheme that was to reward them for their fantastic increases in production.

As part of the "Life is better" bit, Stalin began pushing culture in Russia to the point where he reproved a visitor who was missing a button on his suit. The man apologized by saying it was harder to buy a button than a tractor.

The second Five-Year Plan was aimed at reducing these shortages, and one boost did come from Japan, who sent such luxuries as buttons and shoes in payment for the part of the Chinese Eastern Railway it had acquired from Russia. When such goods hit the Russian market queues formed eagerly. Police shortened them by arresting "speculators," and one luckless woman who bought a pair of shoes for 80 rubles and resold them for a 20-ruble profit ended her venture in jail for five years.

Despite one-time theologian Stalin's permission of sufficient evergreen opium to usher in the new year, Russia continued officially as an antireligious state. February marked the tenth anniversary of the Union of Militant Godlessness and this organization's leaders alternately praised progress and harangued against foot-dragging. Half the Soviet population, they proudly declared, were now "unchurched." And the order was even spreading abroad.

Britishers Lord and Lady Passfield of Passfield Corners had authored a new book called *Soviet Communism* and reported adult membership in the Union of Militant Godless of some five million, in numerous "cells." There were also two million "Junior Godless." On the debit side of the ledger, though Russian priests were resorting to such cheating skulduggery as painting the crosses on their churches red. Clever Orthodox clerics now were preaching the gospel thus:

"Jesus was of proletariat origin, the son of Joseph the carpenter and of a toiling woman. Jesus was a good Socialist and Communist predecessor of the Communist Party."

Back in 1933, when Franklin Roosevelt recognized Stalin's Russia, he had insisted on and received from Foreign Minister Litvinoff the assurance that there would be churches for U.S. citizens who might go to Russia in line with such diplomatic recognition. By 1936 the intent of the Soviet to honor the pledge was in some doubt. The United

States had sought to erect its own church in Moscow but abandoned the idea when it learned that "taxes" on a church to cost only $4,000 would amount to $100,000.

There was, however, one Protestant minister in Moscow, the Reverend Streck, and he preached so often for Americans that he became known as the "Diplomats' minister."

When American civil servants George Minor and Mildred Wright decided that it would be romantic to be married in Moscow, then, Reverend Streck was the logical and only candidate for the ceremony. Came the big day, and the reverend was nowhere to be found until he was at last turned up, in jail. While the nervous bride and groom chewed their fingernails, another minister was flown in from the nearest source—Leningrad, some 500 miles distant. The crime of Reverend Streck was unannounced, being left to the judgment of the religious and the godless of the world.

Russia's foreign affairs got off to a bad start in January of 1936. In the tiny South American country of Uruguay, President Terra decided to break off diplomatic relations with the Soviet Union. His Secret Service, he said, had turned up far too many checks issued by Soviet Envoy Alexander Minkin and payable "To Bearer." The bearers, Terra surmised, were Communist revolutionaries. Citing the recent Brazilian revolt, Terra said that Minkin was planning a similar whoop-de-doo in Uruguay for February or March. So Minkin was told to pack his bags and checkbook and depart.

Premier Molotov had scoffed at the idea that such a thing could be, claiming Russia had more to do than push her beliefs in lands where she was not welcome. The real trouble, he said, was not a planned revolt. Something smelled in Uruguay, maybe, but it was the cheese that that country was trying to blackmail Russia into buying.

Foreign Minister Litvinoff took the squabble all the way to the League of Nations and made the mild Uruguayan delegate, Dr. Alberto Guani, very uncomfortable with his histrionics. Waving telegrams to prove it, Litvinoff said the whole thing started when Uruguay wanted to deport the anarchist Simon Radovitsky back to Russia. Russia declined the honor, and then came the alleged blackmail attempt. Unless Russia would buy 200 tons of cheese to salve the bad feelings, the South American country would break relations.

178

"Millions for revolution," quoth Litvinoff in effect, "but not one cent for cheese!"

Not under the head of meddling, but simply to document the goings-on for the Soviet, a large crew of Tass Information Agency reporters and cameramen were swarming over Ethiopia in January. Their avowed task was an authentic documentation of that situation, perhaps to be used later as evidence against imperialist Italy.

Elsewhere, Russian interest focused on the imminent signing of a treaty. In France debate ran hot on the Franco-Soviet pact, and Léon Blum, leading French Socialist, made the mistake of proclaiming in the street, "Socialism is my religion!" Two young rightists promptly beat the Deputy up "for his religion" and he missed some of the sessions in the Chamber of Deputies.

France had been proclaimed a bulwark of peace by Molotov, and of course Russia was interested in allying herself with peaceful countries against those who were now loudly warmongering. So strongly did the Soviets feel for peace that Foreign Minister Litvinoff was called home to receive the rosette of the "Order of Lenin," about the highest honor his grateful country could bestow. Newspapers featured his picture on the front page with the caption, "The Stalinist Bearer of Peace."

Modestly Litvinoff accepted his kudos and said, "I shall continue to fight against the forces of war and aggression and go ahead with my work for peace, which is the only justification for the activities of a Soviet diplomat."

This was either the understatement of the year or the heralding of a new definition for the word "peace."

Unfortunately there were forces at work in the world which did not have peaceful intentions. Japan was a prime offender, and early in the year she transgressed and felt the wrath of the Soviet Union, through the puppet Mongols. The Japs attacked an outpost on the Mongol frontier and were beaten off by artillery. This happened in the Lake Bor region, and ended with no casualties.

However, when the Japanese drove truckloads of soldiers almost thirty miles inside Mongol territory and near Vladivostok things got hotter. The Japanese claimed that the Mongols started it by staging a bombing raid with twelve planes. Finally, at Pogranichnaya, a frontier station on the

Chinese Eastern Railway, the Japanese again violated Soviet territory and three of them paid with their lives.

In March Scripps-Howard's Roy Howard interviewed Stalin in a three-hour discussion. Stalin told the newsman that his country was prepared to go to war with Japan over Russia's satellite, Outer Mongolia.

In the city of Tokyo four wild-eyed members of the Kenkokukai patriotic society invaded the offices of Tass News Agency and demanded that its reporters leave the country. Things finally calmed down when Japanese Premier Hirota responded to a warning from Russia's Marshal Vasily Blucher by saying he had promised to keep the peace and would live up to his word.

There were rumors that Russia was covering all her bets in Asia by negotiating a pact with China's Chiang Kaishek, a noteworthy feat since one of the Generalissimo's biggest selling points had been his stand-off of the Communists.

What was regarded by cynics as another sly, long-range move was the creation of the Soviet Republic of Biro-Bidjan for Jews. This buffer state alongside the Japanese Manchukuo would be ready-made for atrocity propaganda in case the Japanese started war in that sector.

Russia was actively pushing the Popular Front in France, and she redoubled her efforts when the movement made headway in embattled Spain. Communists had been interested in Spain since the miners' insurrection in 1934 hinted at a coming "dictatorship of the proletariat." When Franco rose, demonstrations began in Russia for aid to the embattled workers of Spain.

Nominally a member of the Committee for Non-Intervention, Russia had to play it carefully, and it was let drop that peace-loving Litvinoff was constantly battling Stalin to prevent sending of aid and possibly touching off World War II. The pressure kept building, until in August thousands of hatless workers milled in Red Square so tightly that dozens were prostrated. The vote was for the party to send $2.4 million in aid to Spain's left-leaning Loyalists.

For some time aid had been sent covertly while Russia feigned nonintervention and protested German, Italian and even Portuguese aid to Franco.

Finally, in October, she threatened to intervene, and at long last the official word flashed from Joseph Stalin. Leading Stakhanovites were rewarded with vacation trips to see Russian steamers like the *Kuban* loading with foodstuffs, and at Barcelona the *Zirayania* was landing 3,000 tons of goods.

Perhaps the biggest thing the Soviet did for Spain was to recruit through the Comintern the International Brigades. Most of the members were not from Russia, but from France, the United States, England and even Italy. As many as 30,000 brigadiers at a time were in action.

Even as Stalin debated open aid to Spain, Hitler talked boldly about moving against Russia. Speaking at Nuremberg on the fourth anniversary of his rise to power, he boasted of all he had done but told his followers of his needs if he was to do what he really wanted to do.

"If I had the Urals and Siberia, if we possessed the Ukraine, then Nazi Germany would be swimming in prosperity!" Stretching a point for effect, he went on. "I am not in the fortunate position of the Soviet Jews." The implication was plain and Russians flinched.

Stalin had been concerned since early in the year that Russia was not included in Hitler's proposed pacts. As the year wore on and actual agreements were made between Germany, Italy and Japan, the concern became anger and alarm.

It began to look as though the Soviet had exercised great foresight in the spring when it had sent an urgent call for blood donors and set up 514 receiving stations throughout the country. To supplement the blood of live donors scientists had found ways of using the blood from the dead, and a continuing program was being carried on. An allotment of two million dollars was made to the Institute for Transfusion of Blood.

Coincidentally, a new technique was adopted for fattening pigs. This consisted of bleeding them periodically, a treatment that made them lazy so that they wouldn't work off the fat. The blood, it was said, could be used for food and fertilizer, but skeptical soldiers may have wondered if they might not someday get a transfusion of pig plasma!

As the skeins of international affairs began to tangle more and more, Stalin managed to keep on the good side of England. He even borrowed the sizable sum of fifty million dollars from her and succeeded in having the interest slashed from the former usurious 11 percent to just half that amount.

181

Since the state sponsored music and the arts in the Soviet, it was natural and expected that it should offer guidance to the artists. The paintings of Matissee and Picasso were on display in Moscow's Museum of Western Art, but art for art's sake was declared to be an outmoded decadent ideal; the new Russian art must be utilitarian.

The works of Dmitri Shostakovich were at that time being received with thunderous ovations in such capitalist dens as Manhattan; this may have had something to do with the sudden reversal taken by critics in *Pravda*. *Pravda*, of course, stood for "truth," and the truth was that Shostakovich's *Lady Macbeth of Mzensk* was not only un-Soviet, but "unwholesome, cheap, eccentric, and even tuneless." Rehearsals of the decaying composer's *Limpid Stream* by the Bolshoi Theatre's corps de ballet were canceled summarily.

Interestingly, the Communist dictator felt himself imbued with the same artistic judgment that Fascist Hitler claimed. Stalin found Shostakovich's work "muddle instead of music, fragments of melody dissolving into a general roar, screech and scream." The dictator much preferred the more traditional *Quiet Flows the Don,* adapted by composer Ivan Dzerzhinskii. It was Cossack and it was something Stalin understood. Thus it became "significant."

Shostakovich escaped arrest, but critics were forced to recant their previous praise of his work and to explain the error of their ways to their readers. Simultaneously, though apparently as belatedly, these same critics were finding much in James Joyce's *Ulysses* to be disenchanted with. The once admired stream-of-consciousness became "confused and obscene," which just showed how wrong a reviewer could be.

There was another purge taking place, one in which the stakes were higher and the players more numerous. In 1926 and 1927 Stalin had purged the left opposition, and in 1928 and 1929 he rid himself of the right. These purge victims, of course, were the very revolutionists who had made it possible for Stalin's big chance. Now in 1936 he set out to purge the last vestiges of the Bolshevik revolutionists. In a move some thought was legerdemain to distract the noisy workers demanding succor for Spain, Stalin dusted off the plotters who with Trotsky had fought him in the old days. Hitler to the contrary, the Soviet Jews were not doing so well. Grigorii Zinoviev, born Apfelbaum, and

Lev Kamenev, born Rosenfeld, were accused with fourteen others of fresh assassination plots against Joseph Stalin, born Yosif Vissarionovich Djugashvili.

Things had been touchy all year. The previous December some 190,000 party members had been dropped for one reason or another. Libraries were constantly being purged of offending books. From February to June, all Communists were required to turn in their old party membership cards and get new ones, so that their social backgrounds and possible deviations could be checked. The week of August 19 to 24, the party got down to business.

Eleven of the sixteen defendants were Jews. Because of the large number of Jews in the party, this figure couldn't be taken for an all-out indictment of anti-Semitism on the part of Stalin but it seemed the dictator was at least beginning to equate his enemies with the Jews.

One damning factor against the Jews was that they had contacts outside Russia. The prosecutor was one Andrei Vishinsky, a sharp party member who had recently made a name for himself in the trial of the lunatic governor of Wrangel Island.

Wrangel Island lies at the tip of Siberia, far north of the Arctic Circle. Experimental truck farming was suggested, with cabbages and potatoes to be grown in the few months of sunshine. Konstantin Semenchuk had taken over as governor some two years earlier and strange stories filtering back home prompted bringing him to trial.

It developed that Semenchuk had indulged in long drunken orgies, raped Eskimo girls, ordered the island's lone doctor killed, and then tried to poison the killer. The governor's wife was of much the same stripe, flogging Eskimo men and trying to starve them to death.

The maximum penalty in Russia for murder was only ten years, but the court was so horrified at Semenchuk's exploits it termed them banditry and, while the demented governor protested that he was really a Martian, sentenced him to death by the firing squad.

The purge trials made much more political hay for Vishinsky. All sixteen defendants confessed to all the charges; one man with some qualifications. The state lost no time executing them, not bothering to answer a plea of leniency by Zinoviev and Kamenev, who decided they wanted to live out their lives at hard labor as penance for their wrongs.

The death of this double handful was only a prologue

to a coming wholesale purge to match the millions of killings carried out earlier. The Soviet vengeance reached almost to Norway, where Trotsky shivered in exile. Dire warnings were given against any more plotting to kill Stalin, who had been earmarked for death in May and then in November when the first attempt miscarried. To prevent such a possibility and the attendant reflection on itself, Norway assigned police to guard the exile. Any false moves on his part would mean banishment from the safety he had found in that country.

There was an immediate stepping up of book reviews to find more traitors in the midst. Critics who played their party cards right managed to clean up on fees, with a record payment of $700 going to the man who reviewed the outsized volume of *Soviet Communism* written by Lord and Lady Passfield.

Casting about elsewhere, the OGPU found "nests of Trotskyites" everywhere. The State Bank harbored them, as did the National Observatory, and even the Army itself. Eventually an estimated half of the Army's officers were purged.

The purge was infectious. The party became suspicious of its own shadows, as shown in the case of young Comrade Gruber in Rostov. A minor deviation was detected in his past, and before it was found to be harmless he had been bounced from the party. The woman who sponsored him for membership got the ax too, along with the union chairman and three members who had accepted Gruber. His brother and sister were ousted not only from the Young Communists but also from school. Things got so bad that it was necessary to caution party leaders to exercise a bit of discretion lest there be no one left in the party except Comrade Stalin himself.

In the case of Journalist Karl Radek, however, the party gave no quarter. This top writer was called the Walter Lippmann of the Kremlin and it was he who gave wit and sparkle to the dull pronouncements of Stalin. He had once taken the Archbishop of Canterbury to task, and his last writings in *Izvestia* were skillful accounts of how he, Radek, foiled the plots of Trotsky. But the secret police dug up too much damning connection between Radek and the Trotsky plotters. He talked himself out of a firing squad, but died shortly in prison.

The year 1936 was big in Russia for more reason than

the purging of "evil" men. There was a total eclipse of the sun in June, broadest in the Lake Baikal area. Part of the preparation for this scientifically interesting event was the sending of teams to lecture the ignorant peasants to whom the eighty-mile swath of darkness might herald an unexpected end of the Five-Year Plan.

But an event to eclipse even this great natural phenomenon was the new constitution. In June, though ratification was months off, several of its important features were "leaked" by Vishinsky and others. One unpopular change was the ruling against abortion, reversing Lenin's decision of 1920. This the people did not want. Another startling revelation was that the new document would correct "basic defects in the criminal code."

This was the first inkling that there *were* any defects, but it was said that the new constitution would protect the individual *"even* against wrongful prosecution by the state." The new constitution would also equate the vote of the peasant with that of the city dweller, where it had previously been worth only one-fifth as much.

In July a mistake was discovered after the presses started to roll. In black and white the constitution solemnly stated that the vote was given only to those in their eighteenth year. The press run of fifteen million was halted while a few heads rolled, and the error corrected so that those eighteen *and older* might vote.

November 25 was the day set for ratification, and Stalin magnanimously asked the 2,500 delegates who were coming to submit amendments as they chose. Taking the leader at his word, the delegates submitted some 43,000 amendments. Since this was an average of seventeen per delegate it was apparent they did not consider the constitution perfect. Eventually a total of 154,000 proposed amendments were received from all over the country.

Stalin read the 146 articles of the document to the cheering assembly, consuming five bottles of mineral water in the process and promising an amended version in just ten days. He kept his word by setting aside 153,993 of the amendments and adopting 7 of them. It was a fitting Christmas gift to his loyal subjects.

Stalin was forced to make another gift, this one to Germany. A German engineer, Emil Ivan Stickling, had been convicted with several others of sabotage in the Soviet Union. The court had sentenced him to death, but word came from Von Ribbentrop that if the sentence were carried out Germany would sever relations with the Soviet Union. In a generous holiday mood, Stalin decided that the court had been a bit hasty and that the sentence could be commuted to ten years.

Another year had gone by in Russia, but it was of course far more than just a year. It was aother fifth of another Five-Year Plan, another twelve months of tribute paid by millions of servile Russians to the mustachioed man in the somberly majestic Kremlin.

Lenin had created Communist Russia. During the next seventeen years Joseph Stalin would make it the second most powerful country in the world before being interred, for a limited time, in that tomb in Red Square with Lenin.

BIBLIOGRAPHY

The Dream We Lost—Utley
The Politics of Totalitarianism—Armstrong
A History of Russia—Lawrence
Stalin's Kampf—Werner
The Life and Death of Stalin—Fischer

Other Highlights of 1936

Aeronautics

Aviation had made some mighty strides in the last ten years and the Atlantic wasn't the awesome body of water it had been back in May, 1927, when Lindy hopped across in the *Spirit of St. Louis.* In 1936 many people flew across. Captain James Mollison, whose wife had set a new record from London to Capetown, Africa, flew from Newfoundland to London. Dick Merrill flew from America to Wales and returned, taking along actor Harry Richman, and 41,000 ping-pong balls for buoyancy! It was no longer a man's ocean, and Beryl Markham made the flight from England to Nova Scotia though she bogged down in the mud there with an empty gas tank.

Such flights were no longer stunts. Germany's *Deutsche Luft-Hansa* flying boat *Zephyr* flew into New York from the Azores, testing a commercial route. And in the Pacific the famous China Clipper made fifty-two practice crossings.

In October Captain Edwin Musick took off from San Francisco on the first scheduled commercial crossing of the Pacific. The 8,200-mile epoch-making flight consisted of hops to Honolulu, Midway, Wake, Guam and finally Manila. With the Pacific whipped, Pan American Airways boss Juan Trippe was going to England to discuss Atlantic flights with adviser Lindbergh. Even the Russians had their eyes on long-range commercial aviation with completion in September of a trail-blazing flight from New York all the way to Moscow.

Humorists were already claiming that air travel was bringing Europe closer to America, and that there were other objections, too. While airplanes were not yet making scheduled trips across the Atlantic, you could fly over in the new German dirigible, *Hindenburg.* For $400 one way, and $700 round trip, a passenger could journey in almost palatial comfort.

On its maiden flight to Lakehurst, New Jersey, with 41 men and 10 women passengers and a crew of 56 including Captain Lehman and Count von Eckener, the *Hindenburg* averaged a speedy 69 miles an hour. Returning to Germany, it carried 150,000 pieces of mail and on other flights its cargo included an automobile and even an airplane.

In 1872, Phileas Fogg had battled his way around the world in a fictional 80 days. Nellie Bly cut that to 72 days by 1889 and in 1907 Colonel Burnley-Campbell made it in just 40. The *Graf Zeppelin* chopped that time in two by 1929.

Now in 1936 three reporters embarked on a round-the-world race to see if they could better that speed. H. R. Ekins of the *World Telegram* was the winner; getting back to his office in 18 days. He had flown from Lakehurst to Frankfurt on the *Hindenburg,* boarded a Royal Dutch Airlines plane to Batavia, changed to Netherlands Indian Airways from there to Manila, where he caught the China Clipper back to Alameda, California. United Airlines took him down to Burbank and he hopped on a TWA plane to Newark. He had covered some 26,000 miles, and the fare was a modest $2,400. Second place went to Dorothy Kilgallen of the New York *Journal,* and Leo Kiernan of the *Times* was third.

High-speed commercial air travel was here with a vengeance, and inevitably an occasional disaster marred the record it was marking up in 1936. During the year there were five crashes on major airlines, and 47 people died in those wrecks. But the odds were heavily against crack-ups, and of course all crashes weren't fatal.

There was even an occasional bit of humor connected with such occurrences, as when an RAF plane piled up on the deck of the liner *Normandie.* The red-faced pilot informed the captain, "I say, I'm terribly sorry about this!"

With airliners flying nearly 200 miles an hour, it was no surprise that the world's speed record was in excess of 440 miles an hour, held by Italy's Francesco Agello in a racing seaplane. So fast had speeds increased that now a battle raged among experts, some of whom flatly stated that man would never fly faster than 575 miles an hour.

Sportsman Howard Hughes set a new record of 9 hours and 26 minutes from Burbank to Newark, and also set new marks for Miami to New York and Chicago to Los Angeles.

An amazing thing happened in the transcontinental Bendix race when women placed first and second. Louise Thaden won the race, and Laura Ingalls was second. There was another woman flier in the news, named Amelia Earhart Putnam. In France Maryse Hilsz set a women's altitude mark of nearly 29,000 feet to go with countryman George Detre's 48,697-foot mark, until Squadron Leader Swain of the RAF reached 49,967 feet.

Another Frenchman named Claisse still held the distance and altitude marks for helicopters, of 1,640 feet and 518 feet respectively, but a displaced Russian named Igor Sikorsky was dreaming up a new design in America and would shortly set the aviation world on its ear.

The autogiro was nothing new, but the roadable giro was. Bystanders gawked unbelievingly at this craft that could chug down the road like a car and then hop into the air like a bird. There was another new plane flying, too. Called the Arrow Flivver, and powered with a Ford automobile engine, it was touted by its builders as the sky flivver of tomorrow.

For sheer sport in the air, though, it was hard to beat gliding. Elmira, New York, was the hub of this activity, and Richard du Pont its most popular exponent. The silent, graceful-winged craft were capable of soaring for miles on currents of air, and of climbing to high altitudes and doing all sorts of stunts. Gliding was popular in Germany, too, having gotten its impetus when the Germans were forbidden to build military aircraft.

Hitler was building bombers now, of course, and the U.S. Army Air Corps was scurrying around trying to get itself some more B-17 bombers—flying giants with four engines and a speed faster than our best pursuit planes. Boeing was building 13 of them for the U.S. and England was talking about buying 300 of them herself.

Elsewhere Elliott Roosevelt was being accused of negotiating a sale of American planes to Russia but the deal did not go through. And an inventor named Hammond was working on a method of using television for an airplane blind landing aid. It was a big year for aviation, but it was obvious that this was only the beginning in the air.

The Armed Forces

In 1936 France had an armed force of 6,134,857. Germany had 2,276,800, and Japan was close behind with 2,175,000. An unconcerned Great Britain numbered its mili-

189

tary at 530,005, and the United States totaled a mere 438,064. One army, the Bonus Army, had been disbanded and when GAR veterans paraded it was found that Civil War survivors were down to 4,500.

The Air Corps was part of the Army, and despite Billy Mitchell and others there was little progress toward building a strong air arm. In 1936 proponents were fighting hard against those in and out of the service who thought buying thirteen of the Boeing B-17 bombers was a ridiculous waste of money. One chore the Army was doing was running the CCC, and when General Hagood protested that too much was being pumped into this and too little into military spending he was relieved of command.

The Army Chief of Staff was General Malin Craig. At the top of the list of generals was Major General Douglas MacArthur, and last on the list of sixty-four brigadiers was a George C. Marshall. Henry H. Arnold was Number 35.

The Navy, under Admiral William Leahy, Chief, Naval Operations, was in better shape. Many complained that this was due to the fact that Roosevelt had once been a Navy Secretary and favored this branch. In 1936 it had 15 battleships, 4 aircraft carriers, 27 cruisers, 181 destroyers and 79 submarines. The total of 306 compared with 309 for Great Britain, 198 for Japan, 195 for Italy, 173 for France, and 53 for Germany.

Total expenditures for the military for the year 1936 were less than one billion dollars.

Art

Along with the work of Thomas Hart Benton, Edward Hopper and Grant Wood, in 1936 much painting was done under the aegis of the federal government in Washington and representing a crop of more than 5,000 WPA artists. Many of these were salvaged from the ruinous chores of ditch-digging and street-sweeping, and though the wages paid for adorning public buildings with their talent amounted to paltry fees it did at least permit them to paint.

Understandably, much of the work decorating post offices, civic centers and the like bore the unmistakable stamp of social significance. Much of it was controversial, like the nude white women being attacked by raiding Indians in one painting, and the statue *Civic Virtue* with a nude male figure stamping on two nude females. But it was a creative outlet, and the artists had their own show in Washington's Phillips Memorial Gallery.

Salvador Dali was in the forefront of the surrealists, and Calder, with his *Mobile 1936* was adding motion to the colors and dimensions of more conventional art. Diego Rivera, who would shortly play host to Trotsky in Mexico, ran afoul of a patron for whom he did a fresco in a Mexico City hotel. The hotel man painted over some of Rivera's more outspoken figures and brooked the wrath of the painter and gun-toting friends.

At the National Academy of Design's 111th show, a nosy reporter spied a painting that had been hung on its side, and in France the Nestlé baby food people were commissioning artists to update the old masters commercially and Raphael's *La Belle Jardinière* was reproduced in magazine ads with the Virgin Mary feeding the infant Jesus with a modern nursing bottle!

Pioneer Charles Boni was broadsiding art lovers of modest means with *Living American Art* series prints for $5 each, but perhaps the newest thing in art was the candid camera craze.

Tired of snapping the children and the family car, shutterbugs were happily experimenting with their new high-quality German Leica cameras and taking a tack somewhat like that of the ashcan school of painters. These new "lens artists" portrayed not only the beauty but the ugliness of 1936. The crumbling tenements, the reliefers and dust bowl victims all were grist for the mill of a breed as honest as Marcus Aurelius and seeing good in rotting fruit and even the slaver on the boar's tusk.

Births

It was a good year for the Roosevelts in many ways, including additions to the family. James Roosevelt and his wife had a daughter, Kate. The Elliott Roosevelts had a boy, Elliott, Junior. The youngsters were the sixth and seventh grandchildren for the President. The La Follettes had a baby, too, and named it Bronson Cutting La Follette for the senator killed in a plane crash a year earlier.

In Italy a baby girl was christened Anna Maria Alberghetti and in Sweden May Britt and Inger Stevens were born. In America James Darren was born to parents who probably didn't suspect he would one day be an actor, but

191

David Nelson's parents may have had such ideas. Baseball profited that year, too, when Don Drysdale and Harmon Killebrew came along. Up in Canada there wasn't much fanfare when a little boy named Joseph was born. His parents were named Dionne. An American baby made some sort of history, though. Mary Gertrude Hughes had a daddy 96 years old—certified by the American Medical Association!

Though the birth rate had declined slightly during the depression, America's population showed a modest increase and in 1936 stood at about 128½ million.

Business

Business in 1936 was good. The stock market was at a five-year high and imports and exports, totaling almost five billion dollars, were the highest since 1930. Auto production was booming, and refrigerators had their biggest year with two million sold. Roger Babson was concerned about all the gold the government was piling up in Fort Knox, and worried about a possible Fascist or Communist revolution to gain possession of it.

Factory workers in the East were getting about $25 a week, and the average monthly rent they paid was some $35. Supermarkets were the big thing and getting bigger all the time. Bread was about 8 cents a loaf and butter 42 cents a pound. Milk was 12 cents a quart and eggs 40 cents a dozen. Potatoes were only 3 cents a pound, but steak to go with them cost 39 cents. Ham was 50 cents, but you could get chicken for about 30 cents. *Paté de foie gras* was going for 90 cents for 2 ounces, but caviar cost the rich $12 for a 14-ounce can!

Airmail postage was 6 cents now, but you could still buy a postal card for 1 cent. Diamonds were popular, and it was evident that somehow people were scraping up millions of dollars a week for legal and illegal gambling. With the low mortgage rates of FHA, home building was picking up dramatically.

In New York City the eleventh of the planned fourteen Rockefeller Center buildings was completed. Originally designed as an opera house, the project was now Radio City. In Philadelphia, advertisers were driving the people crazy with "verbal advertising": actors giving commercials in commuter trains, buses and other public places.

Competition was keen in the cigarette business and

192

Philip Morris had stolen a march by offering dealers a free pack with every carton. In the soup world feisty little Phillips was marketing cans for 5 cents and challenging leaders Campbell and Heinz. Borden and Company found itself embarrassedly boycotted by the League of Women Shoppers for not negotiating with a union.

Zenith Radio Corporation bought a plant from the faltering Grigsby Grunow firm to accommodate its popular line. Elsewhere Philco and RCA were battling it out in court about unfair competition. RCA had retained Joseph Kennedy to work up a plan for its operation—the fee was $150,000. A smaller job Kennedy found time for was a report for Paramount Pictures out in Hollywood; this one paid only $50,000. There was lots of activity in movieland, with Barney Balaban in as new president of RKO and the Schenck brothers working out big deals for MGM and Fox with foreign producers.

Floyd Odlum's Atlas Corporation continued to buy and buy. One acquisition was the big Franklin Simon & Company store in New York, to add to Bonwit Teller, picked up earlier. Odlum had a new wife, too, in the person of flier Jacqueline Cochran. California's Giannini family was making its Transamerica Corporation bigger all the time despite internal feuds.

Swift & Company bought out Arnold Brothers, the twenty-first competitor it had acquired. Nash and Kelvinator merged and people wondered if the next move would be refrigerators in automobiles. Fairchild Aviation was getting so big that boss Sherman Fairchild was splitting the aircraft interests from the cameras. Schick and Dictograph were fighting over patent rights on the new and booming dry shavers. Out west, Sinclair and Richfield were combining, and in Detroit Henry Ford was talking about building car bodies out of soybeans.

There was trouble in the business world, of course. Charles Kettering was admitting that he had somehow parlayed an investment of $260,000 into a final value of $20,000. Financier Samuel Insull was stepping down as president of Affiliated Broadcasting Company. In 1936 there were 9,185 business failures, but there had been more than 11,000 in 1935. There were strikes too, principally the disastrous maritime battles on the Pacific, Atlantic and Gulf coasts, as well as the bitter Remington Rand dispute and the New York building service shutdown. John L. Lewis was not exactly endearing himself, and there were still millions of unemployed, but things were definitely picking up. Prosperity was, as always, just around that elusive corner but at least there weren't quite so many apple sellers blocking the way.

Crime

1936 was a year to restore the faith of those who believed crime didn't pay. J. Edgar Hoover's G-men were having a field day with public enemies, whose numerical ratings changed almost hourly as criminals were rounded up. So effective was the FBI that by 1936 it had solved nearly all the kidnapings that took place since enactment of the "Lindbergh Law" in 1932.

Even as Anna Sage, the "woman in red" who trapped Dillinger, was deported to Rumania, other big guns in the criminal world like Alvin Karpis were being captured. Picked up in New Orleans, Karpis was whisked by plane to St. Paul in connection with the kidnaping of brewer William Hamm, Jr. Newspaper writers speculated that after St. Paul would come St. Peter.

A week after Karpis was captured, G-men took in Harry Campbell for the Bremer kidnaping and William Mahan, who was involved in the Weyerhauser abduction. A few days later Thomas Robinson, who had kidnaped Mrs. Berry Stoll, was caught. It was as though the flight of the Lindberghs to England had inspired the lawmen to sudden action.

Edward G. Bremer was a bank president in St. Paul Minnesota. He was abducted and held for payment of $200,-000 in ransom. The money was paid and Bremer was released unharmed. George Weyerhauser was the 9-year-old son of a Tacoma lumberman. He was kidnaped and also held until payment of $200,000. Eight days after the abduction he was freed and returned to his family safely. Alice Stoll, 26-year-old socialite wife of Berry V. Stoll, wealthy oil man, was kidnaped from her home in Louisville. The abductors demanded $50,000, which was paid, and the woman was freed. The kidnaper, Thomas Robinson, was apprehended quickly and it was learned he had been in an insane asylum earlier. His wife was jailed for her part in the crime, but Robinson managed to jump bail and evade officers for some two years.

While the FBI ranged the country, another proponent of

194

law and order waged a more localized crusade. Young Tom Dewey, 32-year-old special prosecutor, was making it rough on organized crime in New York. It was a bad year, some said, for snow and vice in the state. Of 73 racketeers indicted by Dewey, 71 were convicted. Lucky Luciano was among those who met his Waterloo and was sentenced to 30 to 50 years in the penitentiary.

There were other names in the crime news, too, names that had been on the public's lips for some time. Richard Loeb, who with thrill-killing partner Nathan Leopold had murdered Bobby Franks, made an indecent proposition to fellow prisoner James Day. Day knifed Loeb to death and was acquitted for his act.

Out in San Jose, California, David Lamson was free following his third trial for the murder of his wife, whose butchered body was found in the family bathtub. Tom Mooney remained in jail for a bombing he claimed he didn't do, and in the meantime bombs were still killing people. In Wilkes Barre unknown persons mailed six bombs to union officials, killing two and injuring the other four.

A wierd cult called the Black Legion flourished briefly, culminating in the shooting of WPA worker Charles Poole on suspicion of beating his pregnant wife. Nancy Titterton was attacked and murdered by upholsterer John Florenza in a crime of passion. In another kind of passion John Keogh lost a mortgage suit in court and shot and killed the lawyer who opposed him, then tried to kill the judge, too. Student Wesley Clow of Lehigh University shot and killed his teacher and then himself after the teacher gave him a failing grade.

For another kind of crime, that of negligence, the acting captain and the chief engineer of the ill-fated liner, *Morro Castle*, were sentenced to two and four years respectively in prison. The unlucky acting captain could blame a weird fate that had killed the real captain with indigestion just before the ship caught fire.

Mail robber Joe Bowers was killed when he tried to break out of prison on Alcatraz, and in New York a dog named Idaho was saved from the death penalty in a "murder" charge. The seven-month-old dog was accused of pushing a boy into a canal where he drowned. The judge hearing the case sentenced the animal instead to two years of confinement.

The illegal weed, marijuana, was growing up all over the

place and authorities were doing their best to destroy the plants before they could be made into "reefers." Gangsterism was on the decline, but there was a disturbing new element in crime of great concern to lawmen. Pointing out that there were 12,000 young killers in the country, and that youth was responsible for 20 percent of crime, J. Edgar Hoover was campaigning against the new menace.

"So long as we fail to recognize that discipline is an essential part of human development," he said, "just so long will we have an aimless, directionless milling of the herd which can result only in mental panic and a thorough disregard for the rights of society to peace and order."

Deaths

Millions of people were born in 1936; millions died, as they must each year. All who die are mourned, of course, but some of those who were no longer alive were noted more in their passing than others. Perhaps the greatest figure to pass from the scene was King George V of England. Another king died that year, too—Fuad of Egypt. President Gomez of Venezuela was on the obituary list, as was Don Alfonso Carlos, pretender to the Spanish throne.

In America Governor Floyd Olson of Minnesota died and so did Governor O. K. Allen of Louisiana. Senator James Couzens of Michigan passed away. Presidential Secretary Louis Howe died, and New York's Caroline Hoffman, one of the country's oldest voters at 103, would not cast a ballot in November.

It was an especially tragic year for literature. Venerable Rudyard Kipling died just days before his king did. G. K. Chesterton and A. E. Housman were also lost forever to the English and the world. Russia's Maxim Gorky died, along with American authors Finley Peter Dunne of Mr. Dooley fame, Chic Sale and Lincoln Steffens. In Germany Oswald Spengler died. The publishing firm of Brett-Macmillan seemed all but wiped out with the death of G. P. Brett in America and three Macmillans in England. And baseball veteran O. R. Casey who had been the model for *Casey at the Bat* died, too.

Movie idol John Gilbert died at the age of 38, and another Hollywood loss was 37-year-old producer Irving Thalberg. Dancer Marilyn Miller died at 37, too. Circusman John Ringling, Thurston the Magician and French aviation pioneer Louis Bleriot did not live out the year 1936. Another airman, Juan de la Cierva, who had invented the auto-gyro, died in the crash of a conventional plane.

French General Baptiste Etienne, inventor of the tank, died, along with fellow inventors Hiram Maxim and Cyrus McCormick, as well as Francois Marcel, who created the Marcel hair wave. E. R. Thomas, who in 1908 had won the New York-to-Paris auto race, died at 85, and so did polo-playing Serge Mdivani, who was only 33.

William Candler, Vice President of Coca-Cola died, as did John Harold Dollar of the Dollar Line steamship firm. Thomas Jefferson Foster, founder of International Correspondence Schools, passed away in 1936. A great loss to the medical profession was that of Dr. Joseph Graham Mayo, who perished in an auto accident.

The god of war lost its best salesman when Sir Basil Zaharoff died. Other military men were America's Admiral Sims and General Sherrill of the Olympic Committee. Composer Ottorino Respighi and singer Madame Schumann-Heink ended their days on earth.

Mrs. Macy who had taught Helen Keller, died, as did Sir Thomas Cullinan, the diamond man, and Alexander Berkman, the Russian anarchist who had shot steelman Frick during the Homestead Strike in 1892. Professor Pavlov, whose dog was perhaps as well known as the psychologist himself, died and so did "Ma" Streeter, ex-Vice President Charles Curtis, and the widow of Eugene Debs.

Now all who died did so naturally, or by accident. Some were put to death legally by society. Among these was Arthur Gooch, the first man to be executed under the Lindbergh Law for kidnaping. Gooch was hanged.

Disasters

There were holidays on banking, on debts, and some other things, but there was no moratorium on death. In 1936 you could still get killed and many people did. Despite the grisly and thought-provoking article titled "And Sudden Death" that the *Reader's Digest* had printed and which became a movie this year, automobiles continued to be major killers. Some 40,000 victims would die, plus a million more maimed or otherwise injured.

The Fourth of July holiday accounted for deaths that by grim coincidence totalled 444. Only seven of these were caused by fireworks; 254 died in auto wrecks and another 104 drowned. On Labor Day only 20 drowned, but the highways took another 244. And on Thanksgiving Day the nation could be thankful that only 80 perished in wrecks. People perished in trains, too. Sixty died that way in China in a single accident. The sea was a killer, and a Japanese steamer sank in a typhoon with the loss of 60. A French exploration vessel went down with 31 off Iceland and a German liner sank off England taking 39 lives. A British boat foundered in the West Indies drowning 21, and in the United States 19 died in a single sinking on Lake Erie and 15 in a Lake Michigan disaster.

America was not alone in plane accidents. In the world's history there was a record 48 dead in the crash of one plane—Russia's huge Maxim Gorky. Thankfully, no such tragedy took place in 1936, but in the aggregate, many more lives were lost.

The crashes in America of airplanes were typical of those in the rest of the world. Juan de la Cierva, inventor of the flying machine called the autogyro, perished with 13 others in a commercial airliner when it faltered on takeoff from London's Croydon Airport.

A German government plane smashed into the ground and wiped out 11 more lives, while in Norway an airliner ran into a mountain with an unlucky 7 on board. A Mexican commercial craft went down, killing 14. In Colombia an Army plane wreck took 9 dead, and a flying boat plunged into the sea near Trinidad and killed 3. Skeptics shook their heads and repeated the adage about what went up having to come down, vowing to keep both feet planted on solid ground.

Of course, even solid ground was no guarantee of safety. Earthquakes killed 300 in Colombia and another 100 in El Salvador. In Alaska a landslide buried 14, and a Colorado avalanche wiped out 6 victims, while one in Norway claimed 70. Men died underground, as they did every year. In India 205 miners died and an additional 19 were killed in Belgium. A Chinese fireworks factory exploded in Taipan and killed 23 workers—a warmup for a blast in France that saw 53 die. Movie film caught fire in Chile and 31 perished in the resulting holocaust.

Sometimes man's structures topple like a house of cards. An apartment house under construction in New York crushed 17 workmen, but this seemed a minor disaster compared with the horror of the celebration of the accession of King Carol to the throne in Rumania. A grandstand gave way and plunged 60 to their deaths and injured 700 others. And at the Shamrock Club on San Francisco's Geary Street, a patron laughingly tried to light his cigarette from a torch carried by dancer Peggy Blossom. In the resulting inferno four died and a dozen more were burned.

These statistics pale when nature takes a hand in the disaster columns. October storms killed more than a thousand in the Philippines. In this country, spring floods sent water twenty feet high into Washington, D.C., and Pittsburgh. More than 170 Americans had died in floods by March. Later in the year the blazing sun took a hand and nearly 3,000 died from the heat, 560 of these in Minnesota alone. Cold, too, could kill and among those who froze in 1936 were two couples marooned in their car near Gillette, Wyoming.

Another victim of the snow was Delmar Fadden, a 23-year-old climber who set out to scale Mount Rainier. He was the thirteenth person to die in the attempt. Alongside the impact of a single death like this, the news from Japan that 700 people had perished in a sea of mud when a dam collapsed blurred meaninglessly. More poignant, despite their numbers, were those Japanese who didn't merely die but committed suicide. In 1936 more than 600 young lovers leaped into volcanoes to die rather than face their unhappy futures. Some 500 of these leaps were double suicides.

Closer to home, Americans read of another suicide. Trouble-plagued Congressman Marion Zioncheck had been spirited out of Washington because of his escapades there. In Seattle the young lawmaker plunged to his death from a window of an office building.

But Zioncheck did not go out with the flourish of 22-year-old Robert Erskine, who commited suicide that same sweltering month of August. Erskine, a graduate of Williams College and a member of the staff of *Newsweek*, bid farewell to the half-dozen or so sight-seers on the observation deck at the eighty-sixth story of New York's Empire State Building. "Well, so long folks," he said pathetically. Then he climbed over the wall and dived into space. It was a strong jump, and Erskine cleared all of the obstructons between him and hit the street 1,048 feet below.

Education

In 1936 there were 29 million children in grade school, a drop of some quarter of a million occasioned by the declining birth rate. The classics were still losing out, with Greek all but vanished and Latin not far behind. With returning prosperity some "frill" classes were coming back, though.

Government agencies like the CCC were teaching some Americans, and others were helped by Federal Vocational Education Act funds, which were matched by the states. Teachers' pay was pathetically low, with some getting less than $700 a year.

It was still hard to afford a college education, and some wondered why they should bother. But educators persisted in upgrading higher learning, with Chicago's Robert Maynard Hutchins proposing the most sweeping changes. Harvard, under President James Conant, was celebrating its three hundredth year. Venerable Heidelberg was 550 years old and invited many Americans to participate in the occasion. Many deplored the direction the German university had taken under Nazi influence.

Educator Horace Mann was honored with a centenary celebration, but writer John R. Tunis came out with a book called *Was College Worthwhile?* In Alabama children of union members "struck" when several teachers attempting to organize were dismissed. Another thorn was the loyalty oath, and some teachers refused to sign, until their pay was withheld.

Despite the difficulties, education went on apace. The U.S. Office of Education listed close to 700 American colleges and universities, with total enrollment of 1,250,000. And honors went to the learned. Notre Dame's Laetare Medal was given to Richard Reid, a Georgia law educator. The Franklin Institute Medal, for the physical sciences, was shared by George Curme, Jr., and Robert Van de Graaff. And National Institute of Social Sciences medalists were Nicholas Murray Butler, Mrs. Harrison Eustis, J. Pierpont Morgan and William Edwin Hall.

Something new was being tried in Boston. Educational radio station WIXAL boosted its power and received the blessings of the educational fraternity and government as it beamed programs not only to America but to much of the world. And out in Caifornia the Dean of the Stanford Engineering School was retiring. His name was Theodore Jesse Hoover, and he planned to fish a lot with his unemployed brother Herbert.

200

Fairs and Celebrations

There were two big expositions in 1936, the Great Lakes Exposition and the Dallas Centennial. President Roosevelt opened the former by pushing a button in Washington, D.C. Some 6½ million visitors saw the show in Dallas, a big crowd, even for Texas. For a commemorative in New England half-dollars were struck off bearing the likeness of P. T. Barnum. The coins sold for a dollar and cynics said this followed since Barnum had said there was a sucker born every minute. Other Americans honored during the year on coins or stamps were Stephen Foster and Susan B. Anthony.

In Atlantic City, Rose Veronica Coyle of Pennsylvania was crowned Miss America and reaped a harvest of prestige and dollars. Los Angeles celebrated the bringing of electric power to that city from distant Hoover—or Boulder, depending on your politics—Dam.

Farther north, San Francisco was jubilant over its newly opened Oakland-San Francisco Bay Bridge which had cost $77 million. New York opened its $60 million Triborough Bridge in 1936, too, and was already making plans for the big 1939 World's Fair.

International Relations

By 1936 Iran recalled her Foreign Minister from the United States following an incident over a speeding ticket. The Philippines won their independence, and Panama was wondering what its status was now that Uncle Sam did not again guarantee *its* independence as was customary.

Not just in Spain and Japan and Russia and Germany, but all over the world there was strife and unrest. In Palestine the Jews and Arabs and British fought. Mahatma Gandhi and Jawaharlal Nehru pretended not to be enemies in India as riots and killings took place.

In Mexico President Cárdenas distributed eleven million acres of land to the poor, and the rebel Chief Ramirez was caught and his severed head perched atop a pole in the public square as an object lesson. Many were killed in tiny Macedonia and there were revolts in Bolivia, Cuba, Puerto Rico and Paraguay.

It was a busy year for bloodshed and it must have taken some soul-searching charity for the Nobel Committee to award the Peace Prize to the least of many evils—Argentina.

201

Literature

Among the 7,000 or so books published in 1936 some stood out above the rest. *Honey in the Horn* by H. L. Davis won the Pulitzer Prize for the best novel. Other prize winners were Van Wyck Brooks' history, *The Flowering of New England*, Ralph Barton Perry's biography, *The Thought and Character of William James,* and poet Robert P. Tristam Coffin's *Strange Holiness.* It was no great surprise that Eugene O'Neill won the Nobel Prize for Literature that year.

Inspirational books were big. *Live Alone and Like It* by Marjorie Hillis and Dorothea Brande's *Wake Up and Live* were popular examples, and there was one called *How to Win Friends and Influence People* by a man named Dale Carnegie. John Gunther's latest was *Inside Europe* and there was a swashbuckler titled *Drums Along the Mohawk* by Walter D. Edmonds for lovers of popularized American history.

John Dos Passos was represented by *The Big Money* and Dorothy Parker had written *Not So Deep as a Well.* Carl Sandburg had done *The People, Yes,* filled with social significance, and John Steinbeck's *In Dubious Battle* was in the bookstores. He was flexing his knuckles and thinking about another book—one about the westward migration from the Dust Bowl.

William Saroyan came out with *Inhale & Exhale* and brash Aldous Huxley's *Eyeless in Gaza* hinted at second thoughts since that intellectual had published *Brave New World.* The South's William Faulkner wrote *Absalom, Absalom!* and even the philosophers were writing novels. Venerable George Santayana produced one called *The Last Pilgrim.*

There was a big, lusty historical novel that seemed to be doing well when it finally found a publisher. Written by an Atlantan, Margaret Mitchell, it was called *Gone With the Wind* and some hopefuls said it might even rival Hervey Allen's *Anthony Adverse.*

A newcomer named Ayn Rand had written a book about the individual versus the collective, set in Russia, and called it *We the Living.* David Lamson, just out of prison after his third trial on charges of murdering his wife, had written one titled, *We Who Are About to Die.* Sidney and Beatrice Webb had written a big book called, *Soviet Com-*

munism: *A New Civilization?* in which they predicted that Stalin's Russia might not only last, but prosper as well.

The publishing firm of William Morrow had a new kind of book for mystery fans. Called *Crime File,* the "book" not only described an exciting case but provided the amateur detective with a packet of actual clues to be used in working out a solution—things like bits of burned material, human hair, and so on.

"Edgar Guest Day" was celebrated in Michigan in honor of the folksy poet, and Booth Tarkington was predicting that the novel and the poem might well be dealt a death blow by radio and the coming of television.

Medicine

In 1936 the Nobel Prize went to Sir Henry Hallett Dale of England the Professor Otto Loewi of Austria for their work showing that human nerve impulses were based on chemistry and not electricity. Doctors, psychiatrists and psychologists were arguing the merits of the drastic new "lobotomy" technique that seemed to be helping mental patients. Other researchers claimed that insulin shock was helpful in treating schizophrenics. Meantime, the number of patients in mental hospitals was growing.

Doctors at Mayo Clinic were assuring the country that about half the victims of heart attacks made recoveries and lived for some time afterward, often usefully. Diabetics were being given new treatments, including one medication that was a derivative of barley. Eye surgeons were doing wonders with frozen eyes, donated by those passed away, and some Americans were seeing through dead men's corneas. The contact lens was being improved, and a pair sold for about $100.

Flight surgeons were reporting a new ailment among fliers, known as "aeroneurosis," that was going to be a growing problem. Margaret Sanger was successful in having customs authorities admit Japanese contraceptives to this country, while the victim of another kind of birth control was also in the news. Ann Hewitt Cooper, the last of the Cooper family, sued her mother for $500,000 for allegedly sterilizing her daughter.

At the convention of the American Medical Association, presidential candidate Alf Landon drew rousing cheers when he said, "Medicine will not willingly be made the servile instrument of politicians or the instrument of domineering bureaucrats."

Dr. Dean of the U.S. Health Service reported that naturally fluorinated water in hundreds of areas in the country was permanently disfiguring the teeth of residents. Experiments were being conducted on ways to filter out the fluorine by passing the water over beds of activated aluminum.

Radium was being used to treat cancer, and the disease was now being investigated as hereditary, with conflicting reports from the various scientists engaged in the problem. Infantile paralysis broke out in Alabama in 1936 and a new picric-acid sodium-alum nasal spray was tried out as a preventive. Vaccines, too, were being studied, including a formaldehyde vaccine developed by Dr. Maurice Brodie in New York.

At Rockefeller Institute, Doctor A. B. Sabin, who had come to this country from Poland, reported a discovery in work with mice that might lead to a "barrier" against the virus that caused infantile paralysis. Other researchers were now theorizing that the common cold was caused by a filterable virus, chemical rather than animal in nature. Meanwhile, the cold continued to be quite common among Americans regardless of what caused it.

Movies

Hollywood was enjoying its most prosperous year since 1929. The talkies were firmly established by now and there was an innovation called Technicolor for those producers who could afford it. Five hundred films were made during the year, though of course the men responsible claimed they lost money on four out of five. An additional two hundred films were imported.

There was much talk of censorship of sexy films to protect the country's morals, but President Roosevelt refused any government action. The movies themselves entrusted the job to "Czar" Will Hays and Joseph Breen, and the the Catholic Legion of Decency further rode herd on Hollywood. A young reviewer for the *New York Times*, 28-year-old André Sennwald, deplored the excess of torture and brutality for its own sake in movies. Apparently he was a voice in the wilderness.

Academy Award-winning stars for 1936 included Luise Rainer in *The Great Ziegfeld,* Paul Muni in *The Story of*

Louis Pasteur, Gail Sondergaard in *Anthony Adverse*—the movie some said gave author Hervey Allen a crackerjack idea for a new novel—and Walter Brennan in *Come and Get it.*

Other big movies were *The Green Pastures*; *Mr. Deeds Goes to Town,* with Gary Cooper; *Romeo and Juliet*; *One Hundred Men and a Girl,* with Deanna Durbin and Leopold Stokowski; *Modern Times,* with Charlie Chaplin and Paulette Goddard; *Dodsworth, The Garden of Allah* and *A Tale of Two Cities.*

Stars ranged from Mae West of "come up and see me some time!" fame whose current movie was *Klondike Annie,* to saccharine-sweet curly-headed Shirley Temple, who was making *Captain January* and other movies. Freddie Bartholomew, currently seen in a movie with two youngsters named Mickey Rooney and Jackie Cooper, was having family troubles and being "kidnaped" by his Aunt Cissie.

Harold Lloyd made *The Milky Way* and Joe E. Brown was starring as Alexander Botts in *Earthworm Tractors.* Jean Harlow was sultry as ever in *Suzy* and an import named Simone Simon appeared in *Girls' Dormitory.* Warner Oland was popular as the Oriental sleuth in *Charlie Chan at the Race Track,* and *These Three,* freely adapted from Lillian Hellman's controversial play, *The Children's Hour,* was a box office smash.

War pictures were popular, including *The Road to Glory* and *The General Died at Dawn.* David Lamson's film, *We Who Are About to Die,* was a hit, and among the "social significance" movies was *Winterset,* based on the Sacco-Vanzetti case. Even the *Reader's Digest* article, "And Sudden Death," had been made into a movie in 1936. Fred Astaire and Ginger Rogers were a popular duo in *Follow the Fleet* and another winning couple was Nelson Eddy and Jeanette MacDonald.

Airplane films were a sure bet, and among them were *Ceiling Zero* with young Jimmy Cagney, and *China Clipper.* Universal scooped the field, however, by previewing its *Flying Hostess* 7,000 feet over New York. Inviting a planeload of critics aloft, the company showed the film on a special screen in the cabin of a TWA airliner.

Pioneer cartoon-maker Walt Disney got an Academy Award for the fifth straight year, this time for *Country Cousin.* The newsreel, "March of Time," thrilled audiences with its confident and authentic tone and received a special award. There was an innovation called "Visual Music" that matched changing patterns of light to sound and gave moviegoers a new thrill.

Even President Roosevelt "wrote" a movie. When he suggested to *Liberty* editor Fulton Oursler a plot for a mystery he thought would make a good story, Oursler took him up on it and had professional writers do the yarn. It was then made into a movie called fittingly, *The President's Mystery*. Another government entry into the movie world was more of a thorn in the side to Hollywood—the documentary film, *The Plough That Broke the Plains*, filmed for Washington by ace director Pare Lorentz.

All in all, the flicker business was looking up and even better times were ahead for the cinema world. Nobody even worried about the suggestion made that "home movies"— transmitted there from a radio station—might compete with the Hollywood product.

Music

Tin Pan Alley was still grinding out popular tunes. Sung and whistled in 1936 were such favorites as *The Way You Look Tonight, Moonlight and Shadows, I've Got You Under My Skin, I Can't Get Started with You* and *I'm Putting All My Eggs in One Basket*. Relaxed Johnny Mercer wrote *I'm An Old Cowhand* and there was a zany one called *The Music Goes Round and Round*.

Rudy Vallee, minus the megaphone of earlier days, revived *The Whiffenpoof Song* and Bing Crosby was singing *Pennies from Heaven*. Also current were, *Is It True What They Say About Dixie?, You, There's a Small Hotel, When My Dreamboat Comes Home* and *You Can't Pull the Wool Over My Eyes*.

Another kind of tune, *Stompin' at the Savoy*, was a clue to a fairly new kind of music. Jazz improvisations, the jam session, had been taken over from Negro musicians by white bandleaders like Benny Goodman, Tommy Dorsey, Jack Teagarden and Artie Shaw. Now, along with Count Basie and Louis Armstrong, any band that was hep was sending the kids with swing. Benny Goodman was the acknowledged "King," and appearances featured mobs of *aficionados* with police on hand to keep order.

There was other music, too—long-hair music that not just operagoers but everybody was learning to like because there was lots of it on the radio. There was the New

York Philharmonic and the Metropolitan Opera and the Ford Hour's Detroit Symphony. Toscanini and Stokowski were known over the land.

Chicago's Civic Opera House kicked off its season with stars like Galli-Curci—back after a long absence—Lawrence Tibbett, Lily Pons and Ezio Pinza. Yehudi Menuhin thrilled lovers of the violin and blind pianist Alec Templeton continued to amaze his audiences. José Iturbi had the misfortune of being injured in a plane crash that took the lives of some of the others aboard.

The WPA brought music to the man in the street—live music played by real musicians at admission prices most could afford. It was estimated that some 15,000 of these government-paid artists entertained twenty million in concerts all over the country. Without doubt the biggest of these productions was that of Erno Rapee conducting the huge WPA Symphony in Madison Square Garden. For their *1812 Overture* a huge seventeen-inch cannon was fired, abetted by rifle fire from a special guard of sixteen soldiers. Down in Memphis, the town turned out to honor blues-man W. C. Handy.

Strangely it was a boom year for phonograph records, too. Instead of being killed by radio as predicted, the platters were selling in 1936 at double and triple the rate of a few years before. Radio's *Hit Parade* helped, and the dime stores carried cheap, expendable editions of popular songs. At the same time quality records boomed because of the growing interest in classical music fostered not only by radio but by live performances as well.

The Press

There were still lots of newspapers in America—almost 13,000 of them in 1936. But many cities now had only one morning paper and one in the evening. Wages were miserable and competition was keen for the jobs there were, with perhaps only publishers and topflight snydicated columnists making good money. The big names ranged from Dorothy Dix to Dorothy Thompson, and Walter Winchell to Walter Lippmann. O. O. McIntyre's beat was Broadway and Pearson and Allen covered Washington. Heywood Broun and Westbrook Pegler had big followings and so did a newcomer to the writing game—Mrs. Eleanor Roosevelt.

William Randolph Hearst was the most controversial publisher of the day, and his troubles included the strike that shut down Seattle's *Post-Intelligencer*. Moses Annenberg bought the Philadelphia *Inquirer*, and down in Chattanooga the *Free Press* was going great guns for a new paper.

Pulitzer prizes went to Will Barber (posthumously) for his work as war correspondent in Ethiopia, a task that killed him. Deac Lyman copped the prize for reporting with his story on the Lindberghs' flight from America, and the Cedar Rapids *Gazette* was awarded the honor for public service.

While most employees writing for the paper were probably New Deal sympathizers, the publications themselves were predominantly conservative in tone and thus pro-capital and anti-Roosevelt. Most magazines, too, were in this boat, even the popular *Saturday Evening Post*, despite the fact that most of its readers were for the President. Advertising controlled the editorial policy as a matter of cold hard fact. Long-time Editor George Horace Lorimer stepped down for newcomer Wesley Winans Stout.

The once proud *American Mercury*, Mencken's "Green Badge of Courage," was dying and so was the *Literary Digest* with its wrong-way political straw vote that indicated a nonexistent Republican wind. Several liberal and radical publications fell by the wayside. But *Reader's Digest* was prospering on its policy of condensed, simplified reading, and already England's *News Review* and *Cavalcade* were copying it. *Time* was going great guns and the fledgling *Fortune* was becoming a showcase of significant research and opinion edited by bright and tactful liberals. There was a big new magazine with the name *Life*, inherited from the moribund humor book. It was a picture magazine and would inspire a wave of imitators. And *Esquire*, basking in success, was launching a companion publication in the pocket-sized *Coronet*. Another newcomer to the publishing scene was called *The Pawnbroker's Journal*, undoubtedly filling a long-felt need.

Radio

If the movie people were little concerned about "movies transmitted by radio stations," neither were the radio stations themselves. To be sure, some tinkerers here and in England were claiming results with televising pictures through the air, but the whole thing smacked of black magic. Even if it worked, all the manufacturers could never agree on standardization. So radio was strong and growing stronger all the time.

Kate Smith was still getting the moon over the mountain and Amos and Andy had a following of millions. Rudy Vallee was popular and so was Bing Crosby. George Burns and Gracie Allen vied with Edgar Bergen and Charlie McCarthy. Jack Benny announced that he was going to start writing his own gags, but Fred Allen stuck to using writers. Goodman Ace was writing and starring in the friendly, whacky *Easy Aces* and there was Major Bowes' *Amateur Hour*, that was even whackier if less talented. Contestants regaled listeners with Jew's harps, yodeling, one-man bands and animal imitations. The worst got the gong and the best got votes. One commentator said that America was the place where a citizen cast ten votes a week for the amateurs and forgot to go to the polls on Election Day.

Soap operas brightened the housewife's day at the ironing board and horse opera, too, had taken to the air. *The Lone Ranger* was the most successful example and sound effects men became virtuosos with hoofbeats.

For the more serious-minded there were news commentators, including Boake Carter and H. V. Kaltenborn and Lowell Thomas. The Columbia Workshop was pioneering radio drama and CBS shook up the populace now and then by letting controversial figures like Communist Earl Browder speak their pieces. Lux Theatre was popular, too, along with Lucky Strike's *Hit Parade* and Lanny Ross' *Maxwell House Showboat*. And for those listeners who went in for violence and excitement there was a program that came on like gang busters. It was, in fact, *Gang Busters*.

Religion and Morals

Church membership was growing during the thirties but there were cynics who questioned whether Americans were becoming more religious. Surely most churches except the fundamentalists were becoming increasingly liberal. This was perhaps a natural reflection of the times and of a society whose morals had lapsed somewhat with the hardships of depression.

In 1936 there were an estimated 33 million Protestants, 21 million Catholics, and 4½ million Jews in America. Even with this membership, the Protestants were concerned, however, and the Federal Council of Churches of Christ in

209

America typified their feeling. Dr. E. Stanley Jones, renowned missionary, was called home to lead a huge tour of twenty-five religious centers in the U.S. asking for moral rearmament. There were other concerns, too. The Presbyterian Church ousted Dr. John Machen in a squabble over his insistence on orthodox teachings.

Leader of the Catholics in America was Pope Piux XI, Achille Ratti of the Vatican. During the year the Pope created the new Bishopric of Los Angeles, over which John Joseph Cantwell was made Archbishop. Another act of the Pope was to despatch Cardinal Pacelli to the U.S., where one of his tasks was to try to curb Father Coughlin.

At a gathering of some 2,000 Jews in the East, Rabbi Stephen Wise, was made President of the Zionist Organization of America and pledged himself to work for the good of that body.

Out West the Mormons applied their religion to their everyday life and decided to get their people off the relief rolls before the year was out. It would take a million dollars and a lot of hard work, but it would show the country that the Mormons could stand on their own feet in bad times. And in Chicago the Mormons established a new "stake" for that area.

Religion was strong among the Negroes, too. In addition to the more traditional groups, there was Father Divine smilingly cutting a wide swath among the faithful in Harlem and elsewhere.

Prohibition and its aftermath of bootlegging had created cynicism in the minds of many Americans, and the inability of many young people to marry because of financial reasons had weakened conventional restraints on sex. Migration, due to poverty or wanderlust, contributed further. According to a *Fortune* poll, however, sex wasn't big news to youth any more; not something to flaunt as the rebels of an earlier generation had done. Another poll showed that two-thirds of the people in America favored birth control, and with the marriage rate down, so too was the birth rate. Yet divorces were decreasing, too, and sentiment seemed opposed to easy dissolution of marriage.

Despite repeal there was still widespread bootlegging and even rum-running as the unscrupulous sought to dodge the stiff government tax on liquor. With drinking permitted, college youngsters were not as bibulous as they had been

210

during Prohibition. Coca-Cola was gaining in popularity and even milk was getting a big play. Smoking was on the rise and in 1936 there were 158 *billion* cigarettes manufactured in this country. As with their drinking, women were more open about smoking. Another fact of life was the increase in drinking in mixed groups, while men's clubs seemed on the decline.

Science

1936 was a year of "atom-smashing" as scientists around the world built huge, expensive machines for this purpose. Their "cyclotrons" accelerated particles to fantastic rates of speed and were used in studies of the structure of the elusive atom. Cosmic rays came in for much investigation, and balloons and aircraft carried instruments high into the atmosphere.

Among radiation experts were Drs. Robert Millikan and Carl Anderson of California Institute of Technology. Anderson received the Nobel Prize in Physics for 1936. Stanford University build a "rumbatron" for use in not only atom-smashing experiments but television work.

Einstein's theory of relativity was being confirmed in part by an observed "red shift" in the spectrum of certain stars. Astronomers also sighted the smallest known asteroid. Dubbed "Anteros," it measured only a third of a mile across. In contrast they also discovered the huge exploding star, "Super Nova Virginia 1936," in the Virgo cluster.

More big news was the successful cooling and transportation of the second 200-inch "big eye" for the Palomar Observatory telescope. The first mirror had been faulty but this replacement was found perfect when it cooled. Its huge size, double that of any existing mirror, was expected to increase greatly the distance man could peer into space.

Scientists were learning that an elephant's heart beats faster when he lies down, and that they could grow tobacco plants 22 feet tall in tanks of water containing chemicals. This new science was called hydroponics. Another new field was called "chemurgy," the use of farm products in industry.

Dr. C. G. Abbott of the Smithsonian Institution, who thought there might be a connection between sunspot activity and business ups-and-downs, put the sun to a more immediately practical use. He built himself a solar engine

211

that converted about 15 percent of the sun's heat into usable energy. Dr. Abbott was taken about as seriously as Dr. Robert H. Goddard, whose rockets were whizzing about the landscape.

Goddard's rockets were propelled by liquid fuels and their motors developed 200 horsepower per pound of weight. Already they had attained speeds of 700 miles an hour and Goddard had proposed sending a rocket to the moon with an explosive charge that would cause a flash of light to prove the device had reached its goal. His rockets had progressed to the sophistication of gyroscopic control for stability, and some visionary enthusiasts were proposing them for carrying the mail. Early abortive attempts prompted jokesters to say that rocket mail was fast enough but that you couldn't be too particular about where your letters went.

A book titled *Rockets Through Space,* published in 1936, vaulted the concept far past that of mere earthbound mail. Its author seconded Goddard's proposal of a moon rocket but realistically pointed out some of the big problems involved. For each pound of payload, for example, it would take thousands of pounds of fuel. In fact, it might well cost something like $100 million to hit the moon!

Closer to home, and delving into "inner space," Simon Lake was using one of the submarines he had invented to seek out the sunken British frigate *Hussar* in the East River. The ship had been there since 1780 and reportedly carried four million dollars in gold and silver.

Dr. V. K. Zworykin of RCA demonstrated an invention of his using "infrared" rays that would penetrate haze, smoke and even darkness. Another device involving light rays was the "Polaroid" lens of Edwin Land. The new glass seemed to be a natural for cameras, sunglasses, auto headlights and so on. Elsewhere, glass was being used for everything from erasers to razor blades, and airplane builders and others were using new plastics like Bakelite and Micarta.

A scientist in a more esoteric field was Dr. J. B. Rhine, who was investigating something called "extrasensory perception," or ESP, at Duke University. Many laymen couldn't take it too seriously since the experiments seemed to consist of playing cards and rolling dice. And in France another "scientist" was predicting the end of the world—in September, 1936.

Sports

The big sporting event of 1936 was the Olympics, of course, but there was still plenty of everyday sport to make life interesting for participants and spectators alike.

Big League baseball opened the season on April 13 when President Roosevelt tossed out the first ball in Washington. A total of 204,000 fans were on hand for the various opening games. Several months later the New York Yankees beat the New York Giants four out of six to take the World Series. The last game was played at the Polo Grounds with a score of 13 to 5. Yankee mainstays included Gomez, Dickey, DiMaggio, Crosetti, Rolfe, Gehrig and Lazzeri. With the Giants were names like Terry, Ott, Mancuso, Schumacher and Hubbell.

The Yanks' Lou Gehrig proved himself the grand old man of the game. He led the American League for homers, hitting 49 of them. He also ran his string of consecutive games played to more than 1,800! In the National League Mel Ott hit 33 homers. Paul Waner of Pittsburgh had that league's highest batting average with .373, and Luke Appling of Chicago paced the American League.

Carl Hubbell was the stand-out pitcher of the year. His earned run average was 2.31, and he won 26 and lost 6 for the Giants. He won his last 16 games in 1936, and went on to win the first 8 in 1937 for a record string. Monte Pearson of the Yanks was the American League's top pitcher with a won-lost record of 19 and 7. Grove had the best earned run average at 2.81.

The St. Louis teams led their leagues in stolen bases, with Pepper Martin of the Cards getting 23, and Lyn Lary of the Browns stealing 37.

Most valuable players of the year were Hubbell and Gehrig, with Stew Martin of the Cards and Joe DiMaggio of the Yanks the prize rookies.

Football's Big Ten were Minnesota, Louisiana State, Pittsburgh, Alabama, Washington, Santa Clara, Northwestern, Notre Dame, Nebraska and Pennsylvania. Minnesota, Alabama and Santa Clara were unbeaten and untied, Louisiana was unbeaten, but tied once. The All-America selections, made by Grantland Rice, were as follows:

E	Gaynell Tinsley	Louisiana State
T	Dick Smith	Minnesota

G	John Weller	Princeton
C	Darrell Lester	Texas Christian
G	Inwood Smith	Ohio State
T	Truman Spain	Southern Methodist
E	Jim Moscrip	Stanford
Q	Riley Smith	Alabama
H	Jay Berwanger	Chicago
H	Bobby Wilson	Southern Methodist
F	Bobby Grayson	Stanford

Stanford beat Southern Methodist in the Rose Bowl in 1936 with a score of 7 to 0. In other bowl games Texas Christian beat Louisiana State in the Sugar Bowl, 3 to 0; Catholic University eked out a 20 to 19 win over Mississippi in the Orange Bowl; and at the Sun Bowl Hardin Simmons and New Mexico State battled to a draw. As the year ended Washington invited Pittsburgh for the next Pasadena fracas and would be royally trounced 21 to 0.

Pro football's Boston Redskins and Green Bay Packers dominated the field, and in the All-Star Game the Detroit Lions tied the All-Stars 7 to 7. Individual players singled for honors included:

Arnie Heber, Green Bay Packers—Passing
Don Knutson, Green Bay Packers—Receiving
Tuffy Leemans, New York Giants—Ball carrying
Earl Clark, Detroit—Scoring

At the AAU's forty-eighth annual meet at Princeton, the following were the results:

100-meter dash	J. Owens	10.4
200-meter dash	R. Metcalf	21.2
400-meter dash	H. Smallwood	47.3
800-meter run	C. Beetham	1:50.4
1500 meters	G. Cunningham	3:54.2
5000 meters	D. Lash	15:04.8
10,000 meters	D. Lash	31:06.9
3,000 steeplechase	H. Manning	9:51.1
110-meter hurdles	F. Towns	14.2
200-meter hurdles	J. Hucker	23.8
400-meter hurdles	G. Hardin	51.6
Pole vault	G. Varoff	14' 6½"

Broad jump	J. Owens	26' 3"
Hop, skip, & jump	B. Brown	49' 2"
Shot put	D. Zaitz	50' 7⅝"
Discus	K. Carpenter	166' 2"
Hammer throw	B. Rowe	175' 7"
Weight throw	L. Lepis	35' 1⅛"
Javelin	J. Mottron	214' 7⅜"
400-meter relay	Marquette	41.3
1600-meter relay	N. Y. Ath. Club	3:51.1

At the Western Conference, these were the winners:

100-yard dash	Owens	9.5
220-yard dash	Owens	21.1
440-yard dash	Ellinwood	48.4
880-yard run	Beetham	1:52.4
One Mile	Lash	4:10.8
Two miles	Lash	9:19.9
120-yard hurdles	Osgood	14.2
220-yard hurdles	Owens	23.5
High jump	Walker	6' 6"
Broad jump	Owens	23' 5"
Shot put	Kregowski	48' ⅞"
Discus	Etchells	146' 9½"
Javelin	Lamb	194' 4"

In hockey, the Detroit Red Wings beat the Montreal Maroons to win the Stanley Cup. The final game lasted 2 hours, 56½ minutes of actual playing time before the Red Wings managed to score for victory. Two weeks later they bested the Toronto Maple Leafs to win their first world championship.

American polo players did well in 1936, too, winning the International Polo Cup Series at Hurlingham, England, 2 to 0. At the U.S. Polo Association Championships, Greentree beat Templeton 11 to 10.

The winners at the American Bowling Congress Tournament were the following:

Individual	C. Warren	735
All Events	J. Murphy	2006
Two-Man Team	A. Slanina, M. Straka	1347
Five-Man Team	Falls City Hi Bru	3089

In archery, Gilman Keasey was Man Champion in the National Archery Association competition. Gladys Hammer was Woman Champion.

Cochran won the billiard championship, with Willie Hoppe winning the challenge match. J. Cavos won the pocket billiard championship, and amateurs E. C. Rogers and E. Soussa won the amateur pocket and balkline titles, respectively.

At Indianapolis, Louis Meyer won the 500-mile classic in 4:35:03.39, for an average speed of 109.069 miles per hour. And for the second consecutive year Killian and Vopel won the German Six-Day Bike Race Championship, pedalling 2,572.5 miles. At Madison Square Garden, the race was won by Walthour and Crossley.

Joe Louis was the big gun in boxing and he got off to a flying start in January by KO'ing Ratzlaff in a single round. Then on June 12 Germany's Max Schmeling upset Louis and practically every sports writer in the country with a knockout win in the twelfth round. A flabbergasted Louis salved his pride by flooring three opponents before the end of the year. Each of them was polished off in three rounds: Sharkey in August, Ettore in September, and Brescia getting the treatment in October. By then Louis was a much wiser fighter, with a defense against a solid right, as he would demonstrate when he again entered the ring with Schmeling.

Giant Primo Carnera, whom Louis had demolished in their fight, continued his losing ways and was trimmed by Leroy Haynes twice during 1936. In fact, when it was learned that Italy was drafting Carnera, sports writers opined that if he was as bad with a rifle as he was with his fists the Ethiopians had nothing to worry about.

Hard times or no, horse racing continued in the United States as a popular sport. Betting went on to the tune of millions, and Bold Venture was the big horse of the year, winning the Kentucky Derby and Preakness, while Granville took the Belmont Stakes. Over in England the Aga Khan's Mahmoud won the Epsom Derby.

In college basketball the top teams included Columbia, Indiana, Kentucky, North Carolina, Kansas, Utah State and Stanford.

Golfdom's greats were Tony Manero in the National Open, John Fischer in the National Amateur, Ralph Guldahl in the Western Open, and Byron Nelson in the Metropolitan Open. A phenomenon was taking place in American golf in the decline of private clubs and the rise in public links. In 1936 there were twice as many municipal courses as there had been ten years earlier.

The National Doubles tennis champs were Don Budge and Gene Mako, and Bobby Riggs won the Clay Court championship. Alice Marble was the Women's Singles champ. Gaining on tennis in popularity was the revived sport of badminton. Thousand of fans were putting in their evenings in gymnasiums chasing the feathered shuttlecocks and getting cricks in necks and sacroiliacs in the process.

Another once expensive and inaccessible sport was being made available to thousands by ski trains and buses. Equipment was offered at popular prices and new slopes were being carved out on mountainsides across the country. Of course, you could break a leg on a ski slope, but you could have a lot of fun, too, and people who had never before been closer to a snowy hillside than watching a newsreel of ski jumping were now awkwardly trying it themselves.

Swimming pools, bathing beaches and ice rinks were all on the increase at the public level. While private beaches like Bailey's Beach in Newport hung on, municipal resorts like Jones Beach were hosts to as many as 100,000 more democratic swimmers on a good Sunday.

Spectator sports were still popular, too. There were the old stand-bys like six-day bike races, and the newer roller derbies and midget auto races. Also getting a play were "Bank Night" at the movies, along with free dishes and other prizes. There were mild gambling games like Bingo and Keno, plus the diversions of slot machines, punchboards and pinball. And chain letters were still taking in the gullible who didn't realize how fast the pyramiding chain called for new suckers.

Bridge was more popular than ever, and more people played for money. In Madison Square Garden French and American experts played a tournament with assistants juggling huge seven-foot cards as the contestants played their hands. Eli Culbertson was in charge of the spectacle and the Americans won the match.

For the man who could still remember being wiped out in 1929 there was a game that gave the vicarious thrill without the danger, and players gleefully ruined competitors on the Monopoly board.

There was another game current, too—one called "Knock, knock," and it went like this:

"Knock, knock."

"Who's there?"

"Delia."

"Delia who?"

"Delia cards off the bottom."

Other versions were: "Boo-hoo." "What are you crying about?" "Opportunity." "It can't be, 'cause opportunity only knocks once." And such horrors as: "Eskimo, Christian and Italian—Eskimo Christian, and Italian no lies." Mercifully, "Knock, knock" was knocked out in short order by such puns.

Americans were also playing "Handies," a type of one-man charade in which, for example, two fingers held up before the nose and the other hand above the head represented an Indian driving a Ford V-8.

Even in their adversity, the depression proved, Americans were a fun-loving bunch who would somehow manage to play.

Styles and Fashions

Thanks in part at least to Mae West, curves were coming back. Mature female figures were the thing in 1936 and only little girls looked like little girls any more. Even daytime dresses were quite long. Schoolgirls favored tweed skirts and sweaters, with ankle socks and saddle oxfords. Long hair was the style and the page boy was popular.

Fall fashions decreed dignified suits and dressy afternoon frocks. Evening gowns were long, with a slim, full-skirted, broad-shouldered silhouette. Necklines were low. Black, rust and beige were leading colors with reds, yellows and greens following. Velvet and lace were big news due to the Coronation. The close-fitting helmet sort of hat was losing out to larger and floppier headgear.

Sought-after designers included such mainstays as Schiaparelli, Mainbocher and Raphael. John Frederics was a big name in hats, but Agnes and Molyneux and Maria Guy had a following. J. Suzanne Talbot earned a feather for her own cap by styling headgear for the glamorous Wallis Simpson who would soon be the Duchess of Windsor. There were Creed suits and Guerin bags and Bentivigna shoes. Few European designers knew their time was about to run out.

218

Women bought a variety of new "play clothes": rompers, shorts, play suits, mandarin coats, beach dresses and pajamas, slacks, and even plus fours. Sandals and "wedgies" were worn just about everywhere.

Men's styles changed little, though. Vests were seldom seen now, and garters were a bit stuffy since even the new King of England had publicized elastic-topped socks. Another item of clothing that seemed on the wane was the undershirt, perhaps in part because of virile Clark Gable's undressing scene in *It Happened One Night*. The "King" wore no undershirt, and garment manufacturers could only chew their nails and hope for the day when another actor would return such apparel to a place of rugged honor.

Theater

It was natural that the plays on Broadway reflect the times. Robert Sherwood's *Idiot's Delight*, the Pulitzer Prize winner, was a warning of the dangers of Fascism, as was Sinclair Lewis' novel, *It Can't Happen Here*. There were plays like *Johnny Johnson* and *Bury the Dead* protesting the senselessness of war, and many playwrights dwelt on themes of social consciousness.

In a more conventional vein were John Gielgud's *Hamlet* and Helen Hayes' *Victoria Regina*. At the Metropolitan Opera Rosa Ponselle was doing *Carmen* and Flagstad and Melchior were stars of the Wagnerian roster. Shaw's *Saint Joan* starred Katherine Cornell, and *Ethan Frome* set a sober tone. *Brother Rat*, *The Women* and *You Can't Take it with You* were popular and so were revues like *On Your Toes*. The Ziegfeld Follies featured Fannie Brice and another comic named Bob Hope.

Federal theater players, to quote some cynics, were not so much reviving the legitimate stage across the country as demonstrating why it died. Nevertheless, many were seeing live theater for the first time and enjoying it. And besides the documentary pageants based on news events like *Court Kill Triple-A*, government-supported actors were doing more artistic things such as the federal Negro Theater's presentation of *Macbeth*.

In London, besides Noel Coward's *Tonight at Eight-thirty*, Robert Sherwood's *Tovarich* was popular. Eliot's grim *Murder in the Cathedral* was contrasted with P. G. Wodehouse's *The Inside Stand*. *Storm in a Teacup* was

219

doing well, and King Edward went to a private showing of this Bridie and Frank play. Showing the range of English productions were the classic *Mary Tudor*, an experimental play, *The Dog Beneath the Skin* by Auden and Isherwood, and the Dobie Smith comedy, *Call It a Day*.

Transportation

In 1936 one writer found cheering news in the reported holdup of a train. "At least it was running," he said gratefully. But despite the fact that the railroads were not bouncing back as fast as the auto industry, they did seem at least to be on the right track. The five-day week hurt commuter business, so some railroads put on ski trains to take up the slack.

The revolutionary Union Pacific aluminum train had started something with its streamlined good looks and high speed. The Burlington *Zephyr* wasn't aluminum, but stainless steel, and it made the run from Chicago to Denver at a blinding 83 miles an hour.

By 1936 there were more than 350 streamlined cars being built and President Pelley of the Association of American Railroads could say we had more trains running faster than 60 miles an hour than any other country. However, Germany had made a record run of better than 124 miles an hour with a streamlined three-car train!

This idea of streamlining had caught on in the automobile field, too, and was rounding and softening their lines. The new curves were more for style and selling points than actual speed increases though. A current cartoon showed the driver of a sleek new model bragging, "We've got wind resistance licked!" His car was stalled in a traffic jam.

Cars were selling though, and in 1936 there were more than 3½ million manufactured. There was a boom in highways, too, and in a few spots drivers were getting a look at the roads of the future with banked curves and cloverleaf intersections with multilevel traffic. There was talk of experimental roads built of aluminum or rubber, and one wild scheme used molasses in the paving material! There was something new *on* the highways, too, sometimes sleek and streamlined, but more often boxy-looking. It was the house trailer.

In 1929, before the crash, a man named Sherman had nailed together a neat little house for a vacation cabin.

Lots of handy men had done this before, at the beach or up in the mountains. But Sherman did it at home. To get his cabin where it would be useful he added wheels, hitched it to his car and took to the road. The trailer was born and the highways became a "Nomad's land" with some 160,000 of the contraptions in use in 1936.

Jokes were cracked about trailerites returning home and getting lost in their living rooms, but trailers grew bigger and more luxurious. Some brave souls were staking their trailers out in parking lots to test the legality of such residences, and no less an authority than Roger Babson sagely predicted that half the population would be living in them within twenty years.

There was a weird, huge-tired vehicle being used in the South and called a "marsh buggy," capable of navigating land, swamp or open water. And experts ventured a guess as to what the car of the future would be like. It would have six wheels, with four in the rear, and the tires would be blowout-proof and self-inflating. Air-conditioning would be provided for the teardrop-shaped body and there would be just two instruments on the dashboard—speedometer and fuel gauge. Other instruments would be replaced by lights that would wink red to indicate trouble.

There was one development being watched with a jaundiced eye by automobile owners. The "Park-O-Meter," invented by Carlton Magee, charged the motorist just for leaving his car at the curb. And the worst part of it was that if you didn't pay the required coin it would cost a lot more—down at City Hall!

221